Elizabethan stage conventions and modern interpreters

ELIZABETHAN STAGE CONVENTIONS AND MODERN INTERPRETERS

ALAN C. DESSEN

Professor of English
University of North Carolina, Chapel Hill

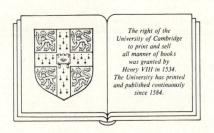

The right of the
University of Cambridge
to print and sell
all manner of books
was granted by
Henry VIII in 1534.
The University has printed
and published continuously
since 1584.

CAMBRIDGE UNIVERSITY PRESS

Cambridge
London   New York   New Rochelle
Melbourne   Sydney

Published by the Press Syndicate of the University of Cambridge
The Pitt Building, Trumpington Street, Cambridge CB2 IRP
32 East 57th Street, New York, NY10022, USA
10 Stamford Road, Oakleigh, Melbourne 3166, Australia

First published 1984
First paperback edition 1985

Printed in Great Britain at
the University Press, Cambridge

Library of Congress catalogue card number: 83–23970

British Library Cataloguing in publication data
Dessen, Alan C.
Elizabethan stage conventions and modern
interpreters.
1. Shakespeare, William – Criticism and
interpretation
I. Title
822.3'3   PR2976
ISBN 0 521 25912 6 hard covers
ISBN 0 521 31161 6 paperback

CE

To Shirl

Contents

Preface

This project was begun in 1976–7 during my term as a National Endowment for the Humanities Senior Fellow at the Folger Shakespeare Library. Earlier versions of some sections have since appeared in print, so for permission to incorporate such materials here I wish to thank the editors of the *Yearbook of English Studies* (and their publishers, the Modern Humanities Research Association), *Renaissance Drama, Renaissance Papers,* and *Elizabethan Theatre IX.* In addition, parts of this argument have been presented to various scholarly gatherings, so for helpful comments my thanks are due to colleagues at the Folger Institute Colloquium; the Southeastern Renaissance Conference; several seminars of the Shakespeare Association of America; the NEH Symposium on 'Shakespeare in Performance' (Urbana, 1977); and, in particular, the 1981 International Conference on Elizabethan Theatre at Waterloo, Ontario (with special thanks to G. R. Hibbard). Of the many people in the academic and theatrical worlds who have been generous in sharing insights and responding to my questions, let me single out Homer Swander, Audrey Stanley, Bernard Beckerman, David Bevington, Michael Warren, Steven Urkowitz, Gary Taylor, G. R. Proudfoot, Pat Patton, Denis Arndt, James Edmondson, Martha Henry, Urjo Kareda, Ian Richardson, Terry Hands, and Patrick Stewart.

Note on texts and old spelling

Unless otherwise noted, quotations from Shakespeare are taken from *The Complete Pelican Shakespeare*, general editor Alfred Harbage (Baltimore, 1969). Elsewhere, whenever possible I have used facsimiles of the earliest texts (as in the Tudor Facsimile series), diplomatic editions (as with the reprints provided by the Malone Society), or later editions that, for the most part, faithfully reproduce the original stage directions (e.g., the six volume 1874 edition of Thomas Heywood or the ten volume Waller and Glover edition of Beaumont and Fletcher).

To avoid a cumbersome apparatus, I have not provided a footnote or endnote for each of my many citations from the plays but instead have included line, signature, or page numbers in my text (for example, *Alphonsus, King of Aragon*, ll. 2109–10; *The Merry Devil of Edmonton*, Blr), and then listed the plays cited and editions used at the end of the book. For the many references to Heywood and Fletcher in the editions cited above (which do not provide line numbers), I cite volume and page numbers (for example, *The Fair Maid of the Exchange*, II, 41).

Since Shakespeare is almost always read in modern spelling, I have chosen to modernize the spelling of many non-Shakespearean passages both from the plays and from Sidney and other contemporary spokesmen. To avoid some obvious inconsistencies in my own text, moreover, I have also regularized the use of italic and roman type in my presentation of stage directions. Any minor distortions caused by such changes are more than offset by the added ease for some readers and, in symbolic terms, the presentation of Shakespeare and his contemporaries as orthographic equals (as opposed to 'modern' Shakespeare versus 'primitive' Heywood).

1 · The arrow in Nessus: Elizabethan clues and modern detectives

Did you ever hear of a sleepwalker carrying a light?

Shakespeare's plays continue to fascinate – and puzzle – the modern reader. Actors, directors, editors, critics, and teachers all wrestle with the words that have come down to us in the quartos and the Folio, seeking clues to pluck out the heart of Hamlet's mystery or answer Lear's question: 'Who is it that can tell me who I am?' But anyone familiar with the wide range of interpreters and interpretations can attest that the solutions advanced or even the questions asked reveal as much about the modern detective as about the Elizabethan dramatist. Like Orlando bearing old Adam on his back, we too bring luggage with us to any reading of Elizabethan plays; or, to use Bernard Beckerman's image, when we pick up a book containing the printed words of a Shakespeare play we simultaneously put on a pair of spectacles 'compacted of preconceptions about what constitutes drama and how it produces its effects.'[1] To the modern reader, the luggage or spectacles of an earlier age may appear ridiculous. Thus, we can chuckle at Nahum Tate's decision 'to rectify what was wanting in the regularity and probability of the tale'[2] in *King Lear* by adding a love affair between Edgar and Cordelia and a happy ending, or we can look askance at Dryden's 'improvement' of *Troilus and Cressida* 'to remove that heap of rubbish under which many excellent thoughts lay wholly buried.'[3] But to recognize the assumptions and predispositions that control (and sometimes distort) *our* view of Elizabethan drama is far more difficult, even at times impossible, especially in our age of demystification in which the responses of the reader or the formulations of the theorist often take precedence over the 'intentions' of the author.

For an especially astute critique of the modern literary detective dealing with Shakespearean clues, consider James Thurber's 'The Macbeth Murder Mystery.'[4] At an English hotel, Thurber's narrator encounters an American lady addicted to murder mysteries at bedtime who discovers to her horror that inadvertently she has purchased *Macbeth*. Stuck with the bard, she grudgingly reads the tragedy and, as an experienced sleuth, becomes firmly convinced that Macduff rather than Macbeth is the murderer of Duncan. In her reasoning lies Thurber's insight. First, Macbeth could not be the murderer because: 'It would spoil everything if you could figure out right away who did it. Shakespeare was too smart for that.' Banquo was a suspect until he too was killed ('That was good right in there, that part'). Macbeth's suspicious behavior in the banquet scene is attributed to his attempt to 'shield' Lady Macbeth, but she too must be innocent because, in the sleep-walking scene, she carries a taper. Says the American lady: 'Well, people who walk in their sleep *never carry lights*! . . . They have a second sight. Did you ever hear of a sleepwalker carrying a light?' Rather, she declares Macduff the culprit because of his hyperbolic reaction to Duncan's death, for she notes that 'he comes running downstairs and shouts, "Confusion has broke open the Lord's anointed temple" and "Sacrilegious murder has made his master-piece" and on and on like that.' Our amateur detective observes shrewdly: 'All that stuff was rehearsed . . . You wouldn't say a lot of stuff like that, offhand, would you – if you had found a body? . . . You wouldn't! Unless you had practiced it in advance. "My God, there's a body in here!" is what an innocent man would say.'

With a fine comic touch, Thurber here demonstrates how the introduction of irrelevant evidence and inappropriate questions can distort a Shakespearean scene or character or problem. Thus, his American lady brings her lore about sleep-walkers, her awareness of mystery story conventions, and her sense of realism about language and human reactions under stress to bear upon a poetic tragedy where a sleep-walker *can* carry a taper and an innocent figure, confronted with the murder of his saintly king, *can* state that 'most sacrilegious murder hath broke ope / The Lord's anointed temple.' At such moments in an Elizabethan play, another kind of literary or theatrical logic – call it symbolic or imagistic or presentational – can take precedence over the interpretative logic or generic expectations supplied by the devotee of Agatha Christie (or Henry James or Henrik Ibsen or Sigmund Freud or A. C. Bradley).

To see such interpretative logic in conflict on stage, consider a moment from the Oregon Shakespearean Festival production of

King Lear in 1976. Here, in a rendition of III. iv, Denis Arndt as Lear took upon himself the role of a lecturer with Poor Tom as his visual aid ('consider him well') in order to raise an essential question ('is man no more than this?') by placing particular emphasis upon nakedness ('uncovered body,' 'the thing itself,' 'unaccommodated man,' 'a poor, bare, forked animal'). At the same time, Ron Woods as Tom was building his characterization upon his iterated line 'Tom's acold' and was therefore shivering, 'playing cold,' grasping at anything that would provide warmth. As a result, at one performance the two actors engaged in a strenuous struggle for Tom's blanket (his only possession other than a loin-cloth), with Lear trying to pull it off in order to display a naked or nearly naked figure (to establish his thesis) while Tom, with equal vigor, sought to pull the blanket around him (to gain warmth). Tom won – perhaps at the expense of the larger implications of Lear's speech.

Note that the two actors were responding to two different sets of signals that then led them in two different directions. Woods, as a modern actor conditioned by the logic of naturalism, was reaching out for appropriate stage business to resolve the question: how would a nearly naked man obviously suffering from the cold 'behave' in a storm? In contrast, Arndt was drawing upon previous speeches about naked wretches in the pitiless storm and was therefore treating Tom as a theatrical expression of images crucial to this part of the play ('is man no more than this?,' can 'man' be reduced to this?). The two different kinds of interpretative logic (physiological-naturalistic versus imagistic-symbolic) are not necessarily incompatible but were at odds in this wrestling match where Poor Tom as stage image linked to the particular coordinates of this scene did not mesh comfortably with Poor Tom as a 'man' or 'character' responding to blasts of cold. The actor's choice, moreover, to play 'cold' rather than 'nakedness' may be a subtler version of what I am terming the *logic* of Thurber's American lady, who 'knows' that in 'the real world' sleep-walkers do not carry candles and thanes who discover dead bodies do not react in highly imagistic blank verse.

To see such a logic of interpretation in action in yet a third arena, let me turn now to two problems involving stage directions – one omitted, the other inserted. First, at the moment that Romeo threatens to commit suicide in III. iii the second or 'good' quarto of 1599 (presumably the version closest to Shakespeare's draft) provides no stage direction, but the first or 'bad' quarto of 1597 (presumably based upon an actor's memory of some production) reads: '*He offers to stab himself, and Nurse snatches the dagger away*' (G1v). Some modern editors incorporate the signal from Q–1 into their texts (usually putting it in square brackets to show it is not to be found in Q–2), but in his recent New Arden edition Brian Gibbons rejects the Nurse's intervention as 'neither necessary or defensible.' Rather, for this editor 'this piece of business looks like a gratuitous and distracting bid on the part of the actor in the unauthorized version to claim extra attention to himself when the audience should be concentrating on Romeo and the Friar.'[5] Given his sense of what 'the audience should be concentrating on,' Gibbons therefore relegates the Nurse's intervention to his textual notes and footnotes. No distractions here.

Like Poor Tom 'playing cold' or the American lady reading *Macbeth* as a murder mystery, this editor is invoking a logic of interpretation that then determines for him what evidence shall be included or excluded, what is deemed 'necessary' or 'defensible' as opposed to 'gratuitous' or 'distracting.' Since many readers concentrate upon the text rather than the notes, such an editorial decision (especially in this prestigious series) can have a greater impact upon future interpreters than an equivalent choice by an actor or critic. Granted, if an Arden editor omits such a signal, it has not ceased to exist: other editors will make different decisions; some readers take the notes into account; other readers go back to facsimiles of the earliest texts. But this editor's decision (noted with approval by at least one reviewer)[6] has made it easier for future interpreters of this scene to ignore the Q–1 stage direction – indeed, has made it more likely many will not know of its existence.

The reader may well ask: why all the fuss? In what sense can the Nurse's intervention be seen as meaningful or consistent or 'Shakespearean'? In response to Gibbons, one scholar has noted that, later in the play, we learn 'that Romeo carried his dagger scabbarded on his back,' so, given proper positioning on stage, the Nurse could readily have prevented his access to the weapon, perhaps with 'a genteel hammerlock.'[7] For me, the Q–1 version makes excellent sense in imagistic or symbolic terms. After Mercutio's death, Romeo had cried out: 'O sweet Juliet, / Thy beauty hath made me effeminate / And in my temper soft'ned valor's steel!' (III. i. 111–13). Then, after Romeo's aborted attempt at suicide, the Friar's long moralization starts:

> Hold thy desperate hand.
> Art thou a man? Thy form cries out thou art;
> Thy tears are womanish, thy wild acts denote
> The unreasonable fury of a beast.
> Unseemly woman in a seeming man!
> And ill-beseeming beast in seeming both! (III.iii. 108–13)

The spectator who sees Romeo's self-destructive violence interrupted by the Nurse and then hears the Friar's terms (e.g. 'Art thou a man?'; 'Thy tears are womanish'; 'Unseemly woman in a seeming man') is thus confronted with the question: what kind of man *is* Romeo at this point in the play? Like other moments of stage violence (to be discussed in chapter six), the woman's intervention here may set up a powerful and meaningful stage image at the heart of the tragedy. What may seem by one logic of interpretation 'gratuitous and distracting' or 'out of character' or 'unbelievable' may, by a somewhat different logic, appear imagistically or symbolically consistent or meaningful. Indeed, how *would* a dramatist in the mid 1590s (the age of *The Faerie Queene*, *Doctor Faustus*, and *Titus Andronicus*) have acted out on stage the 'womanish' behavior of his protagonist?

For a second example, consider the context of one of the most famous moments in Shakespeare, Macbeth's 'to-morrow, and to-morrow, and to-morrow.' The scene starts with the entrance of Macbeth, Seyton, and soldiers. Seven lines later a stage direction calls for '*a cry within of women*' (v. v. 7. s.d.); Macbeth asks 'What is that noise?' and Seyton responds: 'It is the cry of women, my good lord.' After a powerful short speech ('I have supped full with horrors') Macbeth asks again: 'Wherefore was that cry?' to which Seyton responds: 'The Queen, my lord, is dead' (ll. 15–16), a revelation that elicits the famous speech. The Folio, however, provides no exit and re-entry for Seyton between his two lines, so the only authoritative text gives us no indication how he finds out that the queen is dead. Few editors (or directors or critics) can abide such an untidy situation (especially since the original texts *are* erratic about indicating exits and entrances), so the Pelican, Riverside, Signet, and New Arden editions (to cite only four) include an exit for Seyton after his first line and an entrance before his second (with the insert usually, but not always, enclosed in square brackets). A director may have Seyton exit or may have him send off a lesser functionary who then returns or may have Seyton walk to a stage door, confer with someone off-stage, and return to Macbeth. As Gibbons might argue, the focus here is upon Macbeth, not Seyton, so the editor must decide what is 'necessary' and what is 'distracting.' If we are to understand that Lady Macbeth has died at the moment of the cry (which would then rule out Seyton knowing of her death at the outset of the scene), the announcer of the news presumably must have some means of learning the news. Therefore, our prevailing logic of interpretation calls for an exit or some other visible means of getting the news on stage.

Without further evidence, we will never know whether or not such an interpretation is correct.[8] Regardless, given the widely shared assumptions about what is 'necessary' to make such a scene 'plausible,' editors undoubtedly will continue to insert the two additional stage directions, a self-fulfilling action that in turn validates the interpretation and keeps us comfortable. But how valid *is* this logic of interpretation? Can we imagine the scene as presented in the Folio? Macbeth would ask his first question ('What is that noise?') and get the answer ('It is the cry of women'). No one leaves the stage; Seyton remains by his side. After his ruminations about fears and horrors, Macbeth asks again: 'Wherefore was that cry?' and Seyton responds: 'The Queen, my lord, is dead.' In this rendition, the audience cannot help seeing that Seyton (to be pronounced *Satan?*) has no normal (earthly?) way of knowing what he knows. But he *does* know. Macbeth may be too preoccupied to notice the anomaly, but, if staged this way, the spectator cannot help being jarred. Indeed, the anomaly then becomes a major part of the context for the nihilistic comments that follow. Such a staging (which adds nothing but rather takes the Folio at face value) strikes me as eerie, powerful, perhaps quite unnerving. A focus upon *how* Seyton knows of the death almost inevitably leads to the addition of stage business that can provide a practical explanation for that 'how,' but such literal-mindedness may, in fact, end up masking a truly distinctive Jacobean effect linked to a mystery behind that 'how.' After all, how do Enobarbus and Iras die in *Antony and Cleopatra*? How does Henry VI know of the murder of his son in

3 Henry VI, v. vi? Or, much closer to home, how do the witches know what they know in this play? In this, Seyton's last specified appearance, are we being encouraged to grasp larger meanings in his name? Most important, where does one draw the line between 'editing' and 'interpreting' such a moment?

That my two examples of editorial logic have to do with stage directions is no coincidence. Every Shakespeare play has its share of much discussed problems involving which *words* were intended by the author. Thus, in his third soliloquy at the end of Act II, does Hamlet compare himself to a 'scullion' (a kitchen wench) or a 'stallion' (a male prostitute) or (perhaps looking forward to Cleopatra's 'salad days') a 'scallion' (the delectable reading from the 'bad' quarto)? Even in a play like *Macbeth* which survives in one rather than three versions many such decisions must be made. But the editor's rigor in decisions about the prose and poetry is rarely matched by an equally careful treatment of stage directions. Rather, like many critics and teachers, editors regularly envisage Elizabethan plays as literary texts rather than theatrical playscripts, with predictable results. Those readers (e.g., theatrical professionals) who do read the plays as scripts often end up viewing the original effects through invisible barriers set up (often unwittingly) by the modern editor. Thus, the actor or director, although bringing valuable know-how to the reading of Elizabethan playscripts, is nonetheless conditioned both by the logic of the editor and the prevailing assumptions of much twentieth-century theatre (as with Poor Tom playing cold) with significant results for contemporary productions (as I will argue at length in my chapters on lighting, locale, and violence). The Nurse's intervention or Seyton's missing exit may puzzle or provoke the theatrical professional as much as the editor or critic.

Herein, then, lies the many-headed problem to which this study is addressed. Let me clarify my working assumptions. To avoid the trap epitomized by the American lady's wrenching of *Macbeth* or the tug-of-war at the Oregon *King Lear*, the modern interpreter should make every possible effort to sidestep inappropriate assumptions, conventions, or expectations. A major part of this effort involves conceiving of the plays as staged events and consequently viewing the surviving documents as theatrical scripts rather than literary texts (thereby drawing upon the

province of the theatrical professional) but with the understanding that the logic of the staging then (as with the Nurse's
intervention as a 'womanish' side of Romeo or Seyton's possible
continued presence) may differ significantly from the logic of
staging or 'realism' now (thereby drawing upon the province of
the critic or historian). Any inferences or conclusions, moreover,
should be based upon the original evidence (thereby drawing
upon the province of the editor), but that includes the original
stage directions, not the adjustments made by editors and other
scholars who may not be sympathetic to theatre then or now.

To some readers, my assumptions or precepts may sound
straightforward, even self-evident, but, in fact, they create many
problems (some of which I will address in this study) and considerable controversy. Critics, editors, theatrical professionals,
stage historians, teachers – all constituent parts of the enormous
'Shakespeare industry,' all confident that they know perfectly
well what they are doing – often show minimal patience with or
tolerance for alternative views. Attempts to build bridges are not
always welcomed. My claims, moreover, posit a large role for the
historian of drama who should be providing firm evidence about
the original staging and conventions, a role that has not always
been carried out successfully, both because of the nature of the
evidence and, at times, some questionable assumptions on the
part of the practitioners. So Shakespeare studies move (and will
continue to move) merrily along – on parallel tracks to infinity.

But if we *start* with the assumption that there is much we will
never know (e.g., what the stage at the Globe actually looked like
to a spectator), we may be able to ascertain what *can* be discovered or recovered. Hence my second chapter will be devoted to
a fresh look at the basic building block for any detailed investigation of Elizabethan playscripts and theatrical practice – the
stage direction. But before delving into those materials, let me first
confront some general problems – again, with little hope of any
definitive solutions.

A particularly disturbing feature of any study of staging and
stage practice is that, quite simply, we have no way of knowing
how much we do not know. When a word unknown to modern
philologists survives in a Shakespeare play (e.g., the 'prenzie'
Angelo, Caliban's 'scamels'), the critic or actor at least is aware of
a gap in our knowledge (or a textual crux) and can consult learned

notes in editions or journals. Similarly, we know we are missing something when we hear Pistol twice call out 'have we not Hiren here?' (2 *Henry IV*, II. iv. 145, 158–9), apparently a famous line from a lost play, as well known then as 'To be or not to be' now. Again, when Hamlet tells Rosencrantz: 'Ay, sir, but "while the grass grows" – the proverb is something musty' (III. ii. 329–30) or when Lady Macbeth castigates her back-sliding husband for 'letting "I dare not" wait upon "I would," / Like the poor cat i'th'adage' (I. vii. 44–5), we know that Shakespeare is expecting us to fill in the blanks with a proverb well known then albeit obscure today ('while the grass grows, the horse starves'; 'the cat would eat fish yet dare not wet its feet'). A reader without access to notes or Tilley's dictionary of proverbs[9] may have some difficulty making full sense out of these moments, but no alert reader will be unaware that something beyond the words themselves is being invoked or assumed, something presumably accessible to most of the original audience.

But when one turns to the stage practice and theatrical conventions of the past, especially in the plays of Shakespeare (which seem to speak to us so readily across the wide gap of time), the historian or director or critic or editor can never be sure when we are talking the same language, when we are sharing the same assumptions. To be sure, few readers today have difficulty with soliloquies, asides, disguises, eavesdropping scenes, even perhaps alarums and excursions (i.e., regular and recognizable features of Elizabethan plays), but even these well-known practices can cause problems for some sensibilities. Thus, several scholars have challenged modern 'realistic' assumptions about the aside. In his seminal study of the Globe plays, Bernard Beckerman notes that 'many asides give the actor neither time nor motivation for creating verisimilitude.' We often assume that, to deliver an aside, a Richard III or Hamlet or Othello must be distanced from the other figures on stage, but, drawing upon examples from *Pericles* and *Othello*, Beckerman argues that 'the Globe players, in the staging of asides, did not think in terms of creating an illusion of actuality but of relating the crucial elements of the narrative to each other.'[10] Or, as Ernest L. Rhodes has noted, 'the important thing was not the distance but the signal for the "aside," regardless of whether it was given by a movement on the stage, a gesture, by a special tone of the voice, or by all of these.'[11] The modern sensibility may expect some visible separation between the speaker and potential listeners, but if the deliverer of the aside is quite close to the other actors, the emphasis may fall not upon his deceptive speaking but rather upon their faulty listening, an effect demonstrably present in many moral interludes and used adroitly for sardonic comic purposes repeatedly in *Volpone*. Is, then, the gap between aside speaker and listener 'real' or conventional or symbolic?

To confront this and other such questions one must first arrive at a working definition of 'theatrical convention,' so let me turn to the useful discussion of that term by Raymond Williams.[12] A convention, for Williams, 'is simply the terms upon which author, performers and audience agree to meet, so that the performance may be carried on.' Such agreement, he notes, 'is by no means always a formal or definite process' but rather 'is largely customary, and often indeed it is virtually unconscious'; this consent, moreover, 'must usually *precede* the performance, so that what is to be done may be accepted without damaging friction.' Those attuned to a set of conventions (e.g., 'that the speech and action should as closely as possible appear to be those of everyday life') often do not recognize their conventions as such, rather equating their familiar procedures with 'what a play is like' or 'the sort of thing a play tries to do,' yet, as Williams notes, what could be more illogical than seeing actors who supposedly 'represent people behaving naturally, and usually privately,' standing in front of 'a large audience, while all the time maintaining the illusion that, as characters, these persons are unaware of the audience's presence.' Similarly, an actor 'can speak to us, acknowledging his most private thoughts, and we will agree that while we hear him from the back of the gallery, he cannot be heard by a man a few feet away from him, or waiting in the wings.' Although in the cold light of day we might question these and other effects, in the theatre 'we do not challenge them. We accept; we agree; these are the conventions.'

Consider the many cinematic conventions to which we give such unthinking consent. To audiences today, cinema may represent the epitome of realism, yet if we can, for a moment, examine our own assumptions, what is 'real' about sitting in a darkened auditorium, watching figures larger than life (especially in 'close-ups') projected onto a flat screen and seen through camera angles that often do not correspond to our normal viewing range, while listening to voices, not from the lips of the speakers, that boom around us in stereophonic sound accompanied by music from a full orchestra? Yet 'We accept; we agree; these are the conventions.' Again, modern readers of Elizabethan plays may chuckle at the narrative shorthand provided by a choric figure like Time in *The Winter's Tale* or a stage direction like *exit at one door and enter at another* (to indicate a quick change in time or locale), but at the cinema that same individual will have no difficulty recognizing moving calendar pages as the passage of time, accepting necessary exposition from the headlines of newspapers, or inferring the whole of a journey from seeing a figure get on a plane in one airport and get off in another. Granted, the camera can provide far more detail for the viewer of cinema or television than could be presented on the Elizabethan stage, but complex events (a long journey, the flight of an arrow) still require a selectivity in presentation that enlists our conventional responses, while in any medium exposition of essential information without some form of narrative shorthand proves very cumbersome.

One of my goals throughout this study therefore is to reconstruct or recover some Elizabethan playhouse conventions in the hope of determining more fully the terms upon which dramatists, actors, and spectators 'agreed to meet.' My emphasis will not be upon familiar devices that function relatively smoothly in modern productions (e.g., the soliloquy, the aside, impenetrable disguise) but rather upon techniques or procedures that appear to us odd, illogical, or intrusive. In such anomalies may lie important clues to the basic assumptions that characterized theatregoers in the age of Shakespeare.

To clarify such assumptions, however, is no easy matter. The original playgoers have left us little evidence; the extant comments from the dramatists about their craft (e.g., various prefaces, Heywood's *Apology for Actors*) are not especially revealing or instructive. Certainly, the most telling insights are to be found in the choric passages of *Henry V*. In the justly famous Prologue, Shakespeare's spokesman apologizes for the limits of 'this unworthy scaffold' in conveying 'so great an object' as Agincourt; still, the players can 'on your imaginary forces work' if the viewers are willing to 'suppose,' to 'make imaginary puissance' by dividing one man into a thousand parts, to 'think, when we talk of horses, that you see them / Printing their proud hoofs i'th'receiving earth,' in short, to 'piece out our imperfections with your thoughts.' Again, the Chorus to Act III pleads with the audience to 'suppose,' 'behold,' 'do but think,' 'grapple your minds,' 'work, work your thoughts, and therein see a siege,' and, finally, 'still be kind, / And eke out our performance with your mind.' Before Agincourt, the Chorus to Act IV apologizes in advance for disgracing this great event 'with four or five most vile and ragged foils, / Right ill-disposed in brawl ridiculous,' but asks the audience: 'Yet sit and see, / Minding true things by what their mock'ries be.' Repeatedly, Shakespeare asks his audience to accept a part for the whole, to supply imaginatively what cannot be introduced physically onto the open stage.

This apologetic stance, especially when coupled with the strictures of purists like Sidney and Jonson, would seem to suggest severe constraints upon what could be introduced onto the Globe stage. But given the available conventions or shared assumptions (at least in the public theatres), such limits seem to evaporate. For example, consider battle scenes, surely among the most difficult to realize effectively on any stage. Sidney could mock 'two Armies ... represented with four swords and bucklers';[13] Jonson could sneer at the players who 'with three rusty swords, / And help of some few foot-and-half-foot words, / Fight over *York*, and *Lancaster's* long jars: / And in the tiring-house bring wounds, to scars' (Prologue to *Every Man In His Humour*, ll. 9–12). Shakespeare himself, as already noted, was conscious of the danger of lapsing into the 'brawl ridiculous' in presenting Agincourt through only 'four or five most vile and ragged foils.' Nonetheless, rather than avoiding battle scenes, the Lord Chamberlain's Men and the other companies found practical solutions. As Alfred Harbage observes: 'The audience did not see the battles so much as hear them. What it saw was displays of skill by two or occasionally four combatants on that small sector of the battlefield symbolized by the stage.' In addition, the players made adept use of *alarums* or off-stage sound effects ('a gong insistently clanging, trumpets blaring recognizable military signals, then steel clashing, ordnance firing') and *excursions* ('individual pursuits and combats onstage').[14] Thus, from *Captain Thomas Stukeley*: '*Alarum is sounded, diverse excursions, Stukeley pursues Shane O'Neill and Neil Mackener, and after a good pretty fight his*

Lieutenant and Ancient rescue Stukeley, and chase the Irish out.
Then an excursion betwixt Herbert and O'Hanlon, and so a
retreat sounded' (ll. 1170–5). Through such theatrical synec-
doche, the whole of a battle is to be imagined or inferred through
the parts displayed, an approach to mass combat well suited to a
large platform stage and limited personnel.

Not all Elizabethan spectators, however, were willing to make
this imaginative leap and 'be kind' to the 'imperfections' or
'mock'ries' presented on the open stage. Sidney, for one, argues
that 'many things may be told which cannot be showed' if
dramatists would only observe 'the difference betwixt reporting
and representing' ('An Apologie,' p. 198). Some popular dramatists did substitute a Chorus for the sweep of staged action, as in
Henry V or *1 The Fair Maid of the West* where Heywood's
Chorus laments: 'Our Stage so lamely can express a Sea / That we
are forc'd by *Chorus* to discourse / What should have been in
action' (II, 319). Elsewhere, dramatists often used dumb shows to
bring complex events on stage, as in *Edmond Ironside* where the
Chorus would prefer to have the audience 'see the battles acted on
the stage' but since 'their length will be too tedious / Then in dumb
shows I will explain at large / Their fights, their flights and
Edmond's victory' (ll. 970–3). But most popular drama before
and after Sidney's strictures ranged widely in space and time (e.g.,
Shakespeare's *1 Henry VI, Antony and Cleopatra, Pericles*, and
The Winter's Tale) and brought on stage exciting events that
would seem to pose insuperable difficulties. Thus, in his argument
on behalf of the classical *nuntius* Sidney remarks: 'I may speak
(though I am here) of *Peru*, and in speech digress from that to the
description of *Calicut*; but in action I cannot represent it without
Pacolet's horse' ('An Apologie,' p. 198). Yet in the closing
moments of *The Travels of the Three English Brothers*, John Day
does introduce a version of Pacolet's horse: a prospective glass
that enables the three brothers and their father, widely dispersed
in different countries, to see and communicate with each other.
Despite the position taken by figures like Sidney and the practical
limitations of the stage, Elizabethan dramatists, players, and
audiences clearly relished big scenes and effects that would seem
to us to burst the bounds of the unworthy scaffold.

As a representative example, consider a 'mission impossible'
sequence from Fletcher's *The Island Princess* (VIII, 106–18)

where Armusia and his men rescue the King of Sidore from a supposedly impregnable island. First, Fletcher shows us the wicked Governor taunting the king in his prison; next, Armusia and his group appear '*like Merchants, arm'd underneath*' to reveal that they have rented a cellar adjacent to the Governor's storehouse of gunpowder. With their departure the confident Governor enters with a captain; in rapid succession follow an off-stage explosion, a bell ringing, a citizen shouting 'fire, fire,' the returning captain with news of the castle and its wealth in danger, more citizens, a call for buckets, and a mass *exeunt*. Armusia and his men appear for a few lines ('Let it flame on') followed by a brief appearance of captain and citizens ('more water, more water'), perhaps with buckets (none are specified). Then: '*Enter Armusia and his company breaking open a Door*'; they discover the king, break his chain, drive off the guards, and depart for their boat. The sequence concludes with comic comments from some citizens and their wives, followed by a final appearance of the Governor and his men to recount what has happened. The key to the successful plot and rescue is the diversion, but neither the fire nor the quenching of the fire can be shown directly on the Elizabethan stage. But through a combination of sound effects, vivid reports, exits and entrances, and alternating scenes Fletcher has provided all the excitement of such a fire as an appropriate and telling context for the daring rescue. In a good production, a spectator presumably would 'believe' in the fire and the stratagem without actually witnessing the flames, burning buildings, and a bucket brigade throwing water (effects possible in cinema or nineteenth-century theatre).

Or consider *Fortune by Land and Sea* where Heywood brings onto the platform stage a battle between two ships at sea (VI, 410–18). After '*a great Alarum and shot*,' the two pirates, Purser and Clinton, enter with prisoners from their most recent conquest. Once the stage has been cleared, young Forrest appears '*like a Captain of a ship, with Sailors and Mariners, entering with a flourish*'; a boy is told to 'climb to the main-top' to 'see what you ken there'; '*Above*,' the boy calls out 'a sail' and shouts down details; Forrest instructs his gunner, steersman, master, and boatswain; '*a piece goes off*' when the pirates raise their colors (as reported by the boy above). Again, with the stage cleared, Purser and Clinton return '*with their Mariners, all furnished with Sea devices fitting for a fight*'; they urge on their gunner ('Oh 'twas a gallant shot, I saw it shatter some of their limbs in pieces'), and debate strategy. Again, Heywood switches to Forrest exhorting his men not to spare the powder. Finally, '*a great Alarum, and Flourish. Enter Young Forrest and his Mates with Purser and Clinton with their Mariners prisoners.*' As in *The Island Princess*, the key to the effect lies in the combination of alternating scenes and appropriate signals: the boy above, nautical language, costume (e.g., Forrest '*like a Captain of a ship*'), and sound effects, along with the reported action. There is no evidence that shots are actually fired on stage (although there is considerable talk of guns and gunnery), but there is frenzied activity, much noise, and presentation of '*Sea devices fitting for a fight*,' all appropriate for two ships in battle at sea.

My two examples from Fletcher and Heywood display the problems posed by fire and water on the Elizabethan stage and the solutions found if such moments were to be represented rather than reported.[15] Remember too the shipwrecks so important for romance plots but so difficult to present at the Globe. In itself, a storm at sea posed no greater difficulty than a storm on land, calling for sound effects and appropriate acting and dialogue. Thus, Pericles is to enter '*a-shipboard*' (III. i. o. s. d.) and describe the storm for the audience; this storm and its equivalent in *The Tempest*, I. i are then followed by the speeches of figures on shore recounting what has happened. But to provide an actual shipwreck on the open stage is another matter indeed. Thus, at the outset of *The Tempest* Shakespeare provides a shouting match between the boatswain and the courtiers, mariners who enter '*wet*' and crying 'all lost,' hasty exits, '*a confused noise within*,' and Gonzalo's 'we split, we split, we split!' In contrast, Heywood (ordinarily the dramatist least inhibited by the limits of the unworthy scaffold) at least twice conveys a shipwreck by concentrating upon the recently completed action. Thus, in *The Captives* Palestra is to enter '*all wet as newly shipwrecked and escaped the fury of the seas*' (ll. 653–4), while in *The Four Prentices of London* a reported shipwreck is followed by dumb shows that display Godfrey '*as newly landed and half naked*,' Guy '*all wet*,' and Charles '*all wet with his sword*' (II, 176–7). The stage direction from *The Thracian Wonder* is worth quoting at length, if only for its insights into 'playing wet': '*Enter old Antimon bringing in Ariadne shipwrecked, the Clown turning the child up and down, and wringing the Clouts. They pass over the Stage. Exeunt. Enter Radagon all wet, looking about for shelter as shipwrecked. Enter to him Titterus, seems to question him, puts off his Hat and Coat, and puts on him, so guides him off. Exeunt. Storm cease'* (B4v). In these three examples (as opposed to *The Tempest*, I. i), the spectator has been shown not the action itself (the shipwreck) but the results or effects of that action (figures *'as shipwrecked'* or *'as newly landed and half naked'* or *'all wet'*). To borrow terms from *Henry V*, the viewer is being asked to 'work, work your thoughts, and therein see a siege,' a shipwreck, a diversionary fire, or a battle at sea, thereby 'Minding true things by what their mock'ries be.'

Let me conclude with a particularly revealing moment, Heywood's rendition of the death of Nessus the centaur in *The Brazen Age* (III, 180–2). Here, one would suppose, is an event too complex to be enacted on the open stage, for it involves (1) Nessus carrying Dejanira on his back across a river and (2) Hercules then shooting an arrow across that river to kill the centaur. How does Heywood do it? First, after the departure of Nessus and Dejanira, Hercules, alone on stage, describes for the audience their progress through the water ('well plunged bold centaur') but then must rage impotently as he witnesses the attempted rape and hears his bride cry for help (four times). Finally, Hercules announces: 'I'll send till I can come, this poisonous shaft / Shall speak my fury and extract thy blood, / Till I myself can cross this raging flood.' The stage direction then reads: *'Hercules shoots, and goes in: Enter Nessus with an arrow through him, and Dejanira.'* Moments later, 'after long struggling with Evenus' streams,' Hercules reappears to 'make an end of what my shaft begun.' To depict a figure on one side of a river shooting a figure on the other side, Heywood has resorted to rapidly alternating scenes, reported action, off-stage sounds, and, most important (in his version of what in our age has become a stock cinematic effect), a presentation of the initiation and then the immediate resolution of the central event (*'Hercules shoots ... Enter Nessus with an arrow through him'*) rather than the full sequence (the complete flight of the arrow and the striking of its target). If the choric passages from *Henry V* provide the 'theory' behind the open stage (e.g., that the audience is expected to use their imaginary forces to 'eke out our performance with your mind'), the arrow in Nessus provides a telling demonstration of the resulting theatrical practice. The spectator sees (1) the shooting of the arrow and (2) the result but then must supply (3) the connection between the two (I am assuming that Nessus enters immediately at another door), including any sense of the river and the distance involved. For the scene to work, the actors must provide the timing and energy, the audience, the imaginative participation.

To readers concerned primarily with Shakespeare's major plays, my examples from Heywood, Fletcher, and lesser dramatists may appear unrepresentative, tangential, even bizarre. But Shakespeare also provides an arrow-shooting scene, one with a decidedly allegorical emphasis (*Titus Andronicus*, IV. iii), just as he provides off-stage sea battles (e.g., 2 *Henry VI*, IV. i, *Antony and Cleopatra*, III. x, IV. xii), storms, and various spectacular effects. My goal in invoking such moments is not to reduce Shakespeare's plays to their lowest common denominator but rather to establish what effects were possible, even likely, on the open stage and what assumptions were shared then by dramatist, actor, and spectator. What *were* the terms upon which they agreed to meet? And how are we to recognize them? Perhaps we will never be able to recover more than a fraction of what was shared then, but even that fraction may help us avoid indulging in the kind of misguided modern detective work based upon Elizabethan clues epitomized in extreme form by Thurber's American lady.

And herein lies the value of taking seriously the arrow in Nessus. Initially, this stage direction may seem quaint or silly, worthy only of amused contempt, but we should remember that Heywood, like Fletcher and Shakespeare, was a working professional linked to a specific theatrical company who not only knew his craft well but also knew his theatre from the inside, both its potential and its limits. If we chuckle at the arrow in Nessus, we are implicitly asserting our superiority to a 'primitive' dramaturgy ('how could anyone be expected to believe that?') and, in the process, revealing more about ourselves (e.g., how we read playscripts) than about the Elizabethans. If we are not responsive to this and other such moments (e.g., Jupiter descending on an eagle, Gloucester's 'suicide' at Dover Cliffs), are we not in danger of reconceiving the plays to suit our sensibilities, of rewriting the clues to suit our solutions? Certainly, I would not defend *The Brazen Age* as a long lost masterpiece, but it *is* highly representative of one major strain in Jacobean drama (i.e., the kind of sensational play associated with the Red Bull playhouse) and can thereby tell us much about *their* assumptions and predilections. Are we to characterize the theatre or theatrical conventions of another age by the moments that make the best immediate sense to us, that cause us the least discomfort, or, in contrast, can we best understand a theatre other than our own by concentrating upon those moments that do cause us problems and therefore make us conscious of the gaps between then and now (e.g., the wearing of masks in classical drama, the parting of the Red Sea in a Corpus Christi play)? For me, the key to understanding what is distinctive about drama in the age of Shakespeare lies in the anomalies, the surprises, the moments that make us aware of the full stretch of the dramaturgy. To confront the plays squarely, in short, is to confront the arrow in Nessus.

At the risk of indulging in my version of the 'brawl ridiculous,' in the chapters that follow my goal is to introduce examples and raise questions that will challenge the reader to rethink various assumptions about drama then and now. Perhaps my fundamental premise is that such a process, which sometimes involves consideration of obscure plays of questionable merit, is indeed worth the effort if the result is a fuller context for understanding the major works of the period. To grasp what lies behind Hercules 'shooting' Nessus is to forestall the comic depredations of Thurber's American lady and to move closer to an understanding of the terms upon which an Elizabethan audience at a performance of *Hamlet* or *King Lear* agreed to meet.

2 · Interpreting stage directions

Overreach as from dinner
(*A New Way to Pay Old Debts*, III. iii. o. s.d.)

To recover the theatrical techniques and shared assumptions in the age of Shakespeare is no easy task, for such attempts have been and will continue to be frustrated by the nature of the evidence. First, if one excludes descriptions of masques or other special occasions at court, very few accounts have survived of plays in production. Thus, a recent study devoted to 'eyewitnesses of Shakespeare' provides about thirty pages of material written between 1590 and the 1640s, mainly glancing allusions, value judgments, and brief plot summaries (e.g., Simon Forman's accounts of three plays),[1] but included here are few clues about how the plays were staged. Unfortunately for us, contemporary playgoers are rarely informative about what they saw, with the few revealing accounts devoted to lost or little-known plays (e.g., the late moral play, *The Cradle of Security*). Equally limited is the pictorial evidence. Thus, the often-reproduced Peacham drawing may reflect the staging of the opening scene of *Titus Andronicus* or may tell us something about the Elizabethan attitude towards 'period' costume,[2] but it may just as well reflect the artist's own conception as a reader of the scene, just as the illustrations in printed editions (e.g., *Doctor Faustus*, *The Spanish Tragedy*, *Swetnam the Woman-Hater*) may have little to do with stage presentation (or as much as a drawing in an advertisement today).

Any attempt to deal with the original staging or stage conventions must therefore build almost exclusively upon the evidence within the plays themselves. Thus, from dialogue and from the apparent requirements of a given scene much has been inferred about the number of stage doors, the need for stage machinery, and the presence of large properties like tombs or trees, but (as noted in the previous chapter) such inferences can easily be conditioned by the assumptions and expectations of the investigator. To cite but one example, a scholar who starts with firm evidence of the use of castles in some medieval plays can then cite Hotspur's reference to 'yon lime and stone' and Bolingbroke's allusion to 'the rude ribs of that ancient castle' (*Richard II*, III. iii. 26, 32) and then argue that an on-stage castle is 'an indispensable prop' in staging the scene.[3] As a modern playgoer, however, I have seen numerous renditions that conveyed the sense of such a castle merely through the actor's gestures towards the neutral façade of the stage. Then or now, Flint Castle can be 'created' with no strain by words, gestures, and the 'imaginary forces' of the spectator. Similarly, a major bone of contention among stage historians is the number of stage doors in a given theatre, an argument usually keyed to the demands of the most complex scenes known to have been performed in that theatre. Here again, inferences are highly vulnerable to the assumptions of the investigator who must reason: is a third or fourth or even fifth door 'necessary' for a given scene?[4] How can one 'prove' that B cannot enter by means of the door A has just used?

Given the obvious limitations of the external evidence and the dialogue, attempts to reconstruct the original staging and theatrical conventions must depend largely upon the stage directions in the extant manuscripts, the few theatrical 'plots,' and, most abundantly, the surviving printed texts (depending upon chronological boundaries, some three hundred and fifty to five hundred plays). To work with these stage directions, however, especially in the best-known plays, is quickly to encounter frustration and confusion. Thus, many scenes in which meaning is closely linked to decisions about staging have no directions whatsoever (as in the nunnery scene in *Hamlet* where the reader today can never be certain when Hamlet becomes aware of the eavesdroppers, if, indeed, he notices them at all). Moreover, the signals that *are* provided often are uninformative or confusing or inconsistent (as with the many situations where a character is given no *exit* but nonetheless is directed to *re-enter* – e.g., Osric at the close of *Hamlet*). Such murkiness is characteristic not only of printed texts (which may be one or more removes from the playhouse or may show the effects of compositorial error) but also of those texts and manuscripts that actually may have been used as the basis for performance. Thus, I find it chastening to remember that whoever annotated the manuscript of Heywood's *The Captives* for the theatre let stand the marginal stage direction for a murderous assault: '*Either strikes him with a staff or casts a stone*' (ll. 2432–4). At any performance, the actor had to make a choice, but even with what appears to be the playhouse 'book' in front of us we cannot be certain what that choice would have been.

To see a typically murky problem in a well-known scene, consider the question: did or should Hamlet leap into Ophelia's grave? The dialogue establishes that Laertes does make such a leap and that Hamlet and Laertes then grapple with each other, but the reader, looking solely at the words to be spoken, cannot determine whether the tragic hero descends or his antagonist ascends. The second quarto and the Folio provide no stage directions calling for a leap by Hamlet; most modern commentators argue that such a leap would be impractical or out of character or even ludicrous.[5] Yet the first or 'bad' quarto does provide the stage direction '*Laertes leaps into the grave*' and then in the margin '*Hamlet leaps in after Laertes*'; moreover, an elegy for Richard Burbage, the original Hamlet, comments that 'oft have I seen him, leap into the grave.'[6] Note that these two pieces of evidence cannot prove the case. Burbage may have made his leap or leaps in other plays; Shakespeare's company may have played the scene in different ways at different times (such is the nature of theatrical scripts); the first quarto may reflect another version of *Hamlet* (e.g., Polonius here is named Corambis, to note only one of several significant differences). The absence of a conclusive signal in the two 'better' texts may be significant or may only be circumstance; but regardless, a basic problem remains, linked to (1) the murky nature of the evidence; (2) the nature of theatrical scripts; and (3) the assumptions or logic we bring to the plays. In this instance, the choice by editors or directors or critics will probably be based upon their overview of the tragedy and their sense of 'character' – what would Hamlet as I understand him have done in this situation? – but the 'logic' behind this moment could just as well be metaphoric or symbolic. Thus, I can conceive of a Hamlet who here makes a literal and figurative descent to Laertes' level or a Hamlet who here comes to terms with Death or his past or his Nemesis.

To leap or not to leap (like many other problems in *Hamlet*) has elicited more than its share of critical response, but just about any

Elizabethan play provides situations where a reader must wrestle with the evidence provided (or often not provided) by the surviving stage directions. To help in such decisions, scholars have developed some important distinctions. Thus, both editors and stage historians have come to place great emphasis upon the *source* of various stage directions as a by-product of their investigations of the kind of copy a printer may have used to set up the original text of an Elizabethan play. Scholars today therefore try to distinguish among (1) authorial drafts or 'foul papers' that presumably show the dramatist's conception when writing a scene; (2) manuscripts or printed texts used in the playhouse that presumably reflect preparation for theatrical presentation; (3) scribal copies of either of the above in which authorial or playhouse features may have been eliminated or tidied up; and (4) reported texts or memorial reconstructions, sometimes cited as 'bad' quartos (a smaller category with considerable debate over its membership), that record what participants remember as having happened in a performance.[7] Distinguishing among these categories, especially between the first and the second, is a major feature of most textual introductions to modern editions as well as a significant part of many recent theatrical reconstructions, because the scholar's decision about the source of a given stage direction (author, playhouse annotator, scribe, actor) may then determine for him the authority that signal carries.

Editors and stage historians, however, differ significantly about the authority they seek. Quite understandably, most editors link the 'authority' of a given text or manuscript to its closeness to the 'author,' a link that can lead to a prizing of those signals clearly associated with the dramatist and considerably less interest in those associated with the playhouse. Both this distinction and its editorial implications have a long history. Thus, in 1790 Edmund Malone decided 'that the very few stage-directions which the old copies exhibit, were not taken from our author's manuscripts, but [were] furnished by the players.' He therefore announced: 'All the stage-directions therefore throughout this work I have considered as wholly in my power, and have regulated them in the best manner I could.'[8] Although few editors today would make such a forthright statement, many do not value the surviving theatrical evidence any more highly than did Malone (again, literary scholars dealing with theatrical evidence in playscripts), especially in texts somewhat removed from the authorial original. For example, in a carefully reasoned essay Harold Jenkins argues that the many 'little repetitions, interjections, and similar small elaborations' found in the Folio *Hamlet* represent interpolations into Shakespeare's text by the actors – 'stage accretions' that 'have no claim to be admitted into an edition of *Hamlet* which aims at fidelity to its author.'[9] Whether in texts annotated for the playhouse or memorially constructed 'bad' quartos, such interpolations by actors or bookholders represent, for many editors, a contamination of the author's play, with the Folio Hamlet's dying 'O, o, o, o' after 'the rest is silence' often singled out for particular censure.

Conversely, in their attempt to reconstruct stages and staging, theatrical historians attribute the greatest 'authority' to those manuscripts or printed texts that demonstrate not the author's wishes but rather actual playhouse practice. In the most rigorous formulation of this argument, T. J. King has noted that stage directions in printed texts derived from foul papers 'may represent the author's intentions not fully realized on stage.' Therefore, according to King, the principal evidence for reconstructing Elizabethan stages and stage practice should come from 'texts dependent on playhouse copy,' while, conversely, 'texts evidently not derived from the playhouse have no primary value as evidence for the study of staging.'[10] Given the available evidence, King admits two hundred and seventy-six plays from the period 1599–1642 into his charmed circle of 'primary value' and excludes, as having no 'primary value,' such authorial texts as *All's Well That Ends Well*, *Coriolanus*, and *Antony and Cleopatra*.

Anyone tackling a problem that involves interpreting stage directions must heed the distinctions and strictures of both editor and stage historian. Thus, in support of Jenkins' sense of a gap between authorial conception and playhouse interpolation scholars have provided evidence that some Elizabethan dramatists were unhappy with what happened to their plays in the hands of the players. For example, R. C. Bald has noted that both the manuscript and printed version of Sir William Berkeley's *The Lost Lady* contain stage directions that 'must have originated with a prompter or stage-manager,' but 'a fastidious author like Berkeley felt that directions which smacked of the details of theatrical production had no place in a text intended for the reader, and accordingly had them struck out.'[11] More recently, Stephen Orgel has reminded us that a far more significant dramatist, Ben Jonson, 'makes a large point out of insisting that the printed versions of his plays are substantially different from the versions that were staged.' Thus, in the printed version of *Sejanus* Jonson 'has succeeded in *suppressing* the theatrical production, and has replaced it with an independent, printed text, which he consistently refers to, moreover, not as a play but as a poem.'[12] An author's concern with providing an appropriate text for a reader is sometimes reflected on the title page. For example, *The Devil's Charter* is presented to the public 'as it was played before the King's Majesty, upon Candlemas night last: by his Majesty's Servants. But more exactly reviewed, corrected, and augmented since by the Author, for the more pleasure and profit of the Reader.'

But the fastidious Berkeley and the freelance Jonson (who sold his plays to a given company, thereby giving up control over their staging) are quite different from dramatists like Shakespeare and Heywood who were active participants in their companies and could have much to do with production. Indeed, Orgel, drawing upon the work of G. E. Bentley, stresses 'how much the creation of a play was a collaborative process, with the author by no means at the center of the collaboration' and then goes on to argue that, when dealing with 'a performing text,' 'it is a mistake to think that in our editorial work what we are doing is getting back to an author's original manuscript: the very notion of "the author's original manuscript" is in such cases a figment.' For Orgel, Shakespeare's role as actor and shareholder as well as playwright does not make him an exception but merely shows that he was 'in on more parts of the collaboration.'[13] Orgel's position will appear extreme to many editors, especially those who would side with Harold Jenkins in his argument that 'stage accretions' or actor's interpolations should be excluded from an edition 'which aims at fidelity to its author.' But for dramatists like Shakespeare, Heywood, and Fletcher, to assume a disjunction between the virginal work of the author and the subsequent contamination by the players may be to introduce a working model that reveals more about the scholar's assumptions about the artist and the theatre than about Elizabethan practice. If a stage effect was not in Shakespeare's original draft but was seen by an Elizabethan or

Jacobean audience, are we to suppress it as lacking 'fidelity to its author'? Should any valid theatrical signal, whatever its source, that presumably helps us to envisage the play as witnessed by its original audience, be eliminated from a modern edition?

As to playhouse 'authority,' T. J. King's formulation must be weighed heavily, particularly by the historian using playscripts to reconstruct a particular theatre, but is less compelling in reference to matters of general playhouse practice. As one reviewer of King's book asked: 'is the staging projected by an experienced dramatist less reliable a guide to playhouse practice than actual prompt copy?' King may assume 'that demonstration of play-house origin automatically endows a text with theatrical auth-ority greater than that of all other texts,' but, in fact, 'is not the text of a mature Shakespearean play, whether or not of playhouse origin, likely to reflect staging practice more accurately than the prompt manuscript of a relatively inexperienced author such as Henry Glapthorne?'[14] Throughout this study I have kept in mind but have not followed rigorously King's distinctions, but rather have let a wealth of linked examples take precedence over those instances with 'playhouse authority' (of which there are many). The stage historian cannot assume that specific effects or tech-niques remained unchanged over long periods of time or were handled the same way in different theatres, nor should he build any argument upon unique examples (especially from printed texts with no links to the playhouse). But groups of stage direc-tions from a wide range of plays by experienced dramatists (and I have drawn heavily upon Dekker, Heywood, Fletcher, Mass-inger, and Shakespeare) strike me as important basic evidence – indeed, in many cases the only such evidence – for the study of Elizabethan stage practice.

Despite my qualifications about editorial or historical distinc-tions, I would freely admit that some stage directions do sound distinctively authorial, some distinctively theatrical. As examples of the former, perhaps most obvious are the 'open' or 'permissive' signals that give the impression of a dramatist leaving various matters to the players. For example, many entrances do not specify the exact number of actors to be used but rather call for '*and others as many as can be*' (*Titus Andronicus*, I. i. 72. s.d.) or '*as many as may be*' (*Edward I*, l. 51, *The Double Marriage*, VI, 400) or '*as many as may be spared*' (*The Tragedy of Hoffman*, l.

1682). In *Clyomon and Clamydes*, Alexander the Great is to enter *'as valiantly set forth as may be, and as many soldiers as can'* (ll. 358–9); *The Three Ladies of London* calls for an officer with a whip *'or two if you can'* (Flv). Elsewhere, a reader can sense a dramatist slipping into his narrative while writing a stage direction: *'enter old M. Chartly as new come out of the Country to inquire after his Son'* (*The Wise Woman of Hogsdon*, v, 340) or from *All's Well That Ends Well* enter *'divers young lords taking leave for the Florentine war'* (II. i. o. s.d.) and *'Parolles and Lafew stay behind, commenting of this wedding'* (II. iii. 182. s.d.). At times, a reader may get the sense of a dramatist wishing for a more spectacular effect than may indeed be possible: *'exit Venus. Or if you can conveniently, let a chair come down from the top of the stage, and draw her up'* (*Alphonsus, King of Aragon*, ll. 2109–10); enter Jack Cade and his cohorts *'with infinite numbers'* (*2 Henry VI*, IV. ii. 28. s.d.).

Playscripts annotated for the playhouse also have their own distinctive features. R. B. McKerrow has argued that 'copy used or prepared for use at a theatre by a prompter or stage-manager' would be characterized by: 'warnings, either of actors who are to be ready for entry, or of properties which are required for use later' (e.g., sixty lines in advance the warning *'John Bacon ready to shoot off a Pistol'* in *Love's Pilgrimage*, VI, 290, 417); 'the mention, at the time of the entry of a character, of properties which he will require later in the scene, but either must not or need not exhibit to the audience at the time of entry' (e.g., a bloody handkerchief in *Cupid's Revenge*, a letter in *The Spanish Curate*); 'the mention of actor's names as a *gloss*'; and 'the entry of characters before the proper time.'[15] Theatrical annotators, moreover, are often much more specific about sound effects than authors. The 'plot' of *Troilus and Cressida* specifies six alarums, two retreats, and three tuckets; the 'plot' of *The Battle of Alcazar* provides *'sound sonnet'* or *'sound'* eleven times; the Padua *Macbeth* adds marginal notes calling for sounds in the battle scenes, a cry within, thunder, flourishes, and drums. Similarly, several of the extant playhouse manuscripts (e.g., *The Honest Man's Fortune*, *The Captives*, *The Two Noble Ladies*) include elaborate specifications for sound: alarums, flourishes, off-stage shouts, storm sounds, music, even a trampling of horses. R. C. Bald notes[16] that the printed text of *Beggar's Bush* (presumably based upon authorial copy) specifies at one point '*enter Sailor,*' but the manuscript of the same play (presumably a transcript of a playhouse manuscript) provides: '*Drum, flourish, pieces discharge. Enter sailors.*'

Thus, some of the signals in the extant manuscripts and printed texts sound distinctively authorial or theatrical. Nonetheless, nothing prevents a highly knowledgeable professional like Shakespeare or Heywood from conceiving of a scene in theatrical (as opposed to 'literary') terms, nor does the presence of a 'permissive' stage direction necessarily denote an authorial manuscript uncorrected for the playhouse. Earlier I cited Heywood's stage direction in *The Captives* ('*either strikes him with a staff or casts a stone*') that was not changed by the theatrical annotator; similarly, the playhouse manuscript of *John a Kent and John a Cumber* includes the call for a figure to come '*out of a tree, if possible it may be*' (l. 836). In his authoritative discussion over fifty years ago, W. W. Greg noted that playhouse manuscripts 'all preserve stage-directions and other features of a literary type very imperfectly assimilated to the requirements or the point of view of stage representation,' so that 'even when they have been extensively worked over by a stage reviser the assimilation to a technically theatrical type and language has been but imperfectly effected.' Rather, Greg states categorically that the 'assumption that a prompt Book must have been purely and severely theatrical in form and disposition' is 'quite unwarranted,' for the manuscripts from the playhouse 'are full of directions that at first sight suggest a purely literary origin.' Provided the author's signals were 'neither inconspicuous nor too long to be taken in at a glance,' the annotator, according to Greg, left them alone: 'so long as they were intelligible it mattered little to him the form in which they were couched.'[17]

Greg's strictures have not always been heeded by editors and stage historians who would prefer to base their inferences about the nature of printer's copy upon firmer distinctions between author and playhouse than may be warranted by his careful analysis of the surviving dramatic documents (manuscripts, 'plots,' and actor's parts). Also sometimes overlooked is another important distinction, a refinement upon Greg's use of the terms 'literary' and 'theatrical.' Thus, in Richard Hosley's terms, the scholar should distinguish between 'theatrical' signals that 'usually refer not to dramatic fiction but rather to theatrical structure or equipment' (e.g., *within, at another door, a scaffold thrust out, a curtain being drawn*) and 'fictional' signals that 'usually refer not to theatrical structure or equipment but rather to dramatic fiction' (e.g., *on shipboard, within the prison, upon the walls, enter the town*). This distinction, as Hosley notes, 'corresponds approximately to that drawn by textual critics between directions usually written by a book-keeper and by an author,' but for him the distinction lies not in the source but in 'the point of view,' for 'an author may occasionally write directions couched in the technical language of the theatre.'[18]

The failure to observe Hosley's distinction can lead to a misreading or oversimplification of some stage directions. Thus, Hosley briefly confronts the problem: were the public theatres 'permanently equipped with windows over the stage,' a question he terms 'moot.' The pictorial evidence, as he notes, provides no such windows; the 'windows' cited in dialogue and stage directions he finds 'almost invariably appropriate to the fiction.'[19] Consider a cluster of examples (mine rather than Hosley's) from Fletcher's plays. First, in *The Captain* Frank and Clora *'enter at the Window,'* deal with some figures below, and then depart, with the final line from Frank being 'shut the window' (v, 259–61). Here, the stage direction and the exit line *could* support a contention that the King's Men had such a window for this and other scenes. In *The Maid in the Mill* the men below talk of 'this, a goodly window too, / Carv'd far above' and 'hark, hark, a window, and a candle too,' and again the woman's exit line is 'pluck to the windows,' but in this play the two women are directed to enter *'above with a Taper'* (VII, 11–14). In *Wit at Several Weapons* the musicians brought in to serenade a lady are placed 'under her window' according to the dialogue, but the stage direction reads: *'Enter Niece above'* (IX, 98–9). Finally, in *The Woman's Prize* just before Moroso announces that 'the window opens,' the stage direction reads: *'Enter Maria and Bianca above'* (VIII, 15). On the one hand, if a window were available at the Globe or Blackfriars, *'enter above'* could indeed mean *'enter at the Window.'* Yet given the many relevant 'fictional' signals in Hosley's terms, a reference to a window (or a wall, gate, city, or garden) could rather represent an author thinking not of the staging but of the story (see also Brabantio's first appearance in *Othello*, Q–1) as strongly suggested in three of my four examples from Fletcher. Would Fletcher's audience have 'seen' a window? Or were they expected to supply a window through 'imaginary forces'? As Hosley has shown, awareness of the latter possibility can make a big difference in how we read and interpret Elizabethan stage directions.

By calling attention to the many problems, inconsistencies, and anomalies encountered when interpreting stage directions, I do not mean to suggest that nothing can be inferred, that all is lost before the investigation even starts. Rather, my purpose is to take every possible precaution at the outset so not to impose an inappropriate modern 'logic' upon the original logic of presentation (and not fall into the trap epitomized by Thurber's American lady). Behind the many different problems lies one indisputable fact that will continue to bedevil the modern detective: that the signals in the surviving Elizabethan playscripts were not intended for us. Rather, as R. B. McKerrow has noted, the original manuscript 'was merely the substance, or rather the bare bones, of a performance on the stage, intended to be interpreted by actors skilled in their craft, who would have no difficulty in reading it as it was meant to be read.'[20] As emphasized in my previous chapter, those manuscripts were theatrical scripts written to be performed by Elizabethan theatrical professionals, not literary texts written to be read by modern editors and critics. The author or annotator of such a script could therefore assume a language shared by actor and spectator that went beyond the words alone to include stage conventions, emblematic properties, and an overall logic that today we may no longer recognize or appreciate (the arrow in Nessus).

To deal justly with the surviving stage directions is therefore to be conscious of the various pitfalls awaiting the modern detective working with these Elizabethan clues. Like McKerrow, I would assume that the original actors knew their craft well and often did not need specific stage directions from the dramatist to tell them how to achieve particular effects. What may seem murky to us now probably made excellent sense then, with or without specific signals from the playwright. However, without access to that language of the theatre shared then by dramatists, actors, and spectators, the scholar today can only work with whatever scraps of evidence have chanced to survive and then indulge in inference, hypothesis, and conjecture, all to recapture what would have been obvious to an untutored groundling at the Globe. And the only substantial basis for such conjectures and often labyrinthine reasoning lies in those unsatisfying, inconsistent, puzzling, and often tantalizing stage directions.

Obviously, what is needed are ways to minimize the various problems without creating new ones. Thus, Hosley's essays demonstrate the distinct advantages in treating related stage directions as parts of a larger group or genus. Indeed, some of the problems encountered by editors and stage historians have arisen when such evidence has been viewed in isolation, especially one curious signal in one play. Rare or unique examples can easily lead to misleading inferences about stage practice and authorial intentions, whereas missing the fact that a stage direction can be found in a wide range of playscripts can also subvert a scholar's argument. Such a plea for a wider perspective is by no means a new one. Thus, for T. W. Craik the ideal interpreter of stage action 'will read each play with every other Elizabethan play simultaneously in mind.'[21] In a substantial essay, E. A. J. Honigmann has provided several examples of how editors can be misled when they look 'too narrowly at a single play.' Rather, as he observes, 'we are only ready to interpret stage directions when we have identified them as members of a group.'[22] Since philologians, linguists, and iconographers have demonstrated the advantages of such a comparative approach for the reconstruction of lost meanings, should not such a method also be appropriate for recovering the lost language of the theatre?

Much then depends upon what constitutes such a group for the editor or stage historian. As a point of departure, consider the brief stage direction provided by Massinger in *A New Way to Pay Old Debts*: '*Overreach as from dinner*' (III. iii. o. s.d.). Subsequent dialogue establishes that Sir Giles has left the table in anger; thus Marrall enters to say: 'Sir the whole board is troubled at your rising' (l. 13). But, for a modern reader, '*as from dinner*' conjures up no clear picture of stage action. Rather, to the editor or critic viewing this scene in isolation it may appear to be a 'literary' signal geared to a reader rather than a 'theatrical' signal geared to an actor or spectator. Since the dialogue includes the information about the interrupted dinner, why include this stage direction at all?

But Massinger's terse signal makes a good deal more sense when seen as part of a larger group or series in which other examples supply revealing details. For example: '*Enter Tucca brushing off the crumbs*' (*Satiromastix*, III. i. 98. s.d.); enter '*Robin having his napkin on his shoulder, as if he were suddenly raised from dinner*' (*The Downfall of Robert Earl of Huntingdon*, ll. 166–8); enter some shoemakers '*all with napkins on their shoulders*' (*The Shoemakers' Holiday*, v. iv. o. s.d.); '*Enter Master Frankford, as it were brushing the Crumbs from his clothes with a Napkin, as newly risen from supper*' (*A Woman Killed With Kindness*, II, 118); enter Neatfoot '*with a napkin on his shoulder, and a trencher in his hand as from table*' (*The Roaring Girl*, I. i. o. s.d.); enter some nobles hastily '*with napkins on their arms and knives in their hands*' (*Woodstock*, ll. 1–3); '*Enter Petruchio and Nibrassa with napkins, as from supper*' (*Love's Sacrifice*, H1r). In *The Wise Woman of Hogsdon*, figures not included in an off-stage meal are joined by a servant '*with a Trencher, with broken meat and a Napkin*'; finally, '*enter Chartly with his Napkin as from Dinner*' (v, 335–6). From a wide range of plays that spans several decades emerges a shared effect based upon recurring details (real or imaginary crumbs, napkins, trenchers, eating implements) quite practical in the theatre. Initially, '*as from dinner*' may seem 'literary' or impractical to a modern reader, but Massinger (or Munday or Dekker or Heywood or Ford) knew that the actors could act out such a signal simply yet effectively for their spectators. My purpose in citing what may appear to be an excessive number of examples is not to display the number of plays I have read but rather to suggest the presence then of a shared language of the theatre common to dramatist, actor, annotator, and spectator.

Similar '*as from*' signals recur throughout the extant plays, both with and without suggestive details. Thus, figures are directed to enter: '*as newly come from play*' (*The Wise Woman of Hogsdon*, v, 279); '*as at Dice*' (*Valentinian*, IV, 17); '*in their shirts, as from Torments*' (*A Shoemaker a Gentleman*, H3r); '*as robbed*' (*Love's Pilgrimage*, VI, 262); '*as in the field*' [i.e., awaiting a duel] (*The Little French Lawyer*, III, 391); and '*as it were in retire*' from a battle (*Coriolanus*, I. vi. o. s.d.). Some of the more vivid examples include: enter '*as being thrown off his horse, and falls*' (*A Yorkshire Tragedy*, l. 632); '*as out of a cave's mouth*'

(*Sophonisba or The Wonder of Women*, E2v); '*as out of a Bush*' (*The Two Noble Kinsmen*, IX, 325); '*all wet as newly ship-wrecked and escaped the fury of the seas*' (*The Captives*, ll. 653–4); and '*as newly landed and half naked*' (*The Four Prentices of London*, II, 176). The entrance of figures in *Pericles* '*from tilting*' (II. iii. o. s.d.) is amplified by the appearance of King Arthur in *Tom a Lincoln* '*with a spear in his rest, as from the tilt*' (13b). To my knowledge, no play provides '*as from fishing*' or '*as from bowling*,' but Dekker does give us: '*Enter Janicola with an Angling rod, Grissil with a reel*' (*Patient Grissil*, v. i. 56. s.d.); and Field supplies: '*Enter Sir Abraham throwing down his Bowls*' (*A Woman is a Weathercock*, III. iii. o. s.d.). In *The Telltale*, a figure enters with a '*Barber as having trimmed him*' (l. 1773); in *Claudius Tiberius Nero* Caligula is to appear '*with a Racket and Tennis-ball in his hand*' (ll. 1306–7).

A large and distinctive group can be found in the many plays that call for figures to enter '*as from hunting*' (*The Late Lancashire Witches*, IV, 171) or, more commonly, '*from hunting*' (e.g., *The Taming of the Shrew*, Induction, i. 13. s.d.; *The Taming of a Shrew*, A2r; *Titus Andronicus*, II. iv. 10. s.d.; *Demetrius and Enanthe*, l. 187). Even the theatrical 'plot' of 2 *The Seven Deadly Sins* calls for Tereus to appear '*from Hunting with his Lords.*' To achieve this effect, the dramatists and actors relied heavily upon sound effects and costumes. Thus, '*wind horns*' appears in so many plays it is pointless to list titles. For two especially elaborate moments, consider the sequence in *The Shoemakers' Holiday*: '*Hallooing within*'; '*A noise of hunters within*'; '*Hunting within*'; and '*Horns sound within*' (II. i. o. s.d., 9. s.d., II. ii. o. s.d., 9. s.d.); and the stage picture evoked in *Summer's Last Will and Testament*: '*Enter Orion like a hunter, with a horn about his neck; all his Men after the same sort hallooing and blowing their horns*'; these figures then exeunt '*blowing their horns and hallooing as they came in*' (pp. 106, 110).[23] Orion's entrance '*like a hunter,*' moreover, is echoed elsewhere (e.g., *Patient Grissil*, I. i. o. s.d., *The Shoemakers' Holiday*, II. i. o. s.d.); in *The Insatiate Countess* first Guiaca, then Guido is directed to enter '*in his hunting weeds*' (F1r, F2v). Often this costume for the hunt is linked specifically to the color green. Thus, Henslowe's inventory includes green garments for Robin Hood and Marian;[24] then, in Munday's play, the two figures are to enter '*all in green*' (*The Downfall of Robert Earl of Huntingdon*, l. 1260) as are figures in various Heywood plays (*1 Edward IV*, I, 40; *The Silver Age*, III, 146; *The Brazen Age*, III, 187) and a group in Peele's *Edward I* (l. 1368). Many plays, it should be noted, specify no sounds or costumes or colors but rather establish a forest locale or the atmosphere of the hunt by calling for the presence of huntsmen or woodsmen with no further indication of how such figures are to be attired.[25]

Besides sound effects and distinctive costume, hunting scenes often include weapons or other portable properties: a falconer's lure (*Look About You*); crossbows (*3 Henry VI*); various combinations of bows, quivers, and javelins.[26] In *Woodstock*, the treacherous masquers enter '*like Diana's knights led in by four other knights: (in green) with horns about their necks and boarspears in their hands*' (ll. 2119–20). In the quarto of *2 Henry VI*, where the royal party is to enter '*as if they came from hawking*,' the queen appears '*with her Hawk on her fist*' (C1v). To climax a successful hunt, Munday brings on a stag's head (*The Death of Robert Earl of Huntingdon*); Heywood brings on Hercules '*with the Lion's head and skin*' (*The Silver Age*, III, 131); and Fletcher brings on Diocles '*with a Boar*' (*The Prophetess*, V, 325). By far the most elaborate example is the hunt for the Caledonian boar in *The Brazen Age*. Heywood starts with Venus dressed '*like a Huntress*,' horns wound off-stage as 'the summons to the chase,' a group of heroes '*with Javelins, and in green*,' and Atlanta '*with a Javelin.*' Then follow: '*Enter Adonis winding his horn ... a great winding of horns, and shouts*'; cries of 'charge, charge' and reports of wounds and pursuits; '*horns and shouts ... horns ... After great shouts, enter Venus ... A cry within.*' After the dying Adonis is carried on and off and '*the fall of the Boar being winded*,' the successful hunters enter '*with the head of the Boar*' and '*with their javelins bloodied*' (III, 184–94).

What then are the advantages of regarding the '*as from*' or '*from hunting*' stage directions as a group? Readers familiar with Elizabethan plays will have no difficulty compiling a list of banquets and other elaborate events actually presented on stage; nonetheless, certain types of scenes (e.g., hunts, fires, shipwrecks, public executions) often were not displayed, either to increase the narrative flow or to sidestep significant problems. Remember, for the most part we are dealing with repertory companies presenting four to six plays per week on a bare platform stage using mostly portable properties and having no access to formal sets, variable lighting, or a fourth wall curtain. With or without the accompanying details, the '*as from*' stage direction represents an essential part of the strategy for using such a stage, a strategy that builds upon a few clear signals and the actor's skill to convey, deftly and economically, a recently completed or continuing action (again the arrow in Nessus principle). What results is a theatrical shorthand for the spectator, an alternative to a full scene or more extensive narrative detail. To be sure, in a Shakespeare play such details may be part of a larger metaphoric or symbolic effect (so in *Titus Andronicus* the entrance of Marcus '*from hunting*' in II. iv clearly is linked to the maimed Lavinia and the Andronici as prey), but the general usage is more basic, even elementary – a way of telling a story on stage in an economical yet theatrically telling fashion. At its best, such a technique can create for the spectator a sense of a rich, busy, very 'real' world just off-stage.

Obviously, in drawing upon many plays and many stage directions I have not distinguished between authorial and playhouse sources or between 'fictional' and 'theatrical' points of view. Thus, to a discerning eye or ear '*from hunting*' may sound fictional whereas '*as from hunting*' may sound theatrical. Similarly, a general signal ('*as from dinner*') might be deemed authorial while the specific details used to implement the effect might be considered the province of the actor. Although such inferences may be valid, it is also possible (as suggested by Greg, McKerrow, and Hosley) that experienced dramatists like Dekker, Heywood, Fletcher, and Munday (or even an inexperienced dramatist who was a regular playgoer) could have supplied the relevant details, whereas an actor or annotator who knew his craft would have found a general signal adequate in his script. Also to be taken into account are authorial idiosyncrasies. Note that I started with an example from Massinger, brief though it was, but then, despite his canon of seventeen plays, offered no further evidence from him. Massinger's plays do include scenes and entrances relevant to these categories, but, unlike Dekker and Heywood, he apparently left much of the implementation to the players. Thus, in a hunt scene from *The Emperor of the East* a stage direction calls for '*Huntsmen*' (IV. i. 63) and the subsequent dialogue alludes to stags and hounds; then, when the hunt is over, Theo-

dosius orders: 'lay by / These accoutrements for the chase' (IV.
iv. 7–8). Here Massinger specifies no bows, spears, javelins,
horns, or green costumes, but rather leaves the on-stage
implementation of 'accoutrements for the chase' to the actors.
Despite the impression given by my mass of details above, such
lack of specificity is the rule rather than the exception in
Elizabethan scripts. Thus, although I cited various '*as from
shipwreck*' details in the previous chapter, the norm is best seen
in *Twelfth Night*: '*Enter Viola, a Captain, and Sailors*' (I. ii. o.
s.d.).

For the most part, then, in the analyses that follow I will not
be working closely with the sources of the stage directions I cite
(i.e., author, annotator, scribe, or actor) even though I recognize
the potential importance of such distinctions, and, except when
necessary, will not be making fine discriminations about point
of view (i.e., theatrical versus fictional). As seen in the examples
already cited, signals range from the very general ('*as from
dinner*') to the very specific, with many seemingly relevant
scenes providing little or no information. My goal is to use the
evidence that *has* survived to understand better other scenes
where details are lacking, especially those in Shakespeare's
plays. Granted, such a comparative approach has its risks (and
some readers undoubtedly will balk at my conjectures at the end
of this chapter), but, at the least, this method is grounded in
probability (some dramatists or players *did* set up their scenes
this way) rather than solely in flights of modern interpretative
fancy.

To some extent, my claims so far may seem exaggerated, for
many readers, particularly actors and directors, will have had
no difficulty translating '*as from dinner*' or '*as from hunting*'
into appropriate stage action, with or without support from
other plays of the period. Indeed, a recent modern dress production of *Timon of Athens* (Oregon Shakespearean Festival,
1978) used costume and properties to display two of Timon's
false friends entering '*as from tennis*' and '*as from swimming.*'
But some stage directions will call upon associations shared by
actors and spectators then but less accessible, even lost today
(an equivalent, in the popular theatre, to the emblems and icons
in the learned tradition). Deciphering such visual signals today
therefore requires both a good sense of theatre (again, a distinc-

tion between scripts and texts) and fluency in a language for the eye that may at times be as difficult to translate into a modern idiom as Caliban's 'scamels.'

A full account of such potential stage images or conventions as reflected in groups of stage directions would require a separate study, so let me concentrate here upon three categories, each easy to document, each relevant to some key scenes in Shakespeare, but each seldom treated as a meaningful group by modern scholars. Consider first the following series of mostly non-specific signals: '*Enter Ophelia distracted*' (*Hamlet*, Folio, l. 2766); '*Enter Bellafront mad*' (1 *The Honest Whore*, v. ii. 299. s.d.); '*Enter Ann Ratcliff mad*' (*The Witch of Edmonton*, IV. i. 172. s.d.); '*Enter Merione (as newly ravished)*' (*The Queen of Corinth*, VI, 17); enter '*Lavinia, her hands cut off, and her tongue cut out, and ravished*' (*Titus Andronicus*, II. iv. 0. s.d.). This signal even turns up in one of the 'plots': '*Enter Carinus mad; to him Prelior mad*' (*The Dead Man's Fortune*, IV. iii).

Granted, one cannot assume the presence of any one signal or set of signals to denote madness or rape; rather, the responsibility for conveying such an effect must fall largely upon the actor. Nonetheless, a significant number of plays in the age of Shakespeare does provide one such signal, especially for the boy actor playing a female figure distraught with madness, shame, extreme grief, or the effects of recent violence. Most familiar are the Shakespearean examples: '*Enter Cassandra with her hair about her ears*' (*Troilus and Cressida*, II. ii, Folio, ll. 1082–3); '*Enter the Queen with her hair about her ears*' (*Richard III*, II. ii. Folio, l. 1306); '*Enter Ophelia playing on a Lute, and her hair down singing*' (*Hamlet*, IV. v, Q–1, G4v). In the manuscript of *Dick of Devonshire*, Eleonora, who has just been raped, enters '*loose haired, and weeping*' (ll. 687–9); similarly, in the manuscript of *The Swisser*, the ravished Eurinia appears '*with her hair about her ears*' (IV. i. 0. s.d.). In Massinger's *The Unnatural Combat*, after an off-stage rape, '*The Soldiers thrust forth Theocrine, her garments loose, her hair disheveled*' (v. ii. 185. s.d.); in *A Warning for Fair Women*, after the corruption of Anne Sanders has been acted out in dumb show, Chastity enters '*with her hair disheveled*' (E3v). Hair about the ears can indicate public shame (2 *Edward IV*, *The Insatiate Countess*, *The Bloody Banquet*, *The Emperor of the East*) or high passion (*Northward Ho*) or mourning (*Swetnam the Woman-*

Hater Arraigned by Women) or madness (*1 The Iron Age, Tom a Lincoln*). Although one can note an occasional man with disordered hair (Humber in *Locrine*, Saturn in *The Golden Age*), most of the examples are female. One famous modern example can be found in Peter Brook's landmark 1955 production of *Titus Andronicus* in which Lavinia, as played by Vivien Leigh, *did* enter with her hair down in this manner; in contrast, in the 1977 production of *Richard III* at Stratford Festival Canada, Maggie Smith as a grief-stricken Queen Elizabeth did not change her hair for her entrance.

Such choices made in recent productions can be instructive, for what may seem an intrusive or impractical detail to the modern actress may, in contrast, have been easily accessible for the boy actor and visually meaningful for the Elizabethan spectator. Thus, unlike the actress today who must often worry about her coiffure, the original boy actor need only have changed his wig to set up a strikingly different image that, in turn, could convey a severe change in the state of the character. Such an entrance is then particularly effective if previously the viewer had seen the same figure impeccably attired. For example, early in *1 The Honest Whore* Dekker provides Bellafront with an elaborate dressing scene in which, among other things, she '*curls her hair, colors her lips*' (II. i. 12. s.d.). If then in Act v she does enter with her hair about her ears (the stage direction only specifies '*mad*'), this climactic visual configuration would be in striking contrast to our image of her throughout the play. In addition to aiding narrative economy, such an effect can also provide a clear visual display of the falling away from or the destruction of a previous image of order, as with Hamlet's new antic costume in Act II as described by Ophelia: 'his doublet all unbraced, / No hat upon his head, his stockings fouled, / Ungartered, and down-gyvèd to his ankle' (II. i. 78–80). For other clear violations of orderly patterns, remember too the interrupted dance at the end of Prospero's masque in Act IV of *The Tempest* or the opening stage direction of *The Malcontent* which calls for '*the vilest out-of-tune music.*' Without undervaluing the importance of the actor's skill in playing madness or distress, the scholar can still recognize the metaphoric and symbolic potential in 'loose' or 'disheveled' hair, a potential that can extend beyond the psychological state of the individual character.

As with my earlier groups, the extant scripts provide no disheveled hair for some scenes that may have included that detail in the original productions. Thus, in *Valentinian* Lucina enters with her ravisher, the Emperor (IV, 35), but neither in stage direction or dialogue does Fletcher refer to hair or other details, a silence also observed at the entrance of Jacenta after a rape in Rowley's *All's Lost by Lust* (III. i. o. s.d.). Most revealing are the three versions of Ophelia's entrance in IV. v, our first view of her madness. The second or 'good' quarto, the basis for modern editions, provides only '*Enter Ophelia*' (K4r); as noted earlier, the Folio expands this signal slightly: '*Enter Ophelia distracted*' (l. 2766); and the first or 'bad' quarto, presumably drawing upon an actor's memory of how the scene was staged in some production, reads: '*Enter Ophelia playing on a Lute, and her hair down singing*' (G4v). Q–2's minimal signal is typical of Elizabethan practice, for here the author provides a mad scene and leaves the details of the staging to the actors (or, in Shakespeare's case, communicates any further pointers orally to his colleagues). The Folio's '*distracted*,' which to the reader today merely conveys what he or she can readily discern from reading the scene, to the original players may have signaled one or another conventional way of playing madness.[27] What is unusual in this case is the survival of the information in the Q–1 stage direction – in contrast, for example, to the total lack of information in the Folio (the sole surviving script) about Lady Macbeth's appearance at the outset of her sleep-walking scene. Some modern editors exclude the first quarto's details from their texts, reasoning that the 'good' quarto is very close to Shakespeare's draft but a 'bad' quarto that may have been put together from memory cannot be expected to show 'fidelity to its author.' But the details here may be of considerable interest to the historian or the imagist (see chapter seven for a discussion of the lute). How is Baptista to be costumed in the dumb show when she '*makes passionate action*' (III. ii. 129. s.d.)? How is Gertrude to be coiffured in the closet scene or at Ophelia's grave? When investigating this rich, complex tragedy, can one dismiss *any* evidence?

A second category that includes an even larger number of plays further demonstrates the potential meaning in a visible stage detail. Again, to start in general terms, several plays call for figures to enter '*as it were in haste*' (*The Downfall of Robert Earl of Huntingdon*, l. 142) or *'in great haste'* (*Sir John Oldcastle*, l. 1329) or *'hastily'* (*Coriolanus*, I. i. 217. s.d.). Particularly with messengers and clowns, such haste can be conveyed through the speed of the entrance alone. Thus, the call for a figure to enter *'running'* is quite common,[28] while a clownish figure in *1 The Fair Maid of the West* is to appear *'falling for haste'* (II, 315). To convey a hasty arrival is well within the province of the actor (and can be a good source of comedy).

But a wealth of evidence is available to document a specific bit of theatrical shorthand to enhance this effect. Thus, although I have found no examples of *'as from riding'* or *'as going on a journey,'* the dramatists and actors regularly used boots and related apparel to make the same point. For example, in *Sir Thomas Wyatt* Northumberland asks: 'Sir Thomas booted and spurr'd / Whither away so fast?' (I. i. 21–2); in *Sir John Oldcastle* Scroop says of the hero: 'here comes the man himself / Booted and spurr'd, it seems he hath been riding' (ll. 1044–5); in *The Widow's Tears* Tharsalio asks Lysander: 'What, sir, unbooted? Have you been long arrived?' (V. iii. 87). Other items of costume could serve the same function: *'Enter Longueville with a riding-rod'* (*The Honest Man's Fortune*, X, 255); *'Enter Sir Petronell in Boots with a riding wand'* (*Eastward Ho*, C2r). An appropriate signal, moreover, was available for the ladies: *'Enter Winnifred in a riding-suit'* (*The Witch of Edmonton*, I. i. 155. s.d.); *'Enter Jane in haste, in her riding-cloak and safe-guard, with a pardon in her hand'* (*2 Edward IV*, I, 139).[29] But the recurring detail most often associated with haste or a journey recently completed or a journey about to be undertaken is the stage boot. Thus, when a group of figures arrive at an inn in *The Merry Devil of Edmonton*, the stage direction calls for *'the men booted, the gentlewomen in cloaks and safe-guards'* (B1r); in *The Fair Maid of the Exchange*, a figure about to go on a journey is *'booted'* but his friend who remains behind is not (II, 41). For one who reads widely in Elizabethan plays, *'enter booted'* is a very familiar stage direction.[30]

Often the dialogue spells out the associations to be linked to boots and riding apparel. Thus, in *Friar Bacon and Friar Bungay*, the gentlemen arrive *'booted and spurred,'* with Lacy announcing: 'we have hied and posted all this night to Fressingfield' (ll. 1935, 2002–3). *Northward Ho*, with its many journeys and quick exits, has an unusually large number of stage directions that call for boots; at one point Mayberry concludes: 'Come, boots boy, we must gallop all the way' (IV. i. 276–7). Such connotations are best displayed in Act V of 2 *Henry IV*. First, Justice Shallow urges Falstaff not to depart, with the injunction: 'Come, come, come, off with your boots' (V. i. 48). Falstaff's reaction to the news of Henry IV's death then includes 'get on thy boots. We'll ride all night' and 'boot, boot, Master Shallow. I know the young king is sick for me. Let us take any man's horses' (V. iii. 128, ˙131–2). While awaiting the coronation procession, Falstaff argues that his zeal, devotion, and 'earnestness of affection' will be evident in his willingness 'to ride day and night' and 'not to have patience to shift me' but rather 'to stand stained with travel, and sweating with desire to see him' (V. v. 13–27). The boots and travel-stained costume are thereby interpreted by the wearer as an index to his commitment – 'as if there were nothing else to be done but to see him' (ll. 26–7).

My third and largest group draws upon over sixty plays. Thus, twelve of them provide a general signal that figures should enter '*as from bed*' or '*as newly risen*' or '*as newly waked from sleep*' or '*as from their chamber.*' Similarly, figures often are directed to enter '*unready,*' as with a group of surprised Greeks who appear '*half unready, as newly started from their beds*'[31] (2 *The Iron Age*, III, 413). More specific stage directions then suggest various ways to signal unreadiness or '*as from bed.*' Thus, in some morning scenes: enter '*trussing their points as new up*' (*The Merry Devil of Edmonton*, E4r, F2r); enter Moll '*lacing of her clothes*' (*The Puritan*, H2r); '*enter Master Honeysuckle in his night-cap trussing himself*' (*Westward Ho*, II. i. 0. s.d.). On-stage unreadiness can then set up comic effects ('*enter Rusticano with one hose off the other on, without any britches*' – *Tom a Lincoln*, 37a) or contribute to a climate of tension: '*Enter at one door Alexandra in her petticoat; at another, Aristobulus the high Priest in his waistcoat or shirt, both amazedly*' (*Herod and Antipater*, I. i. 0. s.d.); '*Alarum, with men and women half naked: enter two Captains without doublets, with swords*' (*King Leir*, ll. 2476–7); '*Enter Widow undressed, a sword in her hand, and Bould in his shirt, as started from bed*' (*Amends for Ladies*, IV. i. 1–2). As in the example from *Leir*, a failure to 'watch' properly that then leaves one vulnerable to one's enemies often is associated with unreadiness in clothing: in the sacking of Troy in 2 *The Iron Age* (where much is made of 'unready' and 'naked' Trojans); in the capture of Edward IV in 3 *Henry VI* (see especially IV. iii. 27. s.d.); and most clearly in 1 *Henry VI* where, at Talbot's attack on Orleans, '*the French leap o'er the walls in their shirts*' and three French leaders appear '*half ready and half unready*' (II. i. 38. s.d.).

But references to points, trussing, shirts, night-caps, and general unreadiness are far outnumbered by the more than thirty plays with stage directions that call for nightgowns. M. Channing Linthicum describes this Elizabethan garment as 'an ankle-length gown with long sleeves and collar varying in size ... worn for warmth both indoors and out.' She then argues strenuously against those scholars who 'have tried to prove that night-gowns were for night wear in one's chamber'; rather, to 'show the error of this assumption' she cites 'many accounts'[32] (actually three). Linthicum may well be right that off the stage in the 'real world' a nightgown was not limited to a private chamber, much less a bedroom, but, with the possible exception of naturalistic drama, evidence from contemporary life cannot prove conclusively anything about on-stage activity, especially in a drama that draws heavily upon theatrical shorthand and stage metaphor. Thus, although Linthicum can cite a diary reference from Lady Anne Clifford in 1617 that 'I went to Church in my rich night gown,' the Shakespearean can counter with Margaret's comment to Hero that the Duchess of Milan's wedding gown was 'but a nightgown in respect of yours' (*Much Ado*, III. iv. 17–18). Similarly, Linthicum's allusion to Lady Jane Grey wearing a nightgown on the scaffold at her execution in *Sir Thomas Wyatt* does not take into account the potential symbolic value of the costume, a set of associations developed clearly in 2 *Edward IV* where the two little princes enter '*in their gowns and caps, unbuttoned, and untrussed*' (1, 153–4) and then, in their speeches, equate going to bed with going to their graves. Although I cannot offer a detailed description of the stage version of a nightgown, I can demonstrate a clear and consistent connection with night, morning, bed, unreadiness, or some combination thereof.

This ubiquitous garment could serve a variety of functions. On the simplest level, it provided a quick signal that placed the on-stage action at night or in the early morning (either in place of or along with the candles and torches also used to denote stage night or darkness). Thus, a dumb show in *The White Devil* calls for Isabella to enter '*in her nightgown as to bed-ward, with lights after her*' (II. ii. 23. s.d.). Many examples can be cited of such theatrical shorthand: enter the count, in a morning scene, '*in his shirt and night gown*' to spy upon his wife (*An Humourous Day's Mirth*, l. 1); enter the widow '*in her night-clothes, as going to bed*' (*A Match at Midnight*, H2r); enter Psyche '*in night-attire, with a Lamp and a Razor*' to discover the identity of Cupid[33] (*Love's Mistress*, V, 120). To escape pursuit in the middle of the night, enter Sir John Oldcastle '*in his gown stealing*' (l. 2210); to pursue a seduction at night, enter the duke '*in a gown*' (*Rule a Wife and Have a Wife*, III, 229). After the brides have been stolen in *John a Kent*, the bridegrooms come forth in the morning '*in their nightgowns and kerchers on their heads*'; shortly thereafter, two figures enter '*unbraced*,' then a third '*in his night gown*' – all this from a playhouse manuscript (ll. 582, 596, 604). Occasionally, the stage nightgown could convey other associations (e.g., to help characterize the convalescent Dorothea in *James IV*), but a high percentage of the relevant stage directions signal the time (either night or early morning) along with connotations of unreadiness, furtiveness, surprise, or lust.

Not surprisingly, the stage nightgown often turns up in a sexual or romantic context. Heywood, for one, provides several 'morning-after' scenes, as in *The Golden Age* where, after an elaborate seduction that involves lights, a bed, and making unready, Jupiter re-enters with '*Danae in her night-gown*' (III, 70). Similarly, in *The English Traveller* two lovers enter after a night together '*in a Night-gown*' and '*in a night-tire, as coming from Bed*'; after an exchange of pleasantries ('a happy Morning now betide you Lady, / To equal the content of a sweet Night'), the wife is urged to 'retire you / To your warm Sheets; I now to fill my own, / That have this Night been empty' (IV, 70–1). Although no such signals are provided, I suspect that the same effect may have been found at the entrance of Antony and Cleopatra in IV. iv (where the queen urges 'sleep a little' before she helps to arm Antony) and at the outset of *Troilus and Cressida*, IV. ii (where Troilus tells Cressida 'trouble not yourself' but return 'to bed, to bed').

The unreadiness noted earlier in several historical plays can also be found in romantic situations. Thus, in *The Two Maids of More-Clacke*, Sir William calls forth his wife, who appears '*in her*

night gown, and night attire'; a few lines later she brings in her
would-be lover, '*unready, in his night-cap, garterless*' (E3v). In *A
Woman Killed With Kindness*, after Wendoll and Anne have been
surprised in bed off-stage, we see the seducer '*running over the
stage in a Night-gown*'; moments later, Anne enters '*in her
smock, Night-gown, and night attire*' (II, 138, 139). In *The Great
Duke of Florence*, the father of a strikingly beautiful daughter,
roused from sleep by an emissary from the duke, enters '*in a
night-Gown*' (II. ii. 43. s.d.). The emissary asks 'pardon for
disturbing / Your rest at this unseasonable hour' (II. iii. 19–20);
quickly, that disturbance becomes a threat to both father and
daughter.

The associations with interrupted sleep or other disturbances at
night sometimes link nightgowns or unready dress with troubled
consciences. Thus, after Lord de Averne and Dennis have murdered Friar John in *The Captives*, the knight enters '*half unready*';
he is then questioned by his lady about 'these unquiet sleeps' and
tells Dennis that 'strange thoughts solicit me.' After being told to
'awake and rise in haste,' Dennis enters '*half unready,*' complaining that 'my Lord hath done a mischief / And now I must not
sleep for't' (ll. 2464, 2468, 2498, 2491, 2512, 2518–19).
Remember, in the first quarto of *Hamlet* the ghost in the closet
scene is directed to enter not in the armor of Act I but '*in his night
gown*' (G2v), a potentially revealing distinction often ignored in
modern editions, productions, and criticism. Less ambiguous or
puzzling is the situation in *2 Henry IV* where the king enters '*in his
nightgown*' (III. i. o. s.d.) to deliver the soliloquy on troubled sleep
that climaxes with 'uneasy lies the head that wears a crown.'

The ghost's nightgown in *Hamlet*, like Hamlet's leap or
Ophelia's lute and disheveled hair, provides another example of a
potentially meaningful signal of which we hear nothing in the two
'better' texts. Since roughly half of Shakespeare's plays appear for
the first time in the Folio and since some of those texts have sparse
stage directions, we often have no way of knowing how much
theatrical information has been lost for plays with no quartos,
'good' or 'bad.' Where multiple versions of a play *are* to be found,
interesting variations inevitably turn up. In addition to examples
already cited, the second or 'good' quarto of *Romeo and Juliet*
provides only '*enter Romeo's man*' in v. i (K4r), but the first
quarto reads: '*enter Balthasar his man booted*' (I3r); conversely,

the second quarto but not the first has Old Capulet enter in a gown in the opening scene (A4r). Brabantio's nightgown is found in the 1622 quarto of *Othello* but not the 1623 Folio; the hawk on Queen Margaret's fist appears in the quarto of *2 Henry VI* but not the Folio. In the manuscript of *Demetrius and Enanthe*, the hero is directed to enter '*from hunting*' (l. 187), but in the Folio the signal is: '*Enter Demetrius with a Javelin*' (*The Humourous Lieutenant*, II, 285). In the manuscript of *The Woman's Prize*, the opening stage direction calls for a group to enter '*as from a wedding*' but the Folio adds: '*with Rosemary*' (VIII, 2).

Given the wealth of information about some effects, even a silence can be interesting. To focus upon Massinger again, in *The Great Duke of Florence* Cozimo tells Sanazarro, who has just returned from a journey: 'You have rode hard Sir, / And we thank you for it' (III. i. 180–1). Similarly, in *The Duke of Milan* Sforza is told that 'the Marquis of Pescara, tir'd with haste, / Hath business that concerns your life and fortunes, / And with speed to impart' (I. iii. 220–2). Moments later, Pescara announces: 'my haste forbids / All compliment' (ll. 239–40); the message delivered, he is told 'pray take your rest' and responds: 'Indeed, I have travelled hard' (l. 264). Both passages correspond closely to situations in other plays where boots are specified, but Massinger provides no such signals. Nor does Shakespeare call for Leontes to wear a nightgown in II. iii although quite a few lines would suggest such a costume (e.g., ll. 1, 31, 38–9). Similarly, in the Ralph Crane transcript of *The Witch* a servant called forth suddenly in the middle of the night pleads 'give me leave to clothe myself' (l. 1666), but Middleton (or Crane) provides no specific indication of 'unreadiness' or a nightgown. These and other similar examples are typical of many if not most Elizabethan playscripts wherein relatively little information survives about costume, properties, action, and theatrical conventions. The mass of detail set forth in this chapter, culled from a wide net cast out over approximately four hundred plays, can therefore be misleading, for (especially if one discounts the canons of Heywood and Fletcher) the cumulative effect upon the reader quite belies the poverty of documentation within most individual plays including those of Shakespeare. Again, dramatists, actors, and annotators often saw no need to write down for us what would have been obvious to them.

To provide the reader with at least some sense of the implications of both the evidence and the silences, let me offer some
admittedly conjectural suggestions about staging and interpretation in several Shakespeare plays. First, the most suggestive use
of the stage boot is to be found in v. ii of *Richard II* where, after
discovering the plot against Henry IV, the Duke of York calls for
his boots, '*his Man enters with his boots*,' and, after some stage
business involving his servant and his duchess (usually presented
as a tug-of-war over the boots), York puts them on. Although
critics and directors usually treat this scene in terms of its
potential for comedy, York's decision here (strongly linked to the
putting on of boots) and his reappearance booted before the king
in the next scene may form part of a meaningful sequence keyed to
the eye of the spectator. Thus, in ii. i when Northumberland asks
two disaffected lords if they wish to join him in going over to
Bolingbroke, Ross responds: 'To horse, to horse! Urge doubts to
them that fear' and Willoughby: 'Hold out my horse, and I will
first be there' (ll. 299–300). Two scenes later, Northumberland
introduces the two arriving nobles to Bolingbroke with: 'Here
come the Lords of Ross and Willoughby, / Bloody with spurring,
fiery red with haste' (II. iii. 57–8), an introduction that for me
sounds like '*enter booted*.' York's calling for his boots and his exit
in v. ii would then correspond to the departure of the two lords in
II. i, while his arrival, booted, before the king in v. iii would
parallel the arrival of Ross and Willoughby 'bloody with spurring, fiery red with haste' to Bolingbroke in II. iii.[34] Both arrival
scenes, moreover, are about divided allegiances. In the earlier,
York (as Richard II's Lord Governor) had provided only limited
resistance to the returning Bolingbroke; in the later sequence,
however, it is York himself (rather than Ross and Willoughby)
who, through his haste, acts out a spirited commitment to Henry,
now the *de facto* king. The figures who burst in upon the king in v.
iii again act out divided loyalties in England, with the switch in
York's role (as opposed to II. iii) telling us a great deal about new
allegiances under the new king. The one stage direction from v. ii
and the hints in the dialogue would then be the only surviving
evidence of a visual pattern used to link figures who choose the
new king over old allegiances, whether political or familial.

Shakespeare then provides another figure who makes a significant departure to reappear in haste on Bolingbroke's behalf.

Thus, after his brief speech that builds to 'come, let's go' (v. iv. 7–11), Sir Pierce Exton's purposeful exit parallels those at the end of II. i and v. ii. Again, a figure has chosen Henry over Richard, but this choice leads not to a pledge of service or a series of kneelings but to the murder of the deposed king. Certainly, I cannot prove that the arrival of Exton and his men to murder Richard involved booted figures (the stage direction reads: '*the Murderers rush in*' – v. v. 104) any more than I can prove Willoughby and Ross were booted in II. iii, but, on one level, the stage shorthand would suit well the haste and the journeys involved and, on a deeper level, the three booted entrances (including York's in v. iii), all presumably 'bloody with spurring, fiery red with haste,' would link for the viewer's eye three different choices or sets of choosers, each in haste to pick the rising sun of Bolingbroke over the falling star of Richard. Awareness of the wide range of evidence involving boots along with the suggestive silences in some scripts may thus lead to a better grasp of potentially analogous moments in this or other Shakespeare plays.

Such an analogical or patterned approach is particularly rewarding when one considers Shakespeare's use of the stage nightgown in his tragedies. The ghost's nightgown in *Hamlet* remains a puzzle to me; much would depend upon Gertrude's costume in the scene (are she and her first husband being linked through nightgowns?) or perhaps Claudius' costume in the previous scene, a forceful exposition of a troubled conscience. Such links or contrasts are more evident in *Julius Caesar*. Thus, after a troubled night in Rome and just before hearing of Calphurnia's dream, Caesar enters '*in his nightgown*' (II. ii. 0. s.d.). The Folio provides no signal that Brutus also was wearing such a gown in the previous scene, but the dialogue places great emphasis upon night and upon Brutus' troubled sleep. For example, he tells us that 'since Cassius first did whet me against Caesar, / I have not slept' (II. i. 61–2), while Portia twice criticizes him for stealing from her bed (ll. 237–8, 264) in order 'to walk unbracèd and suck up the humors / Of the dank morning' (ll. 262–3). Using other kinds of evidence, critics have linked Brutus and Caesar, whether in these two scenes or in general terms,[35] but parallel appearances in nightgowns could make the connection obvious and emphatic. Such a link would then make more meaningful the aftermath of the quarrel scene when Brutus calls for his gown, Lucius enters *'with the gown,'* Brutus takes it (IV. iii. 231, 236. s.d., 239), and then Caesar's ghost (dressed in a toga? a nightgown?) appears to him while three figures (Lucius, Varro, and Claudius) lie asleep on stage. Brutus' inner turmoil, associated in part with a ghost that identifies itself as 'thy evil spirit, Brutus' (l. 282), is linked, here as earlier, with sleeplessness and perhaps with his own distinctive form of 'unreadiness.' As with the boots in *Richard II*, nightgowns at a Globe performance may have linked these three scenes for the viewer's eye and, in various ways, have enhanced their metaphoric range.

The stage nightgown can also play a significant role in *Othello*. Thus, in the 1622 quarto Brabantio in the opening scene appears *'at a window'* and then enters to Roderigo *'in his night gown'* accompanied by servants *'with Torches'* (B2r, B3r). In a note in his New Arden edition, M. R. Ridley describes the light carried by Othello in the final scene (V. ii. o. s.d.) as 'no more than one of those "code signs", like "night-gowns", of which Elizabethan plays are full, as helps in indicating night-time' (p. 177). Granted, such 'code signs' *are* quite common, but Ridley's quick dismissal does not explain why Brabantio's nightgown should appear well into the progress of a scene that already has been established as taking place at night. Rather, what Shakespeare is setting up here is a Brabantio *'as newly waked from sleep,'* with that awakening caused by a plot set up by Iago (with Roderigo as his agent) that leads to accusations against Desdemona and her lover, Othello. No equivalent stage directions survive from II. iii, but as a result of Cassio's brawling, Othello (rather than Brabantio) is awakened from sleep, again as part of a plot instigated by Iago and using Roderigo, a plot that soon leads to accusations against Desdemona and a supposed lover, Cassio. Neither quarto nor Folio stipulates that Othello is to enter here in a nightgown, but when Desdemona appears, Othello remarks: 'Look if my gentle love be not raised up!'; then tells her: 'All's well now, sweeting; come away to bed'; and concludes at his exit: 'Come, Desdemona; 'tis the soldiers' life / To have their balmy slumbers waked with strife' (ll. 240, 242, 247–8). Brabantio's sleep, interrupted and poisoned by Iago, has now become Othello's interrupted wedding night, again affected by Iago's pestilence, with the two moments perhaps linked by both the nightgown and, equally important, the associations that garment carries – here unreadiness, vulnerability.

The play's final sequence once more alludes to the nightgown. Thus, in the willow scene Desdemona asks Emilia for her 'nightly wearing' (IV. iii. 15), and, moments later, Emilia asks: 'Shall I go fetch your nightgown?' (Desdemona responds: 'No, unpin me here' – l. 33). For me, the key images in the murder scene are the bed and the light, not the nightgown, but for a third time the emphasis is upon interrupted sleep, this time Desdemona's by her husband owing to his tortured, poisoned sense of justice. A different sense of 'unreadiness' is orchestrated here, for Othello wants to be sure that Desdemona has 'prayed to-night' and has reconciled herself 'to heaven and grace' so that he will not kill her 'unpreparèd spirit' (V. ii. 25, 27, 31). As in *Julius Caesar*, strong verbal emphasis upon sleep and sleeplessness (see especially III. iii. 330–3, 338–43) is realized visually and theatrically in three rude awakenings, each a result of Iago's machinations, each linked perhaps by the presence of and associations with the stage nightgown.

What may be the most telling use of the nightgown has no stage directions at all as supporting evidence. Thus, after the murder of Duncan, Lady Macbeth instructs her husband: 'Get on your nightgown, lest occasion call us / And show us to be watchers' (II. ii. 69–70). Presumably, when Macbeth reappears moments later, he is so attired (Macduff observes to Lennox that 'our knocking has awaked him' – II. iii. 39). When the murder is discovered, Macduff awakes 'the sleepers of the house' from 'this downy sleep, death's counterfeit' (ll. 79, 72), thereby bringing onto the stage a group of obviously 'unready' figures (Banquo, Ross, Malcolm, and Donalbain), whether in nightgowns or shirts or hastily donning garments as in my earlier examples. Banquo then calls upon the thanes to reassemble 'when we have our naked frailties hid, / That suffer in exposure' (ll. 122–3), with Macbeth concurring ('let's briefly put on manly readiness' – l. 129). In this first nightgown sequence, the true unreadiness and interrupted sleep of the innocent is juxtaposed with the pretense maintained by the Macbeths ('false face must hide what the false heart doth know' – I. vii. 82).

In subsequent scenes, Shakespeare develops the implications of this murder with particular emphasis upon images of sleep, dreaming, and conscience that coalesce in the justly famous sleep-walking scene. Here, the gentlewoman describes how she has seen Lady Macbeth 'rise from her bed' and then 'throw her nightgown upon her' (v. i. 5–6); for the doctor, 'this slumb'ry agitation' is 'a great perturbation in nature, to receive at once the benefit of sleep and do the effects of watching' (ll. 9–11). The Folio stage direction then notes only that Lady Macbeth is to enter *'with a taper'* (l. 16. s.d.), but the gentlewoman adds: 'Lo you, here she comes! This is her very guise' (l. 17). For me, the 'guise' includes the nightgown just described for us (and also perhaps disheveled hair, a choice often made by modern actresses). In the famous lines that follow, Lady Macbeth echoes her injunctions of Act II ('wash your hands, put on your nightgown, look not so pale!' – ll. 57–8) and builds to a final speech that begins and ends with 'to bed, to bed' (ll. 61, 63). Her assertions of strength and confidence (e.g., 'what need we fear who knows it, when none can call our power to accompt?' – ll. 34–5) are belied by this 'slumb'ry agitation,' whether one ascribes her condition to internal guilt or some higher power or a combination of the two. This rich, complex moment builds upon and recalls some equally telling moments in Act II, so that the presence of the stage nightgown in both segments would reinforce key images and help to signal meaningful connections. Here Shakespeare goes far beyond the conventional stage shorthand to develop his own distinctive links and images close to the heart of this tragedy.

My conjectural readings of moments in *Richard II, Julius Caesar, Othello,* and *Macbeth* have taken me a long way from Massinger's terse *'as from dinner.'* Along that journey, my approach to the evidence and my hesitation about drawing inferences may have struck some readers (especially those who prefer clearcut, 'definitive' answers) as overly cautious. On the other hand, historical scholars who have wrestled with equivalent problems may be dubious about my conjectural readings that may seem to violate my own principles by supplying nightgowns or boots or disheveled hair where no such signals exist in the original texts.

As to the first objection, I too prefer certainties to doubts. Yet so many studies of Elizabethan stages and staging have been diminished in value by inferences and leaps not justified by the evidence or have been undermined by the failure to recognize the problems linked to the sources or point of view behind stage directions or by an unwillingness to confront the special nature of theatrical scripts, especially Elizabethan theatrical scripts as we have them (as opposed to the orderly, meticulously accurate 'prompt-books'[36] some scholars would prefer). As George F. Reynolds, one of the pioneers in this area, has remarked: 'The original contemporary evidence is all that has real authority, and it often speaks with an uncertain voice.'[37] Given the larger goals of this study – particularly the attempt to deal sympathetically with the arrow in Nessus and avoid the misleading 'logic' epitomized by Thurber's American lady – my qualifications and reservations at the outset are necessary so to diminish the possibility of setting up yet another barrier (this time mine) between the Elizabethan logic of presentation and our own. The scholarly rage for order and certainty will, I suspect, always be at odds with something basic in *all* theatrical scripts, imaginative works that never stand still in the manner of a novel or non-dramatic poem.

As for the second objection, I too am uneasy about interpretations based upon boots or nightgowns not specified in the original texts, nor am I advocating such a conjectural approach as my main point of attack. Still, some conjectures or hypotheses *are* given added force when a wealth of evidence from a wide range of plays demonstrates how specific effects often are linked to specific situations. If my conjectures take the cautious reader beyond the bounds of what can be 'proved,' my only defense is that the weight of the evidence overall (and I have spared the reader much documentation) makes my analogous situations at least possible if not probable or likely. In deciding what is necessary or required for a particular moment (e.g., a prison, tavern, tomb, or night scene), the modern scholar should proceed with caution so not to reason by a logic (again, like that of the American lady) that may be at odds with the original evidence and theatrical practice. In this chapter I have therefore paid close attention to the evidence about what actually was provided for the spectator by the actors on the Elizabethan open stage and then, from that evidence, have sought to determine what can be deduced about techniques and conventions in several categories. In a real sense, I did not go out looking for boots, nightgowns, and disheveled hair, but rather, while reading through many, many plays, they found me. How then to use such evidence and such findings remains a central problem. My conjectural approach to some potentially analogous moments in a few major plays represents one kind of implementation, one that may expand the reader's sense of the potential links between historical evidence and interpretation.

A final liability of my presentation in this chapter is that my citations may be leaving the impression of an Elizabethan stage cluttered with crumbs, napkins, javelins, boots, disorderly hair, and nightgowns. In truth, nothing could be farther from my point, for my inclination is to argue for less rather than more detail on the open stage. Thus, the various effects I have been describing require no sizable properties. Rather, most could be achieved with minor adjustments in costume (or wig) in ways that may have been second nature to actor and spectator. As noted earlier, in place of elaborate banquet or shipwreck or bedroom scenes, many of my stage directions help to establish a sense of that world just off-stage, never seen but there to be supplied by the 'imaginary forces' of the audience who implicitly are being asked to 'piece out our imperfections with your thoughts' or 'eke out our performance with your mind.' The key to such effects lies in some significant, visible stage detail that is theatrically practical, that conveys some signal deftly to the viewer's eye, and that, at least in the hands of a Shakespeare, has the potential for some larger meaning or pattern. Clearly, large properties like tombs and scaffolds occasionally could be introduced onto the Elizabethan stage; nonetheless, I would argue that almost all of the scenes could have been staged with recourse only to portable properties, appropriate costumes, and the 'imaginary forces' of the spectator.

To return to where I began, the recovery of the theatrical techniques and shared assumptions in the age of Shakespeare is no easy task. Given the nature of the available eyewitness accounts and pictorial evidence, the investigator has no choice but to build any interpretation upon the surviving stage directions. But to interpret these Elizabethan signals, which (as McKerrow has noted) were meant for Elizabethan theatrical professionals, not for us, is often extremely difficult, at times perhaps impossible. Evidence is commonly lacking or murky; many curious stage directions appear to stand alone with no support from other contexts; the strictures of T. J. King and others about the nature of the evidence must be heeded. Still, students of Elizabethan images and icons have shown how much can be gained from immersion in the literary or learned tradition (e.g., emblem books, mythographers). But need Alciatus and Ripa be the only sources for such a shared language of images? Given the vitality of the developing Elizabethan theatre, the modern scholarly detective should not be surprised to find an evolving theatrical iconography, geared to the exigencies of this particular theatre, with its open stage, its narrative flow, its practical limits upon properties and stage effects (the arrow in Nessus), and its everpresent metaphoric or symbolic dimension (especially in Shakespeare). And where better to find clues for that specifically theatrical imagery or stage iconography than in the evidence provided by the scattered, elusive, murky, but still potentially revealing stage directions?

3 · The logic of 'this' on the open stage

His gesture imports it
(*Othello*, IV. i. 135–6)

Before dealing with a series of problems linking stage directions with differing logics of interpretation, let me focus upon a phenomenon that can bedevil the interpreter of any playscript but, given the absence of clear signals, is especially perplexing in many scenes and passages in the age of Shakespeare. I am referring to the widespread use of gestic terms like *this*, *there*, *here*, *yon*, and *thus* where the meaning of a line or phrase is (presumably) to be completed or fulfilled by a motion or action from the speaker. Indeed, one such passage has achieved a notoriety of its own. Thus, to call attention to the difference between scripts and texts, the 'stage-centred critic' (to borrow a term from J. L. Styan)[1] regularly cites Polonius' line: 'Take this from this, if this be otherwise' (II. ii. 156) where the first *this* refers to 'head,' the second to 'shoulders,' and the third to 'this situation.' Initially puzzling to a reader, the line makes immediate sense to a spectator attending both the words and the gestures of an actor. Equally obvious if less famous is Achilles' appraisal of Hector: 'Tell me, you heavens, in which part of his body / Shall I destroy him, whether there, or there, or there?' (IV. v. 241–2). Here a series of gestures to parts of Hector's body is needed to complete the sense of the passage, but the actor or reader must decide exactly what should be the gesture (with finger? with weapon?) and to which parts of Hector.

The problems in interpreting such passages in Elizabethan scripts vary considerably. Sometimes the accompanying action is quite clear (as with 'take this from this'); often the modern actor or editor must puzzle over the lines; occasionally the meaning remains impenetrable or highly controversial (as with Lear's 'This' a good block'). Thus, the repentant protagonist of *The Miseries of Enforced Marriage*, surrounded by uncle, brothers, sister, wife, and children, exclaims:

53

> Hark how their words like Bullets shoot me through
> And tell me I have undone 'em, this side might say,
> We are in want, and you are the cause of it,
> This points at me, y'are shame unto your house,
> This tongue says nothing, but her looks do tell,
> She's married but as those that live in hell.   (ll. 2815–20)

The editor or reader must work carefully here to reconstruct what would have been obvious to the original spectator watching an actor point to specific figures on stage. Or consider Marlowe's *Edward II* where Isabella provides Matrevis with a hypocritically loving message to be delivered to the imprisoned Edward and adds: 'And bear him this, as witness of my love' (l. 2216). To clarify the unspecific *this*, editors since Dyce have regularly added their own stage direction (e.g., *gives a ring*) even though no such ring is cited in the script. However, at least one recent editor (Russell Fraser) has glossed *this* as 'message'[2] (i.e., the hypocritical words delivered in the preceding speech). Lacking specific internal or external evidence (Holinshed mentions 'loving letters with apparel, and other such things'[3]), can we indeed determine exactly what 'witness' of Isabella's love was delivered in an Elizabethan production? As with Hamlet's leap, the answer today will depend upon the logic or taste of the editor or director, his sense of what would be appropriate or psychologically valid or theatrically effective at this given moment, but, whatever the choice, the speech should *not* be ambiguous for the spectator.

The reader of the Folio version of *3 Henry VI* faces a similar problem. Thus, when Clarence enters '*with Drum and Colors*' (v. i. 75), Warwick addresses his son-in-law and supposed ally with a five line speech, but Clarence responds: 'Father of Warwick, know you what this means? / Look here, I throw my infamy at thee' (ll. 81–2), and, after a substantial speech, rejoins his brothers, forsaking Warwick. From the Folio text alone, the reader gains a sense of some action that symbolizes a rejection of Warwick and the Lancastrian cause ('Look here ...'), an action that appears to involve a throwing of 'my infamy,' but the specific action or the object thrown is by no means clear. Unlike the ambiguity in *Edward II*, however, this puzzle is (apparently) resolved elsewhere. Thus, in the quarto (a memorially reconstructed text that may reflect a performance of a somewhat different version of the play), Clarence enters proclaiming his allegiance to

Lancaster and Warwick, at which point his brother Edward calls for a parley. The quarto stage direction (which has no equivalent in the Folio) then reads: '*Richard and Clarence whispers together, and then Clarence takes his red Rose out of his hat, and throws it at Warwick*' (E2r); the same two lines, minus the 'Look here,' follow. Without the so-called 'bad' quarto, Clarence's 'Look here, I throw my infamy at thee' (like Isabella's 'And bear him this, as witness of my love') would be murky and open to debate.

Situations where the words alone fail to supply all the necessary information are common to all theatrical scripts (and set them off from novels), but the scarcity of stage directions in Elizabethan plays regularly compounds the difficulty. Often, as with Isabella's 'this ... witness of my love,' the choice is between a general sentiment or situation and a specific object or action. Thus, when Iago asks 'is't come to this?' (III. iii. 363), is he referring to Othello's general loss of control or to a specific action (e.g., at this point actors playing Othello often grab Iago by the throat)? When Guildenstern tells Hamlet 'this courtesy is not of the right breed' (III. ii. 301–2), is he referring only to Hamlet's general tone or to a specific action (e.g., a Hamlet who kneels or otherwise exaggerates his 'you are welcome' to parody courtly manners)? When Horatio in the cellarage scene exclaims 'O day and night, but this is wondrous strange!' (I. v. 164), is he referring to the ghost's voice under the stage (other than this line, I see no firm evidence that Horatio and Marcellus hear the ghost) or to Hamlet's behavior?

To glimpse the range of the problem, consider the following passages (in each case the emphasis is mine):

FALSTAFF. Here I lay, and *thus* I bore my point. Four rogues in buckram let drive at me ... These four came all afront and mainly thrust at me. I made me no more ado but took all their seven points in my target, *thus*.
(*1 Henry IV*, II. iv. 184–91)

RICHARD II. Up, cousin, up! Your heart is up, I know,
　　Thus high at least, although your knee be low.
(*Richard II*, III. iii. 194–5)

CASCA. Why, there was a crown offered him; and being offered him, he put it by with the back of his hand *thus*. (*Julius Caesar*, I. ii. 220–1)

HAMLET. Nor do not saw the air too much with your hand, *thus*, but use all gently. (*Hamlet*, III. ii. 4–5)

BOTTOM. Some man or other must present Wall; and let him have some plaster, or some loam, or some roughcast about him, to signify wall;

and let him hold his fingers *thus*; and through that cranny shall
Pyramus and Thisby whisper.

(A Midsummer Night's Dream, III. i. 59–63)

Clearly, for its full effect each passage requires a gesture or
action. Falstaff, using his sword and target, acts out with comic
bravado his supposed bout with the four (quickly seven) attackers; Richard II, addressing a kneeling Bolingbroke, points to or
touches his crown (or head); Casca, with the back of his hand,
mimes Caesar's putting by of the offered crown; Hamlet, in
imitation of the ham actor, saws the air with his hand. When
enacting such gestures, the actor has the same latitude in tone or
degree he would have in any spoken passage, but in these
examples the gestures themselves, the specific stage business
attendant upon the lines, is not seriously in doubt. Thus, the actor
playing Bottom may use the thumb and index finger of one hand
to make the designated 'cranny' or, conceivably, could make a
larger (and more ludicrous) circle with four fingers or even both
hands, but, regardless, the essential nature of the designated
action is clear enough.[4]

But consider the following passages in which the action linked
to a gestic *thus* is less certain. When Othello tells Iago: 'All my
fond love *thus* do I blow to heaven. / 'Tis gone' (III. iii. 445–6),
what should the actor do? How indeed does one 'blow to heaven'
one's love? Again, when Antony tells Cleopatra: 'The nobleness
of life / Is to do *thus*; when such a mutual pair / And such a twain
can do't' (I. i. 36–8), do the two figures kiss? embrace? join hands
in some formal gesture? Few editors can resist inserting a stage
direction here, but most ignore the equivalent problem later in the
play when Eros describes for Enobarbus Antony's reaction to the
death of Pompey and disgrace of Lepidus: 'He's walking in the
garden – *thus*, and spurns / The rush that lies before him' (III. v.
15–16). Particularly puzzling are Poor Tom's actions during the
mad tribunal scene. When Lear in his madness sees (or hears)
barking dogs, Edgar responds: 'Tom will throw his head at them';
in his song he adds: 'For, with throwing *thus* my head, / Dogs
leaped the hatch, and all are fled' (III. vi. 63, 70–1). As with
Othello blowing his fond love to heaven or Antony doing thus to
act out 'the nobleness of life,' Tom's lines call for some distinctive
action, but what action? How does a madman 'throw his head'?
Moreover, is this passage only a bizarre isolated moment or is it

linked to the many other passages and actions in this tragedy dealing with 'the head'? Again, the original spectator at the Globe had no difficulty perceiving the staged action, but the modern actor or reader, privy only to the surviving words, must guess at the gestures that did or should accompany *thus*. And, as emphasized throughout this study, modern conclusions or inferences inevitably will reflect our own logic of interpretation or performance that may or may not be in tune with the shared assumptions of the original dramatist, actors, and audience.

The possible ambiguity in such gestic passages did not go unnoticed in the seventeenth century. Rather, to clarify such moments for the reader or the actor someone has provided marginal notations in various playhouse manuscripts and printed texts. Such notations usually serve as glosses. For example, in Fletcher's *The Pilgrim* when a figure threatens the hero with 'do you see this Sir?' the direction follows: '*Irons brought in*' (v, 214); in the playhouse manuscript of *Believe as You List* when Marcellus asks: 'do you know what this contains?' the marginal note calls for '*the letter*' (ll. 2392, 2390). In *The Two Noble Ladies*, Clitophon's assertion 'who e'er resist the Souldan's passage, this shall be their pass to hell' is accompanied by '*his sword*' (ll. 1358–9); elsewhere in this playhouse manuscript, Cyprian's reference to 'this sacred truth alone' is glossed by '*The Angel's book*' (l. 1902). In *The Wonder of a Kingdom* a former galley slave asserts 'see here the relicts of that misery' (III. i. 95), with the marginal note reading '*Chains.*' Such glosses can also clarify stage metaphors set up by gestures. In *The Fair Maid of the Inn*, after one figure has offered a thousand crowns to free the hero from his situation, a hostile voice counters with 'here's the Physician'; the stage direction reads '*Shows a Poniard*' (IX, 208) – no doctor is needed. Again, at the opening of *A New Way to Pay Old Debts* after Wellborn has been persuaded to stop beating Tapwell and Froth, he responds: 'For once thou hast redeem'd them from this scepter,' with the marginal note: '*His Cudgel*' (I. i. 92). In the 1633 quarto of *The Jew of Malta* Barabas twice refers to the board marked 'thus' under which his gold is hidden with the text including a † after the second *thus* (l. 598). Most of the ambiguities above could have been pieced out by an actor or reader, but the presence of the notations shows an awareness then of the gap between words on the page and words on the stage accompanied by properties or gestures.

The range of gestic passages in Elizabethan plays is quite wide. At one extreme lie phrases that call for a gesture towards a significant property or person. Thus, when Lear asks 'Is man no more than this?' (III. iv. 97–8), clearly he is calling our attention to Poor Tom whose attributes and status are the focus for this part of the scene. At the other extreme lie general references to 'this shore' or 'this coast'[5] where few readers or directors today would expect an elaborate set or diorama but at most would envisage an expansive gesture by the actor. But in between these two poles lie many interesting passages that can reveal a great deal about both Elizabethan staging and the modern logic that can sometimes transform the original effects. In particular, such passages raise important questions about what is essential for stage presentation in the age of Shakespeare, what is 'necessary' for the 'dramatic illusion' as opposed to what is to be supplied by the 'imaginary forces' of the spectators who are being asked to 'eke out' the performance with their minds.

Consider first one of the most revealing of the extant playhouse manuscripts, *The Two Noble Ladies*, a romance replete with magic and supernatural events. At a climactic point, two soldiers drag Justina onto the stage with the intention of drowning her in the Euphrates while two other figures (one of them a conjurer) look on. I quote only the soldiers' lines:

1.	SOLDIER.	Come, now w'are almost at our journey's end;
		This is swift Euphrates, here cast her in ...
2.	SOLDIER.	Come this way, this way, here the stream is deepest.
1.	SOLDIER.	I am enforc'd I know not by what pow'r
		To hale her this way.
2.	SOLDIER.	What strange noise is this?
1.	SOLDIER.	Dispatch, the tide swells high.
2.	SOLDIER.	What fiend is this?
1.	SOLDIER.	What fury seizes me?
2.	SOLDIER.	Alas, I'm hurried headlong to the stream.
1.	SOLDIER.	And so am I, we both must drown and die. (ll. 1150–71)

Here the repeated gestic phrases (e.g., 'This is swift Euphrates, here cast her in'; 'here the stream is deepest') may suggest to the modern reader the presence on-stage of a river or body of water. As G. F. Reynolds has noted, 'if a river was ever represented in any special way' on the Elizabethan stage 'it should have been here.'[6]

Granted such a scholarly inference about what is 'necessary' to stage this scene (on-stage water? trapdoors? wave machines?), the historian conceivably could then move in an orderly progression to an extrapolation of what is necessary or appropriate for other related scenes (e.g., the drowning of Sabren in *Locrine* where there are references to 'this pleasant stream' and 'this River' – ll. 2247, 2252). One on-stage river can beget others.

In this case, however, the manuscript provides specific (and to some readers unexpected) stage directions for this moment (as Reynolds notes: 'no staging could be simpler'). Thus, at line 1166 ('what strange noise is this?') the marginal signal reads: '*Enter two Tritons with silver trumpets*'; next to the subsequent lines we find: '*The Tritons seize the soldiers*' and '*The Tritons drag them in sounding their trumpets.*' Whatever our modern expectations, the original effect was keyed not to an on-stage river but to Tritons and trumpets. The sense of headlong, precipitate action, of drowning in a swelling tide, is conveyed not by the direct representation of water or immersion but by signals in the dialogue and violent stage business in conjunction with the 'imaginary forces' of the audience. In this scene, 'what fiend is this?' *does* refer to a visible on-stage figure, but 'This is swift Euphrates, here cast her in' requires no more than a gesture from the actor towards the stage floor or perhaps the edge of the stage. Within the same passage, one gestic *this* can direct us to a visible Triton or 'fiend' while another *this* can conjure up an imaginary river. But without these informative (and, being informative, atypical) stage directions from the playhouse, the modern reader could easily have reversed the process and postulated a 'real' Euphrates and 'imaginary' fiends.

To see the problems caused by the absence of signals, consider the final moments of *Doctor Faustus* in the 1616 text. Here the Good Angel points to the throne that has descended (l. 2006) and tells the protagonist to 'behold, / In what resplendent glory thou hadst set / In yonder throne, like those bright shining Saints' (ll. 2011–13). Were 'those' saints visible to the original spectator or would a gesture to the throne or the heavens have sufficed? Again, after '*Hell is discovered*' (l. 2017), the Bad Angel enjoins Faustus to

> let thine eyes with horror stare
> Into that vast perpetual torture-house,
> There are the Furies tossing damned souls,

On burning forks: their bodies broil in lead.
There are live quarters broiling on the coals,
That ne'er can die: this ever-burning chair,
Is for o'er-tortur'd souls to rest them in.
These, that are fed with sops of flaming fire,
Were gluttons, and lov'd only delicates,
And laugh'd to see the poor starve at their gates: (ll. 2018–27)

Conceivably, at this point an Elizabethan spectator might have
seen such damned souls in torment (with burning forks, bodies
broiling on the coals, and other nightmare visions out of
Hieronymus Bosch), for the 'Hell' that is 'discovered' could have
been a tapestry. Yet it is also possible that, though Faustus may
share the Bad Angel's vision, the viewer may see only a trap door
(with or without flames) or a hellmouth visible through a stage
door. As with his description moments later of Christ's blood in
the firmament or God's angry arm, Faustus' privileged vision
need not correspond to what is on stage to be seen by the
spectator. Indeed, the final effect of the tragedy can be very
different (and very potent) if Faustus 'sees' but we, aided by the
poetry and the acting, must imagine what lies above and below.[7]
   The moments from *The Two Noble Ladies* and *Doctor Faustus*
help to call attention to a significant problem often skirted by
modern readers of Elizabethan plays. Given the abundance of
gestic phrases (many of them involving *this*), how are we to
determine what is to be seen or included on stage and what is to be
imagined? As noted in the previous chapter, herein lies one of the
dangers of drawing conclusions from the dialogue alone about
stage action or the physical features of the stage, for most
passages are more problematic than 'this coast' or 'this shore.'
Thus, in *Much Ado About Nothing* Hero tells her companions
that Beatrice will overhear their conversation 'as we do trace this
alley up and down' (III. i. 16); in *Twelfth Night* Maria tells her
co-conspirators that 'Malvolio's coming down this walk' (II. v.
13–14). Although nineteenth-century productions could provide
such settings, few scholars today would postulate a visible alley or
walk in the original productions. Most would also doubt the
presence of a special property for Hermia when she says 'for I
upon this bank will rest my head' (*A Midsummer Night's Dream*,
II. ii. 40) or for Lorenzo when he observes 'how sweet the
moonlight sleeps upon this bank' (*The Merchant of Venice*, v. i.

54), even though Henslowe's inventory does include two 'moss-banks.'[8] Indeed, to supply a walk, alley or bank may be to change drastically the nature of the original scene. Thus, Shakespeare has Peter Quince announce: 'Pat, pat; and here's a marvellous convenient place for our rehearsal. This green plot shall be our stage, this hawthorn brake our tiring house' (*A Midsummer Night's Dream*, III. i. 2–4). To include an actual 'green plot' and 'hawthorn brake' is to lose part of the fun; rather, the original audience, looking at a 'real' stage and tiring house, was being asked to imagine an imaginary brake and green plot metamorphosed into what they saw before them.

Rather than introducing special properties, some gestic passages draw upon (or appear to draw upon) fixed features of the stage. Thus, in *Much Ado* Borachio tells Conrade to 'Stand thee close then under this penthouse, for it drizzles rain' (III. iii. 96–7); similarly, in *The Merchant of Venice* Gratiano announces: 'This is the penthouse under which Lorenzo / Desired us to make stand' (II. vi. 1–2). In either instance, the actors need only be standing under something (e.g., the 'hut' above) for the lines to work (and could even deliver the lines with no overhang at all).[9] When Iago tells Roderigo 'Here, stand behind this bulk' (v. i. 1), the modern editor will gloss 'bulk' as a 'projecting shop front' but the spectator at the Globe probably saw Roderigo concealed behind a stage pillar or some other fixed part of the stage. Similarly, the lord who announces that Parolles 'can come no other way but by this hedge corner' (*All's Well*, IV. i. 1–2) probably pointed not to some visible property (that would then have to be brought on- and off-stage) but to the stage railing or empty space. For the original spectator, the penthouse, bulk or hedge corner came into existence when the actor gestured towards something (a pillar, a railing) or some place, thus giving a local habitation and a name to an otherwise neutral area (a technique used many many times in this period to 'create' a city, a cave, a cell, walls, a tree, and more).[10]

Conditioned by the novel, cinema, television, and much twentieth-century theatre, the modern scholar or director may feel impelled to supply a hedge corner or bulk or bank from the property department. But in an appropriate theatrical space, such gestic passages can still work quite effectively today and thereby preserve the Elizabethan flow of action (which did not need pauses to introduce elaborate properties). To take two examples from the 1980 season at the Oregon Shakespearean Festival, when Navarre stepped forth from concealment to confront Dumaine and Longaville, he stated: 'I have been closely shrouded in this bush' (*Love's Labor's Lost*, IV. iii. 132) and pointed to the stage pillar behind which he had been standing. The Oregon audience readily accepted the line without seeing any stage greenery. Similarly, when Hotspur in *Richard II* stated: 'There stands the castle by yon tuft of trees' (II. iii. 53), the actor pointed out over the heads of the audience to a not visible but readily imagined Berkeley Castle (ironically, in this outdoor theatre spectators who turned their heads could have seen tufts of trees in adjacent Lithia Park). If a castle actually figured in the action or interaction (as one does in III. iii), Shakespeare could use a different technique; if a bush or tree or flowers were indeed necessary for Navarre's scene, appropriate stage properties could have been introduced. But, to focus upon the more complex of the two moments, the key to Navarre's situation is the concealment, not the agent of concealment, so that introducing a stage bush for this brief moment in a long scene would not only be superfluous but could be intrusive. Rather, as Neil Carson points out, given dialogue and skillful acting 'the "scenery" on a permanent, non-localized stage can be said to materialize and then melt away in the imagination of the spectators. The effect is a sort of double consciousness in which the stage, without ever ceasing to be itself, becomes also as needed an open field, a stream, a citadel, and so on.'[11]

When a scene *does* demand a strong sense of 'place,' the dramatist will often make substantial use of gestic terms. Consider two scenes from Heywood's *A Woman Killed With Kindness*, each linked to a 'house' (a locale readily achieved in the modern theatre but much harder to realize on the open stage). First, Sir Charles Mountford and his sister Susan enter talking about the 'hard shift' to which they are driven 'to keep this poor house.' Shafton then enters, commenting: 'You have a pretty house here, and a Garden, / And goodly ground about it.' In response to Shafton's offer to purchase house and land, Sir Charles repeatedly invokes the gestic *this*:

> O pardon me: This house successively
> Hath long'd to me and my progenitors

Three hundred years. My great great Grandfather;
He in whom first our gentle style began
Dwelt here; and in this ground, increas'd this Molehill
Unto that Mountain which my Father left me.
Where he the first of all our house begun,
I now the last will end and keep this house:
This virgin Title never yet deflower'd
By any unthrift of the *Mountfords'* line;
In brief, I will not sell it for more Gold
Than you could hide or pave the ground withal.

Sir Charles adds: 'If this were sold, our names should then be quite / Raz'd from the bead-roll of Gentility'; Susan also notes how hard they work 'to reserve to us / And our succession this small plot of ground' (II, 113–15). The house and plot, which cannot be represented in 'realistic' fashion on the open stage but are vitally important to the scene in lineal and symbolic terms, are here set forth largely through repeated use of the gestic *this*, presumably to the otherwise neutral stage floor and façade.

A parallel scene is to be found in the main plot where the threat to the house is sexual rather than financial. To surprise Anne and Wendoll, Frankford and Nicholas steal back into the house; when Nicholas hands his master the key, Frankford responds:

This is the key that opes my outward gate;
This the Hall door; this the withdrawing chamber:
But this, that door that's bawd unto my shame:
Fountain and spring of all my bleeding thoughts,
Where the most hallowed order and true knot
Of Nuptial sanctity hath been profan'd;
It leads to my polluted bed-chamber,
Once my Terrestial heaven, now my earth's hell,
The place where sins in all their ripeness dwell.
But I forget myself, now to my gate.

Frankford's final speech before his exit then begins: 'A general silence hath surpris'd the house, / And this is the last door' (II, 136–7). Like the marriage (and marriage bed) that is being violated, Heywood evokes 'the house' by reference to doors and chambers keyed to the gestic *this*. The extent to which 'real' stage doors are being used to denote the doors of Frankford's house remains unclear, but, as with the comparable scene involving Sir Charles, a combination of language and gesture produces an effect important to the play but difficult to realize without modern sets.[12]

One major function of such a gestic technique, then, is to create for a spectator what cannot actually be shown on the open stage (e.g., the houses of Sir Charles and Frankford). Another equally important (and, for the modern reader, often equally puzzling) function is to establish stage metaphors. Thus, critics accustomed to dealing with literary texts are sometimes not fully attuned to the on-stage situation where an actor can point to an object or person (the tenor) and then describe it in terms of something else (the vehicle). Many straight-forward Shakespearean examples can be cited. For example, Albany, looking at Goneril, refers to her as 'This gilded serpent' (v. iii. 84); Hamlet, meeting Osric, asks Horatio: 'Dost know this waterfly?' (v. ii. 82–3); Romeo begins a complex exchange with talk of profaning 'This holy shrine,' Juliet's hand (I. v. 94). Obviously, the spectator sees not a serpent but a serpent-like Goneril, not a waterfly but a bug-like Osric, not a shrine but a hand venerated by a votary of the religion of love. Similarly, we are not puzzled by the on-stage picture when Mamillius refers to Hermione's ladies as 'yond crickets' (II. i. 31) or when Leontes refers to his son as 'this kernel, / This squash, this gentleman' (I. ii. 159–60) or when Palamon refers to Emilia as 'yon little Tree, yon blooming Apricock' (*The Two Noble Kinsmen*, IX, 316). Elsewhere, traditional associations are invoked at the climax of *The Changeling* when Beatrice-Joanna points to DeFlores and says: 'Beneath the stars, upon yon meteor / Ever hung my fate, 'mongst things corruptible' (v. iii. 154–5) or when the physician in *A Fair Quarrel* introduces his sister to Jane to serve as a confidante: 'Look you, mistress, here's your closet; put in / What you please, you ever keep the key of it' (II. ii. 65–6). For such relatively simple examples, gestures from the actor are hardly necessary, for a reader or spectator has little or no difficulty grasping the analogy or equation.

Equally clear are passages where a property or action is not in doubt. Thus, when Mercutio taunts Tybalt with 'here's my fiddlestick' (III. i. 47), we readily imagine him brandishing his sword; later in the same play the reader should have no difficulty with Juliet's phrase at her suicide: 'O happy dagger! This is thy sheath' (v. iii. 169–70), for that sheath or resting place for the dagger is clearly her body. Sometimes a stage direction helps to gloss the metaphoric equation. In addition to the physician–poniard and sceptre–cudgel examples cited earlier, in *The Devil's*

Law-Case Romelio asks for victuals but the Capuchin responds: 'Here's food for you,' with the stage direction adding '*Offering him a book*' (v. iv. 93). More often the stage business is implicit, as in *The Widow's Tears* where Cynthia tells the disguised Lysander that his punishment will be 'to suffer these soft chains' (v. iii. 43) or in *Edward II* where Isabella tells the king: 'No other jewels hang about my neck / Than these my lord' (ll. 627–8), with the clear sense in both passages of the chains or jewels being arms in an embrace. Although the modern auditor may miss the allusion to the catechism, an actor playing Hamlet can easily make sense of his reference to 'these pickers and stealers' (III. ii. 322) by calling attention to his hands or fingers. Perhaps the most unusual example is to be found at the climax of *No Wit, No Help Like a Woman's* where Mistress Low-Water, disguised as a man, discovers herself, after being threatened with hanging, with the line: 'And I've my neck-verse perfect, here and here' (v. i. 344). The boy actor here 'reveals' his/her breasts as a metaphoric version of pleading 'benefit of clergy.'

As seen in Mercutio's fiddlestick or Wellborn's sceptre, weapons and instruments of death often are granted such metaphoric status. Thus, Webster twice links romantic associations to a noose or strangling cord. In *The Duchess of Malfi* Cariola tries in vain to plead for her life, arguing she is contracted to a young gentleman, but the executioner responds: 'Here's your wedding ring' (IV. ii. 249), presumably showing her the cords. Similarly, in *The White Devil* the murderers who strangle Bracciano tell him: 'This is a true-love knot / Sent from the Duke of Florence' (v. iii. 174–5). The reader may be puzzled when in *The Spanish Tragedy* Hieronimo first talks of seeking justice for Horatio's death and then says: 'Turn down this path, thou shalt be with him straight, / Or this, and then thou need'st not take thy breath: / This way, or that way?' (III. xii. 14–16). But the passage makes excellent sense when one recognizes that he has entered '*with a poniard in one hand, and a rope in the other*' and says, after the passage cited above, 'if I hang or kill myself, let's know / Who will revenge Horatio's murder then?' (ll. 17–18), so he then '*flings away the dagger and halter*' (l. 19 s.d.). This complex moment is part of a problematic scene (where decisions about staging can drastically affect the meaning), but the initial reference to 'this path ... Or this' is not ambiguous if the actor is holding up a dagger and halter as his two alternatives.

An on-stage gesture can thereby clarify, even italicize a theatrical metaphor. But given the frequent absence of stage directions in the extant scripts, the editor, critic, or director often cannot determine from a given passage alone what gesture or action or property (if any) would have been used in the original production. Sometimes, we feel certain that the actor would have pointed to something yet cannot tell what that something would have been. Thus, when Lear in his madness says 'This' a good block' (IV. vi. 180) the spectator at the Globe would not have found the moment ambiguous if the actor pointed to his head or his hat or the stage floor or even to empty space (thereby telling us not about the 'block' but about Lear's state of mind). Lear's (and Shakespeare's) point, whether literal, metaphoric, or illusory, would have been apparent then but is difficult if not impossible to ascertain now.[13] In another puzzling passage the Duchess of Malfi, in despair at the apparent deaths of Antonio and her eldest son, tells Bosola: 'I am full of daggers: / Puff: let me blow these vipers from me' (IV. i. 90–1). In a long and very useful note in his Revels edition, John Russell Brown offers several possible explanations of this passage (including the alternative that 'vipers' is a misprint for 'vapors'), but some gesture that would incorporate the 'puff' with 'these vipers' (fingers? nails? teeth?) would seem a likely solution. As with Lear's block, the answer probably lies in the yoking together of tenor and vehicle by the actor's gesture, a combination not specified in the surviving texts and perhaps irrevocably lost.

Particularly suggestive are those moments when, with the evidence at hand, we cannot be certain if a gestic term is being used in a literal or a metaphoric sense. Thus, during his very funny jealous tirade in *Volpone*, Corvino tells the hapless Celia: 'Then, here's a lock, which I will hang upon thee' (II. v. 57). Editors regularly gloss the 'lock' as a chastity belt (and are probably correct), a fine comic use of such a theatrical metaphor. Yet for a striking and outrageously funny effect, Corvino *could* pull forth an oversized lock to hang upon Celia, an action that would spell out his possessive, mercantile approach to his wifely treasure. Or consider a well-known passage in *Richard II* where the Bishop of Carlisle warns the court of the horrors and 'the woefullest division' that will come 'if you raise this house against this house' by deposing Richard II (IV. i. 145–6). In his New Arden edition (p. 133) Peter Ure links the two houses to Lancaster and York and a general vision of the civil wars to come (while also citing Mark 3:25 on a house divided against itself), and most readers, editors, and directors interpret the two houses in this literal fashion. So did I, until I saw an actor (Laurence Paulsen at the Oregon Shakespearean Festival, 1980) gesture on the first 'house' to the on-stage nobles and on the second 'house' to the heavens, a gesture and a metaphoric link that fit well with his role as bishop and with other passages in the play.[14] To 'prove' the authenticity of this reading is impossible, but when I saw it enacted on stage it made immediate sense and opened up various metaphoric possibilities both in the deposition scene and elsewhere.

Consider another passage from Webster, this time just before the death of the Duchess of Malfi. Thus, soon after the executioners appear with '*a coffin, cords and a bell*' (IV. ii. 165. s.d.) Bosola (in disguise) informs the duchess: 'This is your last presence-chamber' (l. 171). The scene contains many allusions to the values and affectations of nobility and, in particular, to the titles and pomp of the duchess herself, so this line makes perfect sense if Bosola is referring to the room or place signified in general terms by the stage. Yet the 'last presence-chamber' for me makes even more sense and carries more force if Bosola here gestures towards the coffin, thereby linking (as do other moments in this powerful scene) human identity and aspirations with the visible symbol of Death. What may seem subtle in reading can, with a gesture to the coffin, be an expressive symbol for what the duchess confronts when she asserts 'I am Duchess of Malfi still.' Either interpretation fits well with the lines that accompany the coffin, bell, and cords: 'Here is a present from your princely brothers, / And may it arrive welcome, for it brings / Last benefit, last sorrow' (ll. 166–8).

Consider too a much more famous moment, Hamlet's reaction at the departure of the Ghost where his soliloquy emphasizes memory ('Remember thee') and new truths ('That one may smile, and smile, and be a villain'), with particular emphasis upon Hamlet's reason, his faculties, 'the book and volume of my brain' (I. v. 95–112). Given the context, the reader is not surprised to find a telling reference to 'this distracted globe' that surely calls for Hamlet to gesture towards his head. Far less clear, however, is what an actor (then or now) is to do about the 'tables' upon which Hamlet states he will inscribe the new truths, building to 'meet it is I set it down' and 'So, uncle, there you are.' Generations of actors playing Hamlet have carried and used tablets here, but the repeated emphasis upon memory and forgetting throughout the play could suggest (as in 'the table of my memory' in l. 98) that the tragic hero's 'tables' are not literal but rather imaginary or metaphoric. Thus, some actors (including Derek Jacobi in the widely seen BBC Television production) here use their fingers or hands to jab at their heads, thereby signifying that the setting down of the new truths is in the mind, not on a tablet.[15] Either interpretation can work well (for some readers, 'So, uncle, there you are' may make more sense after Hamlet has been engaged in the act of writing), but the fact remains that a choice *is* there to be made, especially if the actor, editor, or critic can go beyond the literal level and see the potential in Elizabethan theatrical metaphors.

Such emphasis upon the choice, not the solution, may frustrate some readers. Nonetheless, in presenting my series of gestic passages my goal has not been to convince the reader of my metaphoric interpretations or my sense of what the original spectator would have seen (or not have seen) but rather (as with my discussion of stage directions) to call attention to a fundamental problem in our prevailing logic of interpretation. If some of my suggestions appear vulnerable, how much more so are the comparable inferences of stage historians, editors, and critics wedded solely to their literal or naturalistic terms and thus divorced from the metaphoric or imaginative potential of the Elizabethan open stage? If we reject the choric pleas of *Henry V* and think instead in terms of property masters rather than 'imaginary forces,' we may end up positing the presence of hedge corners, alleys, walks, banks, hills, walls, caves, cells, trees, and bushes never seen by the audience at the Globe, just as we may blot out some distinctive and meaningful theatrical metaphors. In taking too literally various references in the dialogue, the modern reader may then be acting out a subtler but potentially more insidious version of the American lady's reshaping of *Macbeth*. In many instances, I confess, my persistent question – what would the original spectator have seen? – may be unanswerable, but a repeated raising of this question, whether with gestic passages or, in subsequent chapters, with moments 'in the dark' or scenes *in prison* or stage combats, can remind us forcefully of how much we do not know and how vulnerable our conclusions (and even the questions we ask) are to unacknowledged and often inappropriate assumptions about drama and theatre in the age of Shakespeare. The many perplexing problems raised by the gestic *this* can therefore serve as an excellent introduction to a fuller discussion of some significant gaps between Elizabethan playscripts and the modern interpreter.

4 · Elizabethan darkness and modern lighting

Put out the light, and then put out the light
(*Othello*, v. ii. 7)

Gestic metaphors, hair about the ears, boots and safeguards, the arrow in Nessus – all represent components of that language of the theatre shared by dramatists, actors, and spectators then that may seem primitive, bizarre, or confusing today. Of the many such gaps between the original theatrical 'logic' and our familiar procedures perhaps the most revealing lies in the widely varying assumptions about on-stage night and darkness. For us, 'going to the theatre' (with the exception of outdoor matinees) means sitting in a darkened auditorium watching actors perform in a lighted space. In striking contrast, Shakespeare and his fellow dramatists wrote their plays for an auditorium in which (presumably) viewers could see each other as clearly as they could see the events on stage. The Elizabethan actors then presented their plays in light (whether natural, as at the Globe, or artificial, as at the Blackfriars) that essentially remained constant during the course of a performance, changing only when the sun moved behind a cloud or descended lower in the sky or when torches were carried on stage. In short, variable lighting, one of the essential tools for the modern director, was not available to the King's Men.

Nonetheless, night and darkness play an important part in many Elizabethan plays – for plot, imagery, and general atmosphere. Given an outdoor performance at the Globe by natural afternoon light or an indoor performance at the Blackfriars by unvarying interior light, how then did the King's Men or any other dramatic company distinguish between 'day' and 'night' scenes, between stage 'light' and stage 'darkness'? The first and most obvious tool, of course, is dialogue, for characters often tell us or each other about night or darkness (as in Hamlet's ''Tis now the very witching time of night' – III. ii. 373); as with other kinds

70

of relevant information (e.g., about locale and time), the words spoken by the actors serve as the primary vehicle for signaling stage light and darkness. To enhance the spoken words dramatists could also call upon various conventional stage effects ('the terms upon which author, performers and audience agree to meet' according to Raymond Williams). Often cited by scholars is the introduction of torches or other lights to establish the existence of on-stage darkness (as in the final scene of *Romeo and Juliet* where both Paris and Romeo enter with torches). As noted in chapter two, moreover, dramatists also resorted to costume, especially the nightgown, to denote night or interrupted sleep. Throughout the period, both *enter with torches* (or candles or lanterns) and *enter in a nightgown* are widespread; thus, *Alphonsus Emperor of Germany* begins: '*Enter Alphonsus the Emperor in his nightgown, and his shirt, and a torch in his hand.*'

As demonstrated with other categories in chapter two, moreover, the stage directions and dialogue in the extant plays can provide further clues to how Elizabethan actors 'played' night or darkness. Thus, some scenes place great emphasis upon silence, stealth, even tiptoeing. In *A Woman Killed With Kindness*, Frankford, about to steal back into his house at night, asks for his dark lantern and tells Nicholas to 'tread softly, softly'; the latter responds: 'I will walk on Eggs this pace' (II, 137). In *Captain Thomas Stukeley*, three Irish rebels are directed to enter '*softly as by night*,' with the dialogue emphasizing quiet and stealth ('softly let us creep about by the walls' – ll. 924–5, 957–8). In *Greene's Tu Quoque* a boy who enters '*with a lantern*' is told: 'Softly Boy, softly, you think you are upon firm ground, but it is dangerous; you'll never make a good thief, you rogue, till you learn to creep upon all four' (L2r); the subsequent dialogue then makes much of poor visibility. In Shakespeare's *3 Henry VI* the watchmen guarding Edward IV's tent talk of night and sleep; Warwick and his group then enter '*silent all*,' drive off the guards, and re-enter '*bringing the King out in his gown, sitting in a chair*' (IV. iii. 22. s.d., 27. s.d.). The most revealing evidence about 'playing' night comes from the Trojan horse sequence of Heywood's *2 The Iron Age*. After Synon has called upon 'sweet mid-night' to mask 'mischief and black deeds,' the Greeks come on stage '*in a soft march, without noise*,' while Agamemnon urges: 'soft, soft, and let your stillness suit with night, / Fair *Phoebe* keep thy silver splendor in, / And be not seen tonight.' After Synon appears above *'with a torch'* speaking again of 'horrid night,' Menelaus proclaims: 'March on then, the black darkness covers us.' The stage direction reads: *'They march softly in at one door, and presently in at another. Enter Synon with a stealing pace, holding the key in his hand.'* When Synon unlocks the horse, *'Pyrrhus, Diomed, and the rest, leap from out the Horse. And as if groping in the dark, meet with Agamemnon and the rest: who after knowledge embrace'* (III, 377–80).

Such signals as *'silent all'* or *'softly as by night'* or *'as if groping in the dark'* make immediate sense to the modern reader or actor but are especially revealing when we remember that the *'as if'* action was being presented in full light. Other appropriate conventions also turn up regularly. For example, if a torch or candle was cited as the only source of light in a given scene, to extinguish that light was to indicate stage darkness (an effect readily enforced through dialogue and acting). Thus, in *The Hog Hath Lost His Pearl* Albert climbs to Maria's window *'and being on the top of the ladder, puts out the candle'* (ll. 265–6); with the only light on stage extinguished, Maria then mistakes Albert for her lover, Carracus. In *The Maid in the Mill* Fletcher presents an even more complicated version of the same confusion 'in the dark,' for here Martin (pretending to be his friend, Antonio) *'ascends'* to Aminta (pretending to be Antonio's love, Ismenia). The dialogue reads:

> AMINTA.   *Antonio?*
> MARTIN.   Yes *Ismenia.*
> AMINTA.   Thine own.
> MARTIN.   Quench the light, thine eyes are guides illustrious.
> AMINTA.   'Tis necessary.   *Exeunt* (VII, 59)

Here the quenching of the light *is* 'necessary' to establish the 'darkness' necessary for such mutual confusion to take place. In the scene already cited from *Greene's Tu Quoque*, one figure who wishes to remain unseen by a second group says: 'Out with the candle, who's that asks the question?'; after some dialogue 'in the dark,' another figure directs: 'Boy, up with your lantern of light, and show him his associates' (L2v). In other plays, the 'darkness' associated with the extinguishing of an on-stage light can be linked to a rape (*The Queen of Corinth*, VI, 17) or a murder (e.g., *The Atheist's Tragedy*, II. iv; *Macbeth*, III. iii).

Consider two more elaborate scenes, one tragic, the other

comic, that build upon this convention. First, in *The Atheist's Tragedy* Borachio enters '*warily and hastily over the stage*' (II. iv. o. s.d.); after he descends into the gravel pit (presumably, a trap-door), two servants enter '*drunk, fighting with their torches*' so that their lights are extinguished (one says "'Tis exceeding dark' – l. 8). After the murder of Montferrers has been accomplished 'in the dark,' servants enter '*with lights*' (l. 17. s.d.) and find the body. Later, Borachio notes that, after the lights had been put out, 'then darkness did / Protect the execution of the work / Both from prevention and discovery' (ll. 129–31). Again, in Fletcher's *The Night Walker* Wildbrain meets Mistress Newlove at night while a supposed ghost is roaming the house; she asks him to 'put your candle out' and to 'hold me fast' and he readily complies. After she is frightened off, the clownish Toby enters, saying: 'my light's out / And I grope up and down like blind-man-buff, / And break my face, and break my pate.' The two men hear but cannot see each other, so that, in a very funny sequence, Wildbrain mistakes Toby for a woman, calling him/her 'a hairy whore' when he tries for a kiss (VII, 331–3). Starting with a light, extinguishing it, and then playing darkness could thus be a fruitful way for actors in full light to convey treachery or comic confusion in the dark.

As shown by the scene from *The Night Walker*, such errors and confusion in imaginary darkness are especially appropriate for comedy (as in the long night sequences at the climaxes of *The Two Angry Women of Abingdon* and *The Merry Wives of Windsor*). Often the comic effect is linked to the inability of figures to 'see' what would be clear in a day scene and what *is* clear to the audience (as when Puck gets the four lovers to lie down on stage without seeing each other in *A Midsummer Night's Dream*, III. ii). In Fletcher's *Thierry and Theodoret*, a villain is tricked into an important revelation when he is left on stage, bound, near another figure whom he can talk with but not see (in fact, the other 'victim' is one of the plotters). Similarly, in *Love's Pilgrimage* Fletcher brings on Phillipo and Theodosia as in a room at an inn '*on several Beds*' and in the dark so that she can reveal her plight to a supposed stranger (actually her brother); after the revelations, Phillipo calls for candles, a figure enters '*with a light*,' and Theodosia recognizes her brother (VI, 246–50). In Haughton's *Englishmen for My Money*, a long comic night sequence begins with Vandalle, one of the foreign suitors, suspended in a

basket hanging between the stage floor and the 'above,' a striking
stage picture that remains in full view of the audience for some
time but is not noted by a host of figures who come and go during
the scene. In Davenport's *The City Nightcap*, after a bed is *'thrust
out'* with Lodovico and Dorothea, Francisco is led into the 'dark'
chamber, goes first to the wrong side of the bed ("'sfoot there's a
beard? but all's well yet, she lies on this side sure') and then must
stand by in fear ('How I do dwindle!') when Dorothea wakes her
foolish husband (as part of her plot) who is unable to see the man
standing next to his bed (II. i. pp. 111–14). In such scenes,
imaginary stage darkness sets up that audience superiority in
seeing and awareness basic to many different comic effects.

Two similar comic scenes, each involving violence, show the
lengths to which a dramatist can take this convention. First, in
Fletcher's *Women Pleased* (VII, 275–7) Isabella, knowing she is
about to confront her jealous husband, persuades her servant
Jaquenet to 'sit here, as if thou wert asleep' and then exits with the
candle. The infuriated Lopez then enters in the dark ('have you
put your light out? I shall stumble to ye') and scratches Jaquenet's
face ('has harrowed me, plough'd Land was ne'r so harrow'd'),
but when the husband returns with witnesses to his wife's supposed disfigurement and shame, they find an untouched Isabella
('where's the scratch'd face ye spoke of, the torn garments, / And
all the hair pluck'd off her head?'). In *The Guardian*, Massinger
takes Fletcher's scene several steps farther. Iolante has prepared
a banquet for her supposed lover (actually her brother in disguise)
but is thwarted by the unexpected arrival of her banished
husband, Severino, who threatens her, binds her, and departs
with the taper to search the house ('in darkness howl thy mischiefs' – III. vi. 93). To the rescue comes Iolante's servant,
Calypso ('how's this? no lights? what new device? will she play /
At Blindman-buff' – ll. 107–8), who, like Fletcher's Jaquenet,
trades places with her mistress. Severino reappears *'having a
knife'* (l. 142 s.d.) but without a taper ('it is a deed of darkness,
and I need / No light to guide me' – ll. 143–4) and proceeds in the
dark to stab Calypso and, as emphasized repeatedly in the
dialogue, to cut off her nose ('Oh my nose! I had one' – l. 168).
After Iolante and Calypso again exchange places (significantly,
the noseless servant does not reappear in the play), Severino
enters *'with a Taper'* to overhear his wife's plea to heaven that, if

she has been true to wedlock, 'restore my martyr'd face and wounded arms / To their late strength and beauty' (ll. 230–1); immediately, she finds: 'this minute I / Perceive with joy my orisons heard and granted' (ll. 232–3). Now, in the light, Severino sees blood on the floor but an untouched wife and can only respond: 'I profess / I am astonish'd' (ll. 244–5).

From this range of examples (some of which, like Massinger's sequence, will appear extreme to the modern reader) emerge some significant and revealing differences between our sense of theatre and the logic of presentation in the age of Shakespeare. To convey 'night' today, a director uses lighting to establish stage darkness and then has the actors enter carrying torches or groping in the dark or unable to see something of importance; we thereby *start* with a verisimilar stage night as a justification for confusion in the dark. But an Elizabethan dramatic company would have used dialogue, torches, nightgowns, groping in the dark, and failures in 'seeing' – all presented in full light – to establish the illusion of darkness for a viewer who, presumably, would infer night from such signals and stage behavior. For us, the lighting technician supplies night and the actors perform accordingly; for them, the actors provided the signals and the audience cooperated in supplying the darkness. For us, one figure fails to see another *because* the stage is dark; for them, one figure failed to see another and *therefore* the stage was *assumed* to be dark. Our theatrical sense of cause-and-effect (the stage is dark, therefore a given action took place) may then at times be inappropriate.[1] Rather, at the Globe a greater burden lay upon the dramatist, the actor, *and* the spectator to sustain the illusion of night and darkness through imaginative participation. Again, remember the injunctions from *Henry V*: 'Let us ... / On your imaginary forces work'; 'piece out our imperfections with your thoughts'; 'eke out our performance with your mind.'

To the modern eye, this Elizabethan logic for presenting night and darkness can yield further anomalies. Thus, as R. B. Graves has argued, at the Globe or Blackfriars 'indications of darkness were effected by the introduction of more, rather than less, light onto the stage,' for 'light paradoxically represented darkness.' At the same time, 'the deployment of property lights about the stage was very realistic, because real people do light candles and torches when it gets dark,' so that the on-stage action 'was real enough, even though the illumination on stage was not.' As Graves describes the technique, when a torch or candle was carried on stage to denote night, 'the theatrical statement was that an *instrument* of light had been called into use'; therefore, 'it was the instrument, or rather the imaginary need for the instrument, and not the light it produced that represented the darkness.' Thus, a taper (commonly used as a nightlight in a bedroom) would denote an indoor scene, but torches or lanterns would denote the outdoors. Graves concludes: 'whether the audience was to think of the scene as indoors or outdoors was determined by the *type* of lighting utensil, not by its light,' for the scene was 'set' by 'the shape of the utensils rather than the quality or quantity of the light they produced.' Indeed, given the difficulty of keeping candles or tapers lit on windy days, Graves goes so far as to suggest that the actors may never have bothered to light them 'since the light of the flames added little to, indeed worked against, the evocation of darkness.'[2]

Awareness of the Elizabethan approach to stage light and darkness can have significant implications for modern productions and criticism. As Lee Mitchell pointed out thirty years ago, Shakespeare's 'imaginary darkness' had distinct advantages, especially since 'no matter how deep the imaginary gloom, the audience could always see the performer quite clearly.' With such 'high visibility,' Mitchell argues, 'although characters on stage might not be able to recognize one another, the audience could always recognize the characters. Tragic mistakes could be foreseen in the making, surprises anticipated, and deceptions penetrated.' As Mitchell shrewdly observes, 'many scenes of imaginary darkness actually depend upon daylight visibility for their full effect.'[3] Conversely, modern productions that severely darken the stage may unwittingly bury essential elements of the original scenes, casting shadow rather than light upon their meaning and effect.

Thus, several scholars have commented upon the *dis*advantages of modern lighting in presenting Elizabethan plays. G. Wilson Knight, for one, notes that 'the moment we begin to rely on lighting as a primary aid to significance, the actors begin to dissolve, gesture and facial expression lose value, words are blurred.' Often, he notes, modern lighting has its price: 'the actors become dream figures, invisibility clouds expression. Grouping becomes meaningless; if we clearly see only the chief figures, their positional relation to the rest is blurred or lost; and also the relation of every one to the stage itself, especially its centre.'[4] Similarly, Graves has argued that in the original productions 'the overall, evenly distributed light meant that the audience's attention could not be directed to specific actors or stage properties'; rather, the Elizabethan playwrights 'were free to direct the audience's attention to some telling stage business or to catch their imaginations by the language.' As Graves observes: 'when they soliloquize, our modern Hamlets are usually very alone indeed, visually isolated from the stage scenery, cut off from any sort of comforting relationship with their physical environment,' but Elizabethan actors 'performed in a pleasant, ungovernable light which shone on the tiring-house façade and spectators as well as on the actors' so that 'the overall illumination' allowed 'a sense of continuity between the stage and the auditorium, between the actors and their background.'[5]

Both Knight and Graves cite some specific scenes. For example, Knight observes: 'I have never yet seen a performance of *Hamlet* where the actors facing the Ghost were properly visible.' As he notes, various kinds of stage trickery can make the Ghost impressive, but he laments the absence of that 'greater effect which has the power not just to please with a transient titillation, but rather to transfix the listener and crucify him to an unforgettable experience.'[6] Echoing Mitchell, Graves points out that 'the steady, over-all illumination of the public and private stages, far from imposing a restriction on the actors and playwrights, meant that even in scenes of pretended darkness the audience could see and respond to the visual media of the actor's craft.' For the full effect of various scenes, on-stage figures 'need to be seen while they are supposed to be standing in the dark.' Thus, after looking closely at the moment involving the Duchess of Malfi, her brother Ferdinand, and a dead man's hand, Graves concludes: 'whether the point of the scene was shock or suspense, whether the darkness was only symbolic or was suggested by a slight diminution of light near the actors, the scene works best when played in enough light to allow the audience to see what is going on.'[7]

For me, the most revealing examples of Elizabethan stage darkness are to be found in those scenes in which Shakespeare turns the supposed limitations of his stage to metaphoric advantage. Consider first the murder of Banquo (*Macbeth*, III. iii) where, by the end of the scene, the theatrical darkness is often so deep today that a spectator cannot make out what is happening. Indeed, I recently saw one production in which I *think* that the third murderer's function was to help Fleance escape, but, because the stage was so dark, I could not be sure. But, in a Jacobean production, no such doubt could have existed for a viewer. Moreover, the scene enacts a murder but also enacts an escape that, as revealed by the dialogue, is accompanied by the putting out of a light: 'who did strike out the light?' asks the third murderer; 'was't not the way?' replies the first (l. 19). Thus, the original spectator would have recognized that the three murderers end the scene with the body of Banquo in a conventional darkness (as signaled by the putting out of an on-stage light), but that spectator would also have clearly seen their frustration and failure ('we have lost best half of our affair') represented by their inability to extinguish the light that is Fleance. The killing of Banquo and the putting out of the light help to epitomize what the Macbeths, the creatures of night and darkness, are doing to Scotland (and to themselves), but a modern director's imposition of a verisimilar stage night upon the scene may oversimplify the situation by calling attention away from a significant failure on the part of the forces of darkness. Many modern productions thus realize the rich darkness of the murder at the expense of the glimpse of light in a visible escape.

For a comic rendition of such a metaphoric darkness, consider the confusion in the 'moonlit' woods during Acts II and III of *A Midsummer Night's Dream*. Spectators familiar with modern productions expect to witness some form of stage night (or moonlight) for such moments, but what would have been the effect in the original production when all the scenes in this comedy, whether in Athens or the woods, night or morning, were played in the same light? One result may have been a greater emphasis upon failures in 'seeing' linked not to poor visibility (or even to the love-juice itself) but to the transforming power of love or the imagination, a motif orchestrated throughout the play. Thus, in a major speech early in the comedy Helena notes that 'things base and vile, holding no quantity, / Love can transpose to form and dignity,' because 'love looks not with the eyes, but with the mind, / And therefore is winged Cupid painted blind' (I. i.

232–5). Later, Bottom observes shrewdly that 'reason and love keep little company together nowadays' (III. i. 130–1). Without any verisimilar stage darkness, many of the comic events may appear more clearly linked to such speeches. In particular, the final confusion involving Demetrius and Lysander, in which each takes Puck for his intended opponent and is therefore led astray ('where art thou?' – 'I will be with thee straight' – 'Where dost thou hide thy head?' – 'Yea, art thou there?' – III. ii. 401–11), becomes less a consequence of dim light (this scene is often played in a stage mist or gloom) or even of Puck's magical control but rather acts out in one climactic (and very funny) moment the brand of myopia or blindness everpresent in this part of the comedy. The implicit suggestion in many modern productions that physical darkness causes these and other errors may blur some shrewd comic insights into the nature of love and lovers.

A more complex presentation of such metaphoric not-seeing 'in the dark' is to be found in Act v of *Troilus and Cressida*. First, the Greek leaders escorting Hector to the tent of Achilles enter '*with lights*,' with Agamemnon complaining 'we go wrong, we go wrong' and Ajax responding 'No, yonder 'tis; / There, where we see the lights' (v. i. 64. s.d., 65–6). After this initial confusion of the Greeks lost in their own camp, Hector exits with Achilles, and Ulysses directs Troilus to follow Diomedes' torch to Calchas' tent (ll. 83–4), thereby setting up the much-discussed observation scene in which Ulysses and Troilus 'stand where the torch may not discover us' (v. ii. 6) to watch Cressida and Diomedes and in turn be watched by Thersites. Here, the modern reader or spectator usually takes for granted an on-stage darkness that helps us to believe that the figures being observed (especially Cressida and Troilus) remain unaware of the observers, so, according to the prevailing modern 'logic,' Cressida and Diomedes would be in the light and Ulysses, Troilus, and Thersites in shadow or darkness. But if instead the scene is played in full stage light and 'imaginary darkness,' greater emphasis falls upon the inability or unwillingness of the key figures to see or understand each other. Thus, in her farewell to a Troilus she imagines far away, Cressida comments: 'One eye yet looks on thee, / But with my heart the other eye doth see,' and adds: 'Ah, poor our sex! This fault in us I find, / The error of our eye directs our mind' (ll. 103–6). These lines could be especially telling if she is looking at or in the vicinity of a

Troilus she cannot (or can no longer) 'see.' Moments later, after Troilus has tried to convince Ulysses and himself that 'this [is] not Cressid' (l. 129), Thersites asks: 'Will 'a swagger himself out on's own eyes?' (l. 132), thus emphasizing the disillusioned lover's attempt to block out what actually has been seen. No brief analysis can do justice to this climactic acting out of Troilus' quandary, but a staging in full light would not only make more visible the actors' expressions and gestures but would also heighten various lapses in 'seeing' in both psychological and metaphoric terms.

By far the most complex rendition of such metaphoric darkness can be seen in the final movement of *Othello*.[8] The time of day for the climactic actions is clearly established in the willow scene through Othello's comments (e.g., 'get you to bed on th'instant'), Desdemona's call for her 'nightly wearing,' and Emilia's reference to the nightgown (IV. iii. 6, 15, 33). The imagistic context is then further orchestrated in the banter between Desdemona and Emilia when the former swears 'by this heavenly light' that she would never abuse her husband but the latter responds: 'Nor I neither by this heavenly light. / I might do't as well i'the dark' (ll. 63–5). Metaphorically, the darkness of this play is linked to actions predicated upon the absence of 'heavenly light.'

Readers impatient to get to the moving last scene then tend to skip over v. i, a practice abetted by directors who regularly pare down the lines considerably (e.g., Othello's appearance here is rarely included) and usually present the action in a deep stage darkness to justify the many allusions in the dialogue to night and confusion in the dark. But a spectator watching the scene in full light and hearing all of Shakespeare's lines can get a much richer effect. First, Roderigo, who is prepared to commit a murder because of 'satisfying reasons' provided by Iago (v. i. 9), can emerge as a clear analogue for Othello, especially if the Moor conceals himself in the same place Roderigo had stood 'behind this bulk' (l. 1). Shakespeare also sets up a clear echo of the earlier 'ocular proof' scene (IV. i) where an eavesdropping Othello had seen but not heard Cassio 'confess,' for here the Moor hears Cassio cry out ('O, help, ho! light! a surgeon!' – l. 30) but does not 'see' him (he concludes, wrongly: 'minion, your dear lies dead' – l. 33). Verisimilar darkness may blur some revealing links.

Even more important for the spectator watching the action in 'imaginary darkness' is an increased awareness of the manipulative power of Iago who literally controls the light during much of the scene. With Othello gone, the two wounded figures crying out for help, and Gratiano and Lodovico cautiously proceeding in the dark ('Two or three groan. It is a heavy night. / These may be counterfeits. Let's think't unsafe / To come in to the cry without more help' – ll. 42–4), Iago enters *with a light* (Gratiano comments: 'Here's one comes in his shirt, with light and weapons' – l. 47). Although the two onlookers soon recognize Othello's ancient ('a very valiant fellow' – l. 52), it is Iago who 'finds' Cassio and Roderigo (killing the latter), identifies Lodovico, Gratiano and Bianca, publicly discloses the identity of Roderigo ('Lend me a light' – l. 88), and quickly casts suspicion upon Bianca by controlling how those on stage 'see' her ('Do you perceive the gastness of her eye? ... Behold her well; I pray you look upon her' – ll. 106, 108). If after the initial violence Othello, the two wounded men, and the two Venetian lords are clearly visible to the spectator but cannot see each other, that spectator is far more conscious of Iago's influence upon how people 'see' those around them (going back to the 'satisfying reasons' he has been providing since the beginning of the play) and is painfully aware of the inability of various on-stage figures to grasp what is truly happening. Here, as with the murder of Desdemona moments later, darkness is linked not to verisimilar night or lighting but rather to a failure to 'see' associated both with Iago's poison and a blindness (or vulnerability) on the part of the observer. As with the eavesdropping in IV. i, through Elizabethan conventions the emphasis can fall upon the gaps or spaces between people, the darkness of misperception, the blindness of inner night.

The modern director, conscious of the evocative power of the actors' gestures and expressions, is less likely to play the famous final scene in a deep stage darkness[9] even though the signals clearly call for 'night,' with Desdemona, presumably in her 'nightly wearing,' in bed and Othello, with or without a nightgown, entering *with a light* (V.. ii. o. s.d.). No attentive reader or spectator can miss the metaphoric intensity of light and darkness at this pivotal moment. Thus, with his initial 'It is the cause, it is the cause, my soul,' Othello brings with him (despite the 'light' he carries) an inner darkness linked to his twisted sense of 'cause' and justice ('Yet she must die, else she'll betray more men' – l. 6).

Starting with the Moor's 'Put out the light, and then put out the light,' the 'flaming minister' is at the center of our consciousness, both as a light that can be relit if quenched and as an index to Othello's intentions towards Desdemona's life ('but once put out thy light ...'). But given the orchestration of darkness and not-seeing in the previous scene (as well as the link between Iago there and Othello here as luciferic light-bearers), the light and the metaphoric darkness inform what follows, especially Othello's inability to hear or see the truth in Desdemona. In his terms, Othello is gaining 'justice' by putting out Desdemona's 'light.' For the spectator, who can readily see beyond the Moor's limited sense of 'It is the cause,' the tragic chooser is not only extinguishing a light or life in his innocent wife but, equally if not more importantly, putting out a light within himself ('it is the cause, *my soul* ...'), linking himself irrevocably to Iago and Iago's darkness ('I am your own for ever' – III. iii. 480).

When Othello then regains his 'sight' after the murder (thanks to the truths from Emilia at the cost of her 'light' or life), his anguished comments echo (and provide a Hellish context for) the earlier banter between Desdemona and Emilia about 'heavenly light' and 'i'the dark,' for, thinking forward to the Last Judgment, the Moor foresees that 'This look of thine will hurl my soul from heaven, / And fiends will snatch at it,' and calls out: 'Whip me, ye devils, / From the possession of this heavenly sight!' (ll. 274–9). Moments before his suicide, Othello looks for but cannot see cloven feet on the demi-devil Iago (l. 286), just as he has been unable to 'see' Cassio and Desdemona. The putting out of a light in this scene therefore has little if anything to do with stage illumination. Rather, especially given the careful preparation in the previous scene, the presence and deployment of such a light can generate metaphoric possibilities close to the heart of this tragedy and can help us to grasp more fully the inner darkness and the failure in vision that have led to 'the tragic loading of this bed' (l. 363). The image of something eclipsed from our sight is not linked to on-stage lighting but rather to Lodovico's sense of outrage or horror as he comments 'The object poisons sight; / Let it be hid' (ll. 364–5), presumably ordering the closing of the curtains on the bed. Here, as opposed to earlier actions 'in the dark,' Shakespeare *wants* us to be cut off from sight of the three bodies, whether to stress the horror or perhaps to suggest the inability of Lodovico and the other remaining figures to comprehend or face up to what has happened.

What this final 'Let it be hid' suggests, then, is that Shakespeare carefully worked into his scripts his own strategy as to what his spectator should and should not see. On a simple level, the reader or director who assumes a verisimilar stage night forgets that, in the original productions, the 'over-all illumination of the public and private stages, far from imposing a restriction on the actors and playwrights, meant that even in scenes of pretended darkness the audience could see and respond to the visual media of the actors' craft.'[10] On a subtler level, when we assume that figures on stage do not see each other *because* it is dark we are in danger of translating the action into our own idiom and theatrical language at the expense of the original metaphors. Let me emphasize that I am *not* arguing in favor of a wholesale rejection of modern technology – in this case, lighting – and a return to the conditions prevailing at the Globe. I *am* arguing, however, that we should not become the prisoners of that technology, confined by assumptions about verisimilitude and stage illusion that have accumulated over the last century and a half, thanks, in part, to the effects possible first with gas, then with electric lighting. *Our* sense of 'going to the theatre' – again, sitting in a darkened auditorium watching actors perform in a lighted space – *is* an anachronism and, when thrust upon Shakespeare's scripts, can produce subtle yet telling kinds of distortion. To ignore the conventional or metaphoric basis of Elizabethan night and darkness is to flirt with the danger of transforming Shakespeare's metaphors, scenes, and effects into an experience acceptable to audiences today but greatly diminished from their full potential (and, in *Othello*, perhaps to blur the truly insidious darkness). To fall into this trap is to equate ourselves with Malvolio, who, imprisoned in his mad-house, is told by Feste that 'there is no darkness but ignorance, in which thou art more puzzled than the Egyptians in their fog' (IV. ii. 42–4).

5 · The logic of 'place' and locale

O, this is to be imagin'd the *Counter* belike?
(*Every Man Out of His Humour*, l. 4246)

If theatrical professionals have used a later technology to impose a verisimilar stage night upon imaginary darkness, for an even longer period editors have imposed upon many, most, or all Elizabethan scenes a later sense of 'place' or locale. Behind this insertion of information not in the original texts or scripts lies a long and hallowed tradition dating back to the eighteenth century. Thus, in the Preface to his highly influential edition of Shakespeare, Edmund Malone wrote that his reader will 'be pleased to find the place in which every scene is supposed to pass, precisely ascertained: a species of information, for which, though it often throws light on the dialogue, we look in vain in the ancient copies, and which has been too much neglected by the modern editors.'[1] Malone (like several editors before him) therefore supplied what he felt had too long been neglected, and, until quite recently, most editors have followed his example, even when the dramatist has provided no clear signals. As a result, many of the texts widely used by actors, directors, and critics give prominent typographical position to such locales as 'a wood' or 'a room in the castle,' designations that have no authority other than the theatrical or literary tastes of an early editor. Thanks to generations of editing and typography, modern readers have thereby been conditioned to *expect* placement of a given scene ('where' does it occur?), regardless of the fluidity or placelessness of the original context or the potential distortion in the question 'where?'[2]

But the skeptic may well ask: what exactly does 'another part of the forest' (to cite a notorious example) mean when linked to a production designed for a large open platform where the 'forest' is largely if not totally the product of the 'imaginary forces' of the spectator? I know of no evidence that the audience at the Globe or

Blackfriars shared this obsession with place. Rather, as Gerald Eades Bentley reminds us, Shakespeare 'wrote with the Globe, not the Drury Lane, in mind, and he wrote a drama of persons, not a drama of places' in which, normally, 'the audience is expected to concentrate wholly on words and actions and to ignore the place where the action may have taken place.'[3] Thus, as Bernard Beckerman has demonstrated, scenes at the Globe could be localized (in a specific place) or unlocalized (with no indication whatsoever) or generally localized (about sixty per cent) wherein the stage represents 'a place at large' (e.g., Rome or Troy) 'but not a particular section of it.' According to Beckerman, Shakespeare's stage 'was constructed and employed to tell a story as vigorously and as excitingly and as intensely as possible,' with the spectators informed about the locale 'by the words they heard, not the sights they saw,' so that 'place was given specific emphasis only when and to the degree the narrative required.'[4] To the original audience, 'place' was an adjunct of the narrative, not an end in itself.

For a provocative example, one need only look at the last scene of *Coriolanus* which a majority of editors locate in Antium but others place either in Corioli or 'a Volscian city.' Upon close inspection, the reason for such disagreement is readily apparent. Plutarch, for one, sets this action in Antium, a placement Shakespeare appears to be following in various references during the first part of the scene (see v. vi. 49, 72, 79). Later in the action, however, as J. P. Brockbrank points out in his New Arden edition, 'the dramatic advantage of *Coriolanus*, in *Corioles* proves irresistible, and Corioles remains the setting from then on' (p. 302). Although the modern editor or reader may feel the need to fix upon one place, Shakespeare apparently chose to have it both ways, so that he could establish an interesting link between this moment and our previous view of Aufidius in his native town (IV. v) without losing the opportunity of climaxing his play with an even more revealing comparison between the actions of Caius Marcius here and in Act I when he earned his name (a moment the protagonist so untactfully recalls just before his murder). Without ever being *too* specific, two different parts of the same scene can thereby suggest two different Volscian cities, each useful (for the moment) in setting up a meaningful dramatic analogy (with the links to a third city, Rome, always hovering in the background).

To fix the place as either Antium *or* Corioli is to impose our rigidity upon Shakespeare's chameleon stage and to blunt part of the effect of this climactic scene.

To see further examples of the potential flexibility of the Elizabethan stage, consider several scenes from the early 1590s. First, the shoemaker who picks a fight with Jenkin in *George a Greene* asks: 'Come sir, will you go to the town's end now sir?' and Jenkin responds (with no intervening stage direction): 'Ay sir, come. / Now we are at the town's end, what say you now?' (ll. 1009–11). Presumably, a walk across part of the large apron stage was enough to signal the displacement indicated in the dialogue (a use of theatrical 'space' for journeys characteristic of much early English drama). A different effect is found in *The Massacre at Paris* where the king announces hypocritically 'I will go visit the Admiral' who has been wounded and is 'sick in his bed.' Rather than using an *exit* and *re-enter* to move the king to the Admiral's chambers, Marlowe instead keeps the royal group on stage and '*enter the Admiral in his bed*' (ll. 255, 250, 256. s.d.).

A relevant Shakespearean example is to be found in *Romeo and Juliet* at the end of I. iv (the original texts have no scene divisions here) where the second quarto directs Romeo and the masquers to '*march about the stage*' rather than exiting (thereby signaling a change in locale), while '*Servingmen come forth with napkins*' (thereby establishing the new locale as the Capulet house); then, after some dialogue among the servants, '*enter all the Guests and Gentlewomen to the Maskers*' (I. v. 15. s.d.). The first or 'bad' quarto also provides no *exeunt* for the masquers, omits the servants, and has only '*Enter old Capulet with the Ladies*' saying 'Welcome Gentlemen, welcome Gentlemen' (C2v). As in *The Massacre at Paris* at no point is the stage cleared; rather, in both quarto versions of the sequence the action is continuous, regardless of any change in place. As seen in these examples, the open stage (at least in the 1590s) can be neutral as to place until indicated otherwise by appropriate signals, whether dialogue ('Now we are at the town's end') or properties (e.g., the Admiral's bed, napkins) or stage business ('*march about the stage*'). Indeed, to expedite matters the Admiral's chambers could be brought to the king or Capulet's ball to the masquers (or the wrestling participants and audience to Rosalind in *As You Like It*, I. ii). Our expectation of a 'change in scene' or an exeunt–re-entry to denote a change in locale is here superseded by another principle, perhaps best described as dramatic economy. This particular effect may or may not be widespread after the 1590s but was at least possible or acceptable from the point of view of Elizabethan actors and spectators. Regardless of any modern notions of 'place,' their world picture *could* include such a phenomenon.

Also evident in the sequence from *Romeo and Juliet* is the transition from outside (wherever I. iv, the Queen Mab scene, supposedly 'takes place') to inside (the Capulet house) without any clearing of the stage. Such transitions may be deeply embedded in other Shakespearean scenes only to be teased out by the careful reader (e.g., *Othello*, I. i, *Romeo and Juliet*, I. ii). In contrast, in III. i of *Julius Caesar* the first part of the action clearly takes place outside (so Cassius chides Artemidorus: 'What, urge you your petitions in the street? / Come to the Capitol' – ll. 11–12), but the climactic moments clearly take place 'in the Capitol.' The Folio provides no evidence that Caesar and the others march about the stage, but, with little or no difficulty, the Lord Chamberlain's Men could have signaled a transition from the streets and the crowd to some new place without any total clearing. Significantly, the key issues raised 'in the street' and in the transition (e.g., will Caesar be told of the plot by Artemidorus or Popilius?) are continuous and do not admit of any neat divisions that correspond to outside and inside. Rather, the logic of the sequence supersedes any formal sense of outside–inside, so that a break here would be quite inappropriate, even more so than in Act I of *Romeo and Juliet*.

An especially interesting example of such an outside–inside transition or continuity without a clearing of the stage can be noted near the end of *Henry VIII* (significantly, not a play from the 1590s). At the outset of the climactic sequence, Cranmer is forced to wait outside the door of the council chamber; first Cranmer himself, then Doctor Butts and the king (who end up viewing his plight from above) comment upon his being forced to wait 'at door' or 'at the door' (v. ii. 17, 24, 32). The Folio stage direction is then quite specific: '*A council table brought in with chairs and stools, and placed under the state. Enter Lord Chancellor, places himself at the upper end of the table on the left hand ... Duke of Suffolk, Duke of Norfolk, Surrey, Lord Chamberlain, Gardiner seat themselves in order on each side*' (v. iii. 0. s.d.).

Cranmer, the council is then told, waits 'without' and, moreover, 'has done half an hour to know your pleasures' (ll. 5–6). When the Keeper tells Cranmer 'your grace may enter now' (l. 7), the stage direction reads: '*Cranmer approaches the council table.*' As is evident in my citation, the Pelican editor (like many modern editors) starts a new scene with the entrance of the council, but, as R. A. Foakes points out in his New Arden edition (p. 157), 'the directions in F indicate that Cranmer is on stage all the time, presumably kept waiting outside one of the doors to the stage ... Thus when he is called before the council, all he has to do is to approach the table.' As Foakes sees it, 'an audience would readily accept the presentation of Cranmer as on stage, but *outside* the council-chamber.' As with Marlowe's king or Romeo, a new 'place' comes to a figure already on stage or, in different terms, the door that separates Cranmer from the council has changed from a stage door (for an off-stage council) to the stage space between the waiting figure and the seated lords at the table. Again, a Jacobean sense of continuity or dramatic economy or theatrical 'space' has superseded later strictures about outside–inside or the cleared stage.[5]

Two more examples are to be found in Act IV of *2 Henry IV* which is divided into two scenes in the Folio but five scenes in most modern editions (and, of course, no designated scenes in the quarto). The distinction between the modern IV. iv and IV. v is based upon the king's request: 'I pray you, take me up, and bear me hence / Into some other chamber' (IV. iv. 131–2), for at this point the Pelican editor adds his own bracketed stage direction: '*They bear him to another place.*' But no such signal is provided by the quarto nor the Folio; rather, the king's lines cited above are the beginning of a continuing speech with no indication of such a break. Here and later, the dialogue does support a general sense of various rooms or chambers on or off the stage (see IV. v. 4, 17, 56, 82); later Henry IV asks about 'the lodging where I first did swoon' (l. 233) with the answer calling attention to the fulfillment of the Jerusalem prophecy. Nonetheless, the picking up and bearing of the dying king 'into some other chamber' is accomplished without an *exeunt* or a clearing of the stage or any such break in the continuity. If indeed a new place or 'chamber' is to be signaled, that signal will be provided by movement around or across the large platform stage, probably while the king is speaking, rather than by a modern sense of 'change in scene.'

A similar gap between continuity then and division now can be seen in the modern distinction between IV. i and IV. ii. The relevant dialogue reads:

WESTMORELAND. The prince is here at hand. Pleaseth your lordship
                To meet his grace just distance 'tween our armies.
MOWBRAY. Your grace of York, in God's name then, set forward.
ARCHBISHOP. Before, and greet his grace, my lord; we come.
LANCASTER. You are well encountered here, my cousin Mowbray.
                Good day to you, gentle lord archbishop.

In the quarto of 1600, the stage direction '*Enter Prince John and his army*' appears after Westmoreland's speech above (G2r); in the Folio, '*Enter Prince John*' follows the Archbishop's line. Neither quarto nor Folio calls for or even suggests a change of scene. For the Pelican editor, however, the dialogue provided by Mowbray and the Archbishop 'seems to indicate that the stage was cleared' at this point (p. 728). In contrast, A. R. Humphreys argues in his New Arden edition (p. 126) that 'to mark an *Exeunt* and change of place is misleading'; rather, 'the place changes to "just distance 'tween our armies" with no more ado than that the army present and the army entering take up positions on the stage' (see also the appendix on pp. 240–1). As in IV. iv–v, movement across or around the large platform can establish a new configuration without any clearing of the stage and without any break in the continuity.

Perhaps the most flexible Shakespearean use of 'place' can be seen in the play that least observes neo-classic rules – *1 Henry VI*. Consider IV. iii–iv in modern editions. With York '*and many Soldiers*' on stage (IV. iii. o. s.d.), a figure enters to urge the rescue of Talbot beleaguered at Bordeaux. In the Folio this figure is designated as '*another Messenger*' (l. 16 s.d.) and in the subsequent speech prefix as '2. *Mes.*,' but just before his exit York rejects the plea and says: 'Lucy, farewell.' The messenger or Lucy then stays on stage, delivering a seven line speech on 'the vulture of sedition,' at which point most modern editors indicate a new scene at the entrance of '*Somerset, with his Army*' (IV. iv. o. s.d. in the Pelican). Somerset quickly rejects the pleas of the Captain who then calls upon 'Sir William Lucy' (l. 10) to support his concern for Talbot; the Folio speech prefixes now denote Lucy rather than

Messenger. The point behind York and Somerset's rejections of the parallel pleas is evident to any reader; clearly, Talbot is undone (quite unhistorically) by the internal divisions within the English forces, not by the prowess of the French. To establish this point as emphatically as possible, Shakespeare plays fast and loose with a neo-classic sense of place or scene division by having one figure (Messenger–Lucy) provide two parallel pleas and a soliloquy in between without leaving the stage, while York–army and Somerset–army are moved on and off.[6] Concern for geographical realism has been superseded not just by dramatic economy but also by a kind of symmetry of action or parallel construction that makes the central point unmistakable. Adroit use of stage space or distance could 'soften the blow' for the modern viewer (e.g., in his New Arden edition Andrew Cairncross argues that 'Lucy does not leave the stage and return' but rather 'remains on stage, aside' – p. 96), but I can imagine the scene staged with Messenger–Lucy at stage center so that the parallel generals and armies are subordinated to his pivotal role and point of view. As Shakespeare designed it, whose scene is it, anyhow?

To ignore this flexibility available on the open stage is then to run the risk of distorting Shakespeare's plays by misreading the signals and asking the wrong questions (as in a production of *Othello* where the director inserted a skylight into an elaborate bedroom set in v. ii so that the Moor could have 'chaste stars' to address in his opening lines). Rather, a key question about locale should be: what details are to be supplied by the players and what is to be left to the imaginary forces of the viewer (a question that has recurred in discussion of both the gestic *this* and on-stage darkness)? Thus, Alfred Harbage argues that Benedick's request for his page to bring him a book 'in the orchard' (*Much Ado*, II. iii. 4) 'would be superfluous if the orchard looked like an orchard'; in a similar situation, a modern dramatist would not write: 'Bring it to me here in the living room.' Benedick's subsequent comment that he will hide 'in the arbor' (l. 33) may also 'send our minds seeking for some stage object or recess that looks like an arbour, either because an arbour would normally appear upon a modern stage or because in some other Elizabethan play an arbour was demonstrably employed.' But, for Harbage, 'just as the bare stage became an orchard at Benedick's word, so any part of it might become an arbour at his further word. The arbour is wherever he chooses to stand.'[7] Translating Benedick's 'orchard' and 'arbor' into stage properties or a locale visible to the spectator may therefore misconstrue an essential feature of the open stage and, in the process, change the terms upon which actors and audience originally agreed to meet.

Admittedly, substantial stage properties at times could be introduced onto the open stage. Thus, the annotator of the manuscript of *Sir John van Olden Barnavelt* calls for a bar for the major trial scene and a scaffold for the execution scene (ll. 2160, 2852–3), two sizable properties that recur in the stage directions of printed texts; at appropriate moments, large objects (especially thrones and beds) could be introduced and could bring with them some sense of locale. But a bar is not a courtroom, a throne is not a throneroom, and a bed is not a bedroom, especially when such objects stand alone on an otherwise bare stage and carry with them potential metaphoric or symbolic meanings. Thus, Lawrence J. Ross argues that Desdemona's bed in the final scene 'is not placed in a bedroom' but rather 'brings the locale of a bedroom with it, by implication, and only to that extent.' For Ross, 'the bed is not a necessary "room" furnishing which might *encumber* the action; it is physically and expressively the center of the action and so placed as to be inseparable from it,'[8] a formulation that could apply as well to the bed in *'Tis Pity She's a Whore*, v. v, to many playhouse thrones (e.g., in *3 Henry VI*, i. i), to banquet tables (e.g., in *Macbeth* and *The Tempest*), even to the cauldron in *The Jew of Malta*. Not nurtured by cinema, television, the novel, and naturalism, an Elizabethan viewer would not have moved as readily from the signal (bed, throne) to our sense of 'room' but probably would have inferred a general sense of locale (especially if reinforced by the dialogue and the acting) while being receptive to potential larger meanings. Our sense of 'furniture,' like our sense of 'place' (or 'night'), can lead to subtle distortions (and diminutions) of Elizabethan effects for the open stage.

As a result, even though scaffolds, beds, bars, thrones, and banquet tables could be introduced for major scenes, the comments and caveats of Bentley, Beckerman, Harbage and others, along with the obvious difficulty of getting large objects on and off the platform stage, should encourage us to proceed cautiously in drawing inferences about requisite properties and action when we lack clear evidence. For example, many of the supposed 'tree scenes' cited by Werner Habicht actually do not require a stage tree,[9] any more than *All's Well That Ends Well*, IV. i, requires a hedge corner; thus, at least one manuscript with playhouse annotations in which the dialogue has a figure tied to a tree (*Beggar's Bush*) has no marginal call for such a property and, indeed, no indication that anything other than some permanent part of the stage would have been used. As noted in chapter three, the gestic *this* made excellent sense to the original spectator who saw an actor point to something (an object, a fixed feature of the stage, vacant space) but can cause problems for the literal-minded reader today who reacts to 'this hedge corner' or 'this bulk' with reflexes conditioned by naturalism and by more recent stage pictures. In deciding what and what not to supply to satisfy our sense of locale, the modern critic, editor or director should keep in mind the two poles Shakespeare so tellingly provides in *Henry V* and *A Midsummer Night's Dream*: on the one hand, the player's plea for his audience to 'eke out our performance with your mind'; at the other extreme, the hilarious caveat provided by the hempen homespuns who feel it necessary to introduce onto their stage Moonshine and Wall.

To explore further this relationship between properties and 'place,' let me turn to Sidney's witty and incisive comments on locale in early Elizabethan drama. 'Now ye shall have three Ladies walk to gather flowers, and then we must believe the stage to be a Garden. By and by, we hear news of shipwreck in the same place, and then we are to blame if we accept it not for a Rock. Upon the back of that, comes out a hideous Monster, with fire and smoke, and then the miserable beholders are bound to take it for a Cave. While in the meantime two Armies fly in, represented with four swords and bucklers, and then what hard heart will not receive it for a pitched field?'[10] Despite the tone and implicit criticism, note Sidney's inferences. A sixteenth-century viewer seeing 'four swords and bucklers' in combat would infer an army and, in general terms, 'a pitched field'; given appropriate dialogue and acting, when a monster enters through a stage door, for a moment that door becomes a cavemouth; if ladies gather flowers, even if only in pantomime, the spectator would supply the garden; the sighting of a shipwreck would imply a vantage point near the water, Sidney's rock. His terms ('Now ... By and by ...

Upon the back of that ... While in the meantime ...') adroitly express a witty incredulity that all these events are being presented 'in the same place,' but from another, more sympathetic point of view this chameleon-like flexibility could be seen as a major asset. Like Jonson and Chapman two decades later, Sidney rejects many popular dramatic conventions (what 'the miserable beholders' have to 'believe' or 'accept' if the scene is to work). Nonetheless, his mocking inferences correspond to the audience reactions encouraged by the Chorus of *Henry V*: signals determine locale; a part implies the whole; 'imaginary forces' must predominate; only a 'hard heart' can resist Shakespeare's handling of the flexible, essentially placeless open stage.

Note, moreover, that except for a costume for the monster, none of the different locales cited by Sidney requires significant properties; rather, his garden, rock, cave, and battlefield could readily be supplied through the skill of the actors and the imagination of the spectators. What then are we to infer about the many equivalent scenes in the age of Shakespeare that place figures in specified locales (e.g., prison, tavern, forest, shipboard), but provide no clear indication other than the lines delivered by the players of how such locales are to be presented or elicited? Such scenes often do supply directions for figures to enter '*in prison*' or '*in a tavern*' or '*in the woods*' or, '*a-shipboard*' (*Pericles*, III. i. o. s.d.), but I can find no clear distinction between 'authorial' and 'playhouse' sources in such cases (such signals turn up in manuscripts with playhouse annotations and even in the theatrical 'plots'). Whether such stage directions, in Hosley's terms, should be understood as 'fictional' or 'theatrical' is also much in doubt, for, as with '*from hunting*,' one can interpret the signal either as an author thinking in terms of his story or someone knowledgeable about theatrical practice thinking about the conventional shorthand (or the appropriate properties) for conveying a prison, tavern, ship or forest.

After reading through many such scenes, I have become increasingly conscious of the potential in the term *as* (either explicit or implied) for interpreting such signals. Thus, in *The Shoemakers' Holiday* Dekker directs: '*Enter Jane in a Seamster's shop working*' (III. iv. o. s.d.); at the beginning of *Doctor Faustus* both versions have the protagonist enter '*in his study*.' For most readers, 'shop' and 'study,' especially when coupled with 'in,' conjure up a stage picture that requires significant properties (e.g., a counter, a table, shelves) as well as a discovery space (not too long ago, an 'inner stage') to provide some sense of a room or an interior. But what if the stage direction read (or implied) '*as in a Seamster's shop*' or '*as in his study*'? Thus, in *Greene's Tu Quoque* a figure enters '*as in his study reading*' (B4v). As perhaps suggested in '*working*,' Jane would then enter carrying her sewing and a stool (as in *Coriolanus* where Volumnia and Virgilia enter and '*set them down on two low stools and sew*' – I. iii. o. s.d.). The rest of Dekker's stage direction ('*and Hammon muffled at another door, he stands aloof*') suggests the use of two stage doors rather than a discovery space; Hammon's line that begins the scene ('Yonder's the shop and there my fair love sits') then creates the shop by means of a gestic *yonder*. Similarly, to satisfy the minimum needs of his opening scene Faustus need only enter carrying books (the major properties for his opening speech) and a chair or stool, for the final line of the Prologue ('and this the man that in his study sits') has clarified the 'where' for the spectator. Both stage directions could equally well be considered 'fictional' (in keeping with the story rather than the staging), but both make excellent sense too in terms of *as in*. Despite the first reaction of the reader, neither requires a discovery space or anything other than portable properties.[11]

Actual *as in* signals are less common than the *as from* variety discussed in chapter two (the latter, moreover, usually deal not with a place but with a recently completed action), but they do occasionally turn up. Thus, Davenport has two figures enter '*as in prison*' (*The City Nightcap*, v. ii. o. s.d.); Suckling has Iphigene enter '*as in a Garden*' (*Brennoralt*, III. i. o. s.d.); similarly, '*enter Sir Thomas More, the Lieutenant, and a servant attending as in his chamber in the Tower*' (*Sir Thomas More*, ll. 1728–9); in a related usage, some sailors in *The Two Maids of More-Clacke* appear with digging implements '*as on the sands*' to bury a trunk and refer to 'this golden beach' (F4r). Playwrights sometimes use *as* to cite a specific locale: '*as upon the Exchange*' (*How a Man May Choose a Good Wife From a Bad*, A2r); '*as being at Mile-end*' (*I Edward IV*, I, 25), although such places can readily be established in the dialogue ('we hear the Londoners will leave the city, / And bid us battle here on *Mile-end Green*'). More revealing are '*enter Scudmore, as in his Chamber in a morning, half ready, reading a Letter'* (*A Woman is a Weathercock*, I. i. 1–2) and '*enter two Officers, to lay cushions, as it were in the Capitol*' (*Coriolanus*, II. ii. o. s.d.) where apparently the 'chamber' or 'the Capitol' is conveyed not by furniture but by a figure in unready dress or officers laying down cushions, just as the 'golden beach' was conveyed through figures with digging tools. Thus, appropriate dialogue, costumes, and portable properties (books, sewing, cushions, spades) can readily provide a spectator with a sense of *as in* a chamber, study, shop, or Capitol or *as on* a beach.

Again (as with so many problems cited in this study), the role played by the spectator (as opposed to that of the property master) must be taken into account. Consider a curious moment from Jonson's *Every Man Out of His Humour* where Fallace, visiting Fastidious Brisk in prison, laments: 'what pity is't to see so sweet a man as you are, in so sour a place?' at which point she '*kisses him.*' Since Brisk and Fallace have only just entered, Jonson's two on-stage choric commentators initially are confused about where the action is taking place. Thus, Cordatus reacts to Fallace's line and the kiss: 'As upon her lips do's she mean?' and elicits from Mitis: 'O, this is to be imagin'd the *Counter* belike?' (ll. 4241–6). In this instance, Jonson's quarto (his first published play and one of the longest dramatic works of the period) is undoubtedly far removed from the script performed by the Lord Chamberlain's Men in 1599 (a version now irrevocably lost or buried in the text as revised for publication). Here as elsewhere in Jonson's canon, the scholar looking for evidence about contemporary staging cannot draw upon stage directions and other signals with any confidence, for (as noted in chapter two) this author self-consciously transformed the original playscripts into poems or literary texts. Nonetheless, Mitis' reaction suggests to me that the placing of the action in 'the *Counter*' (missed momentarily by the usually perceptive Cordatus) was not signaled by any significant property (and certainly was not linked to any equivalent to a prison 'set'), but rather was left largely to the previous dialogue (Macilente had just informed Fallace's husband that Brisk was 'i'the Counter' – ll. 4213–14), the behavior of the two entering actors, and, of course, the imagination ('this is to be imagin'd'). Although not specifically noted by Jonson, a sense of '*as in prison*' clearly is attached to the entrance for this scene.

Still, the reader familiar with staging problems, then or now, may well ask: to present a prison, forest, tavern, or ship, why not simply bring on stage some portable property (e.g., a grate for a prison, a tree for a forest, a sign or bush for a tavern, ropes thrown down for a ship)? Such too were my expectations at the beginning of my search, but after looking at a wealth of prison, tavern, forest, and sea scenes (along with the courtroom,[12] the most popular locales), I have found surprisingly little evidence for such shorthand through emblematic properties. Again, what may seem quite logical to us (to use bars or a grate somehow to denote a prison) need not have been part of the shared assumptions or theatrical logic in the age of Shakespeare. Given the nature of the evidence, I cannot prove that such properties were not there, but I have found very little evidence for their presence in my sample of roughly four hundred plays.

Rather, what I have found is suggestive but by no means conclusive evidence that locale was most often keyed to the presence of representative figures whose costumes or accessories provided the major signals for the spectator. As noted in chapter one, sea or shipboard scenes use details suggestively but sparingly (as with Heywood's '*Sea devices fitting for a fight*'), but such moments consistently call for a captain or some other recognizable nautical figure (master, boatswain, lookout, gunner). Even more obvious is the use of a shepherd or rustic to signal a pastoral setting. In *As You Like It*, the first Arden scene calls for '*Duke Senior, Amiens, and two or three Lords, like Foresters*' (II. i. 0. s.d.); a later scene stipulates '*Lords, like Outlaws*' (II. vii. 0. s.d.); Rosalind's arrival in Arden is announced in the dialogue (II. iv. 13–14) and immediately reinforced by the appearance of the two shepherds, Corin and Silvius. In similar fashion, in *Clyomon and Clamydes* a stage direction reads: '*Enter Neronis in the Forest, in man's apparel*'; after one speech, '*in the Forest*' is given visual and theatrical force by '*enter Corin a Shepherd*' (ll. 1254, 1287). *The Thracian Wonder*, like *Clyomon* a play of many locales, signals its numerous switches from court to country through appearances of shepherds, with particular emphasis in the dialogue and stage directions upon their sheephooks (a property also used for the same purpose in *Tom a Lincoln*, 4a). Many plays that evoke a pastoral setting either introduce early in the sequence or start a scene with shepherds, woodsmen, huntsmen, or country fellows, with the father and son of *The Winter's Tale*, III. iii, a representative example.

The principle seems to hold for many different locales. In addition to the bar, courtroom scenes are keyed to the presence of judges and legal personnel in their distinctive costumes; as noted in chapter two, hunts are established by sound effects, weapons, the color green in costumes, and almost always the presence of one or more huntsmen. I have found few actual garden scenes in Elizabethan plays, but the famous one in *Richard II* is keyed to the presence of the two gardeners, not to any discernible stage properties. Evidence about tavern scenes is inconclusive. Some major sequences do apparently require stage furniture, but more common is the situation in *Greene's Tu Quoque* where a group of figures enter with a drawer, reveal verbally that they are in a tavern, ask for wine, and have the drawer exit and re-enter with their drinks (C1v–C2r, D2r). Most tavern scenes require no more than the presence of such a drawer (or host or vintner) along with hand-held bottles and glasses, just as the occasional inn scene needs only a host or innkeeper.[13] For particular stage business a dramatist may require tables and chairs (as in II. iv of *1 Henry IV*) but to provide a general sense of a tavern locale (especially for a brief scene, as in *Look About You*) the players probably resorted to (and audiences accepted) the combination of dialogue, hand-held drinks, and a drawer in some readily recognizable costume (an apron, a distinctive cap).

The locale most often specified in stage directions and dialogue presents the most difficult problem, for I have found evidence to suggest at least four different ways to present prison scenes. A surprisingly large number of plays call for figures to enter '*in prison*';[14] moreover, '*in prison*' is even signaled in one of the theatrical 'plots' (*The Dead Man's Fortune*, III. i). To convey such an effect, today's director can introduce a set of bars (or a barred effect through lighting), but would bars or a grate have been introduced in Elizabethan productions? In his chapter on the staging of such scenes, E. P. Pendry finds 'only scanty evidence' (he cites three examples) for such grating;[15] both of the two stage directions (*Antonio and Mellida*, ll. 844–5; *A New Wonder, a Woman Never Vexed*, p. 59) could easily be 'fictional' ('*Mellida goes from the grate*'; '*above at the grate, a box hanging down*') and need not correspond to any general theatrical practice.

Granted, in general terms grates often are associated with prisons (as in *The Merry Wives of Windsor*, II. ii. 8–9). More specifically, the imprisoned Anne Sanders recalls 'standing at a grate / That looks into the Street' (*A Warning for Fair Women*, K1r); in the Tower, Lady Jane Grey tells Guilford to look 'out of this firm grate' (*Sir Thomas Wyatt*, III. ii. 11); in Massinger's *The Picture*, a figure trapped *'above in his shirt'* complains: 'slight tis a prison ... / The windows grated with Iron; I cannot force 'em' (IV. ii. 130. s.d., 138–9). Such passages, however, quite likely drew upon the imagination of the spectator rather than the presence of such a property, so, despite the sprinkling of evidence, my conclusion is that, on the Elizabethan stage, iron bars did not a prison make.

In contrast, several plays provide solid evidence that a trap door could be used to establish a prison or dungeon below.[16] For example, in the playhouse manuscript of *Believe as You List* the annotator anticipates the temptation of Antiochus in his dungeon with: '*Gascoigne and Hubert below: ready to open the Trap door for Mr. Taylor*' and '*Antiochus ready: under the stage*'; the jailor discusses his tasks 'before I have raised him out of the dungeon'; and the marginal note for the hero's first speech is '*Antiochus below*' (ll. 1825–31, 1877–9, 1926, 1931). In Fletcher's *The Island Princess* the imprisoned king enters '*laden with chains, his head, and arms only above*; no exit is indicated, but the angry Governor says: 'Down with him low enough, there let him murmur,' while an attendant comments how 'quietly he sunk down to his sorrows, / As some men to their sleeps' (VIII, 107–10). Similarly, a jailed figure '*under the Stage*' in Massinger's *The Renegado* is '*pluck'd up*' and has his chain taken off (IV. iii. 4. s.d., 6. s.d., 50. s.d.).

The evidence for grates or traps, however, is overshadowed by the many examples of two other methods particularly suited to the open stage and Elizabethan expectations. First, a convenient way to signal a prison locale (or a general sense of incarceration) is to present a figure bound by shackles, irons, fetters, or manacles. As just noted, the king in *The Island Princess* appears '*laden with chains*' which must be broken to effect his rescue, while in Fletcher's *The Double Marriage* two figures '*in the Bilboes*' are fettered so that a key is needed for their escape (VI, 346). Conceivably, whether or not specific signals are available, such shackles may have been present in most prison scenes as a kind of visual shorthand. Thus, in *Measure for Measure* does the Provost's offer to Pompey to 'redeem you from your gyves' for assisting Abhorson (IV. ii. 8–9) tell us that all the prisoners in this play were wearing gyves or is the line merely metaphoric? When called for, this property can yield a strong effect. In the manuscript of *Dick of Devonshire* the heroic Dick Pike, captured by the Spanish, appears 'in shackles, nightcap, plasters on his face' and later 'shackled'; at his trial he is brought in guarded, 'an Iron about his neck, two Chains manacling his wrists; a great Chain at his heels' (ll. 941, 1447, 1624–5), with the emphasis upon an heroic figure only kept in check by such restraints. Other scenes call for fetters to stress the powers of villains (*Lust's Dominion*), the powers of a magician (*John of Bordeaux*), the blows of Fortune (*A Woman Killed With Kindness*), or the welcome conditions of martyrdom (*The Martyred Soldier*); often the putting on and taking off of chains is important to the plot (*Captain Thomas Stukeley*, *The Two Noble Kinsmen*, *The Island Princess*, *The Double Marriage*). The device is particularly effective when the dramatist wishes to emphasize the degradation of an heroic or worthy figure,[17] or when a sense of imprisonment or bondage, symbolized by such restraints, is also developed metaphorically.

For an excellent Shakespearean example consider *Cymbeline*, v. iv, where Posthumus, in manacles, develops at length a complex sense of the bondage in which he has placed himself through various errors. Bondage, he states, is 'a way, / I think, to liberty' in the sense that death 'is the key / T'unbar these locks'; his conscience is 'fettered / More than my shanks and wrists' so that some 'penitent instrument' is needed 'to pick that bolt, / Then free for ever.' To redress Imogen's death he asks the gods to 'take this life / And cancel these cold bonds.' In Shakespeare's hands, the gyves and the generalized prison locale become part of a larger metaphor that conveys the mental and moral state of this perplexed figure who must come to terms with his past and present bonds before he can rediscover both himself and Imogen and find 'freedom.' In one sense the fetters 'place' the action 'in prison,' but both the gyves and the prison are rich signals that lead us to larger imagistic and psychological meanings. Rather than being a liability, the absence of a verisimilar prison yields greater freedom to the imaginative vision of Shakespeare and his audience.

The large majority of prison scenes, however, provide no evidence for grates, trap doors, fetters, or any other distinctive property. Rather, in keeping with my earlier observations about tavern, sea, hunt, and pastoral scenes, the one common denominator for a wealth of scenes is the presence (along with one or more prisoners) of a jailer, gaoler, keeper, or lieutenant of the Tower usually at the outset of the sequence. Such keepers or jailers can appear outside the prison locale (*The Comedy of Errors*, *Fair Em*, *The Merchant of Venice*); an occasional scene will include only the incarcerated figure (*The Fleer*). But most of the relevant scenes (and there are many) start with a jailer who serves primarily to usher figures on- and off-stage (*Sir John Oldcastle*, *The Fair Maid of Bristow*, *The Fatal Dowry*, *The Honest Lawyer*) and has few if any lines (a silence readily explained by several manuscript references that indicate that these parts were often taken by the stagekeepers). The many historical plays that place prisoners in the Tower of London do so by having on stage a lieutenant whose identity, if not already clear through his costume, is signaled in the dialogue.[18] Typical of the general technique are the situations in *The Wounds of Civil War*, where Marius enters '*with his keeper, and two soldiers*' (l. 913); *A Warning for Fair Women*, where Anne Sanders appears '*and her keeper following her*' (K1r); and 1 *Henry VI*, where the dying Mortimer is brought in by jailers (II. v. o. s.d.) whom he addresses as keepers.

How would a spectator have recognized such a jailer or keeper? Not surprisingly, the detail often specified is a set of keys.[19] Thus, in 2 *Tamburlaine*, when Callapine's jailer, Almeda, reappears as a king, Tamburlaine comments: 'let him hang a bunch of keys on his standard, to put him in remembrance he was a Jailer' (ll. 3640–1); pretending to rebuke the Provost (a term often equivalent to jailer) for killing Claudio, Duke Vincentio discharges him of his office, commanding: 'Give up your keys' (*Measure for Measure*, v. i. 458); the clownish jailer in *The Martyred Soldier* says: 'let us I say, be unbounded in our Authority, / Having the Laws, I mean the Keys, in our own hands' (D2v). As a result, stealing or handing over keys plays an important part in many prisoner sequences (e.g., *Edward II*, *All's Lost by Lust*, *The Wasp*); thus, in three different plays (*Richard III*, 2 *Edward IV*, *The True Tragedy of Richard III*) a hapless Brackenbury hands over his keys to figures about to murder a prisoner in his charge.

For many readers today, one key will not adequately represent *in prison* any more than the presence of a jailer (or drawer or shepherd) will satisfy fully a modern sense of locale. Yet an audience attuned to the open stage, where objects not portable or part of the costumes could pose awkward problems, would have been especially alert to any distinctive detail or item of dress and would have made certain inferences (perhaps unconsciously) not always evident to us today. The fetters, sheephooks, nightgowns, and boots presented to that audience could serve merely as narrative shorthand for the exposition of locale, time, or atmosphere or, when used by a dramatist like Shakespeare, could generate complex and meaningful moments. For example, if 'the convent' associated with the order of St. Clare in *Measure for Measure* is conveyed solely through the costumes of the novice Isabella and '*Francisca, a nun*' (I. iv. o. s.d.), then as Isabella moves through the play she metaphorically carries that convent (and its particular strictness) with her. Her costume (and any significant alterations in it) can therefore become quite significant, whether to demonstrate her continuing rigidity or to act out some significant change[20] (e.g., in the final scene when she kneels at Mariana's request or when she responds to the duke's offer of marriage). The convent as a 'place' (quickly left behind) is far less important to the play as a whole than the habit of mind of the central figure who had chosen it. If both 'place' and choice are epitomized by the same costume, metaphorically the convent has been projected into the streets of Vienna, the halls of justice, and the prison in a fashion easily obscured when we ask the wrong questions about verisimilitude or locale in the original scene.

To see the potential in the Elizabethan approach to 'place,' let me conclude with two scenes that often bedevil the modern interpreter. First, editors and critics of *As You Like It* have puzzled over Duke Senior's 'banquet' that, according to the dialogue, is set up on stage in II. v (see ll. 26–7, 55–6) and then enjoyed in II. vii with no indication that it is removed for the brief II. vi (the first appearance of Orlando and Adam in Arden). In an appendix to her New Arden edition (1975), Agnes Latham argues that 'the simplest explanation is probably the right one, that the attendants unobtrusively remove the feast as part of their comings and goings in the background at the end of scene v, and bring it on again at the beginning of scene vii,' but she is still left with the question: 'why introduce the "banquet" at all in scene v?' (p. 133). In his New Variorum edition (1978), Richard Knowles also asks: 'what becomes of the banquet evidently prepared during the preceding scene?' (p. 109). After reviewing several answers that have been offered (e.g., that II. v and II. vi should be transposed, that an 'inner stage' was used so that the banquet could be concealed), Knowles concludes: 'the early setting of the table seems to me thoroughly puzzling; it is totally unnecessary, for the banquet could have been carried on, as banquets usually were, at the beginning of scene 7.' Directors too must wrestle with this apparent anomaly. Thus, in his 1977–8 production at Stratford Festival Canada, Robin Phillips rearranged the scenes into the sequence II. vi–v–vii, while, in the 1980–1 production for the Royal Shakespeare Company, Terry Hands cut the relevant lines in II. v so that the banquet first appeared in II. vii.

As most editors and critics would agree, Shakespeare did not *have* to introduce a banquet into II. v. Yet he *did*. The result, moreover, as Beckerman has pointed out,[21] is a clear example of the kind of simultaneous staging often found in earlier English drama. Even though prevailing post-Elizabethan assumptions (about locale, scene divisions, and the cleared stage) have obfuscated the issue, can we not consider the *advantages* of having a 'banquet' in full view of the audience during the speeches that constitute II. vi? In particular, consider how the presence of such food affects our reaction to Adam's 'O, I die for food' and Orlando's subsequent 'if' clauses: 'If this uncouth forest yield anything savage, I will either be food for it or bring it for food to thee ... I will here be with thee presently, and if I bring thee not something to eat, I will give thee leave to die; but if thou diest before I come, thou art a mocker of my labor ... thou shalt not die for lack of a dinner if there live anything in this desert.' If the food Orlando will find in II. vii is seen by the audience during II. vi (present but symbolically just out of reach) these 'if' clauses carry a different weight (e.g., compared to comparable speeches during the storm scenes in *King Lear*). To clear the stage in order to satisfy our sense of 'place' or scenic division is to simplify the situation and to run the risk of eliminating a rich and potentially meaningful effect, a good insight into the nature of Arden (or perhaps romantic comedy), especially since the 'if' clauses of II. vi are recapitulated and intensified in II. vii (see ll. 113–26) and then developed at length by Rosalind in v. ii and v. iv. Much virtue in if. And much virtue in the flexible Elizabethan stage and stage conventions.

As a final example consider *King Lear* where, at the end of II. ii, Kent is left alone in the stocks, Edgar enters for a speech of twenty-one lines, and, after his departure, Lear and his group arrive to find Kent. In a variety of ways this sequence has puzzled modern critics, editors, and directors. Readers as diverse as A. C. Bradley and Marvin Rosenberg have mused about 'where' Edgar is to be 'placed';[22] until quite recently, editors provided a heading such as 'the open country' or 'a wood' for Edgar's speech (traditionally designated as II. iii even though no scene divisions are indicated in Q–1 or the Folio); to avoid causing problems for their audiences directors usually use their lighting to black out Kent and highlight Edgar during his speech. To the modern reader or viewer, the presence of the stocks and the recently completed action involving Oswald, Edmund, Cornwall, and others implies one 'place' (e.g., the courtyard of a castle) which proves incompatible with a fleeing Edgar (especially given a lapse of time and the pursuit through open country implied in an escape by means of 'the happy hollow of a tree'). Obviously, many critics, editors, and directors would prefer not to have Kent and Edgar visible at the same time, even though some interpreters of the play have called attention to parallels between these two figures and a few (particularly George F. Reynolds) have posited a stage convention whereby Kent is 'just not there.'[23]

If Kent is eclipsed by modern lighting, neither Edgar nor the spectator is conscious of the figure in the stocks (who also has lost his identity and been subjected to injustice). But what about the original production at the Globe where the King's Men had no way to black out Kent? Can we at least entertain the possibility that Shakespeare, surveying the various options, *chose* to have these two figures visible simultaneously, not only making no effort to hide the juxtaposition but indeed encouraging a staging that would draw all possible attention to it? On the unencumbered Globe stage with few distractions for the eye, such a choice would yield a highly emphatic effect that would strongly enforce any interpretation based upon links between Kent and Edgar, a form of theatrical *italics* that could not be missed by an attentive viewer. The original audience would not have been troubled by the imaginary darkness in which Edgar failed to see Kent; indeed, Edgar's stage behavior in itself could have been a major signal for stage night. Given their conditioning, that audience would not have been concerned with 'place' unless the question had been called to their attention. The stocks would then signal not a courtyard or other specific public locale but rather a general sense of imprisonment or bondage (or the perversion of an instrument of justice, as developed more fully, again with Cornwall and Regan, when Gloucester is bound to a chair in III. vii), just as Edgar would be assumed to be in flight, anywhere. The chameleon-like flexibility of the open stage here makes possible a juxtaposition rich with potential meanings, a juxtaposition (as in *As You Like It*) easily blurred or lost when we, like Thurber's American lady, ask the wrong questions.[24]

In conclusion, our tacit assumptions about 'place' and locale, like our similar assumptions about on-stage night and darkness, can stand between us and the full richness of some major moments in Elizabethan drama, especially in the plays of Shakespeare. The dramatists of this period had at their disposal a highly flexible stage and an appropriate set of conventions, both for darkness and for locale, that could be used to tell a story deftly or to develop some complex effects (as in my examples from *Coriolanus*, *Cymbeline*, *Measure for Measure*, *As You Like It*, and *King Lear*). In particular, the use of costume or significant properties to present 'place' (again, like the use of not-seeing to present 'night') had a metaphoric or thematic potential that could yield rich rewards. To recover and appreciate the original conventions, then, is to expand our awareness of the potential range of the best plays. On the other hand, to impose an anachronistic conception of 'place' (or darkness) upon these playscripts is often to transform the scenes, to delete Shakespeare's *italics*, to deny the choric pleas of *Henry V*, and to supply our version of Moonshine and Wall.

6 · The logic of stage violence

As he raises up the axe strikes out his own brains
(The Atheist's Tragedy, v. ii. 241. s.d.)

A third area where Elizabethan playscripts run afoul of modern expectations is to be found in the many moments of on-stage violence – duels, armed combats of many varieties, murders, even maimings. Although evidence about the original staging of such scenes often is very limited (e.g., *'they fight'*; *'kills him'*; *'alarms and excursions'*[1]), scholars generally have agreed how duels, sieges, and battles would have been presented at the Globe or Fortune or Rose. For example, stage historians argue forcefully that the players would have presented one-to-one fights (Mercutio versus Tybalt, Edgar versus Edmund) as convincingly as possible 'in order to make the fencing scenes in their plays realistic enough to satisfy a critical audience well versed in the use of swords.'[2] As to battle scenes, the platform stage and the size of the companies provided various constraints, but, despite the apologetic stance provided by the Chorus to Act IV of *Henry V*, dramatists and actors were not intimidated by the prospect of lapsing into the 'brawl ridiculous.' Thus, even though some unsympathetic voices sounded out against swords, bucklers, drums, and trumpets,[3] stage battles appealed to audiences for several decades and remained an integral part of Shakespeare's plays from *1 Henry VI* through *Coriolanus* and *Cymbeline*.[4] As opposed to stage duels, such battles placed greater demands upon the 'imaginary forces' of the spectator to 'piece out' or 'eke out' what could not actually be shown (as also with *'Hercules shoots ... Enter Nessus with an arrow through him'*), but, given an appropriate theatrical 'space,' both verisimilar duels and selective stage battles could work effectively then and can still work today, even for that spectator with a penchant for 'realism.'

But the important question remains: need we stop here? Is verisimilitude or 'truth to life' the only yardstick to be applied to

Elizabethan stage violence?[5] Thus, to call attention to the wide-spread appetite for elaborately staged combat, scholars have pointed to tournaments, barriers, and other displays of martial skills, including an elaborate naval show at Deptford in 1550 for Edward VI (that involved a fortress on a boat in the Thames, various galleys and pinnaces, and a series of assaults and counter-assaults) and the Hock Tuesday play performed for Queen Elizabeth at Kenilworth in 1575 (a re-enactment of the English victory over the Danes[6]). But even the battles performed for royal audiences were not limited to verisimilar combats. In 1581 the queen and the French ambassadors watched an assault upon a fortress by a group of attackers supported by cannons mounted upon a rolling platform. But the fortress was the Fortress of Perfect Beauty, while the attackers were led by the Four Foster Children of Desire (one of whom was Sir Philip Sidney). Most revealing, after the long speeches and compliments to the queen, 'the two cannons were shot off, the one with sweet powder, and the other with sweet water, very odoriferous and pleasant, and the noise of the shooting was very excellent consent of melody within the Mount. And after that was store of pretty scaling-ladders, and the footmen threw flowers and such fancies against the walls, with all such devices as might seem fit shot for Desire.'[7] Clearly, the deployment of this battle flowed not from the logic of the battlefield but from the logic of what constitutes 'fit shot for Desire.' To the modern eye the example may appear quaint, but the principle – the presence of an alternative kind of logic for scenes of violence – could be fundamental.

Such an alternative logic is widely available in the English dramatic tradition, especially in the moral plays. An excellent example can be found in one of the earliest extant English plays, *The Castle of Perseverance*, when Superbia, Invidia, and Ira storm the castle only to be beaten back by Meekness, Charity, and Patience. The only stage direction (*Tunc pugnabunt diu*) is unrevealing; as Richard Southern points out, 'the Sins are armed with slings, lances, shot and bows … and the Virtues, it seems, pelt them with the symbolic roses.'[8] After his defeat, each Sin complains for a stanza about how he was 'all beaten black and blue' (l. 2219) or gained a broken head or was undone, all because of the 'fair roses' or 'flowers sweet' or 'a rose that on rood was rent' (ll. 2211, 2213, 2220). The Sins have raged and threatened with conventional weapons but have been bested by the qualities of their opposing Virtues epitomized by the roses associated with the Passion. But the crucial theatrical question, so easily missed or misconstrued (as in Southern's use of 'pelt'), is: how are the roses to be delivered in this stage combat? Although verisimilitude obviously has little relevance to this allegorical play, our habits of thought automatically translate a rose as a weapon into a projectile; we readily assume that the Virtues *hurl* the flowers at the Sins, either thinking in terms of the thorns (never mentioned in the dialogue) or the force of the throw (so that Meekness, Charity, and Patience become fast-balling baseball pitchers). But, quite the contrary, the beauty and spiritual meaning of the scene may lie in the *contrast* between the raging Sins and the calm Virtues who respond to violence and insults by delicately dropping roses (or rose petals) or perhaps by throwing the flowers heavenward to have them descend upon their enemies. Consider the theatrical effect if the colorful flowers float down gently yet wreak havoc upon the assaulters. The illogic in verisimilar terms would then create the logic or force of the scene – the power and the beauty of man's spiritual or virtuous nature.

Although lacking the pageantry and scope of *The Castle of Perseverance*, several moral plays from Queen Elizabeth's reign also provide evidence for an allegorical or symbolic logic behind stage violence. In most of these plays the most notable figure is the Vice who carries a memorable prop, a dagger of lath, that he uses to belabor freely his vice-lieutenants and victims. This dagger can serve both as a source of laughter and 'good theatre' and as a part of a larger pattern in which the comic violence of the Vice (or some other figure) is answered by an alternative spiritual force wielding a sword. In Ulpian Fulwell's *Like Will to Like*, the Vice (Nichol Newfangle) with his wooden dagger is contrasted to Severity, a figure of justice who carries a sword as his major property. In W. Wager's *Enough is as Good as a Feast*, the Vice (Covetous) also uses a great deal of verbal and physical intimidation (one stage direction tells us: '*He fighteth with them both with his dagger*' – l. 440). Then, near the end of the play Worldly Man, who has been corrupted by the Vice and has consistently misused his worldly possessions, ignores the warning of the prophet and goes to sleep on stage. At this point, enter God's Plague to '*stand behind him awhile before he speak*' (l. 1222 s.d.), define himself at length ('I go through all towns and cities strongly walled, / Striking to death, and that without all mercy'), and deliver a blow ('Here thou wicked, covetous person I do strike' – ll. 1245–7). Worldly Man later describes his dream: 'And methought before me the Plague of God did stand / Ready to strike me with a sword in his hand' (ll. 1301–2). The bulk of this play has been concerned with the power of the Vice in this world, a power often represented by his dagger, but the final movement displays the justice awaiting worldly men in the next world, a justice represented by the sword of God's Plague.

Interplay between true and false weapons need not be limited to the Vice's dagger of lath. In Wager's *The Longer Thou Livest the More Fool Thou Art* Moros again and again acts out his foolishness through his inept use of his weapons (e.g., making impossible claims, fighting alone on stage, getting both dagger and sword stuck in their scabbards). At the climax of the play the dramatist then brings on God's Judgment *'with a terrible visure'* (l. 1758 s.d.) and with a sword to tell the audience: 'I represent God's severe judgment, / Which dallieth not where to strike he doth purpose' and to announce that he has been 'sent to the punishment / Of this impious fool, here called Moros / Who hath said there is no God in his heart' (ll. 1763–7). To show the power of God to the fools of the world, this 'terrible' figure strikes Moros 'with this sword of vengeance' (*'strike Moros and let him fall down'* – l. 1791 s.d.). Here a false or limited weapon, which (like the Vice's dagger of lath) has hitherto been a source of laughter, is juxtaposed with a truly potent weapon wielded by a figure who represents a higher power ignored by the foolish protagonist. The various references to the dangers of sharp 'edge-tools' in the hands of a fool or madman (ll. 842–5, 1947–50) further develop this distinction between weapons that are abused and that higher 'sword of vengeance' that awaits erring humanity.

The most interesting use of the dagger and sword is to be found in George Wapull's *The Tide Tarrieth No Man*. Throughout the play Courage, the Vice, indulges in the usual threats and physical action (e.g., *'Out quickly with his dagger'* – l. 200 s.d.) to intimidate allies and victims. In contrast to Courage's ascendancy is the plight of Christianity, who should be exhibiting the well-known Pauline armor but instead is 'deformed' in appearance: *'Christianity must enter with a sword, with a title of Policy, but*

on the other side of the title, must be written God's Word, also a
shield, whereon must be written Riches, but on the other side of
the shield must be Faith' (l. 1439 s.d.). Although Faithful Few
turns the titles so that Faith and God's Word take their proper
place, Christianity is soon forced to resume the burden of Riches
and Policy owing to the continued depravity of Greediness and
the Vice. The restoration of the true sword and shield must wait
until the final scene. Again, Faithful Few is on-stage, this time
with Authority, who bears 'this sword of God's power' (l. 1837).
When Correction tries to arrest the Vice, Courage *draweth his*
dagger and fighteth' (l. 1821 s.d.), once more atempting to assert
his power. But the Vice's dagger, which earlier had dominated the
action, now fails, physically and allegorically, when juxtaposed
with the sword of God's authority and the correction that
accompanies it. With Courage off-stage and under arrest, Christianity's sword and shield can be restored to their pristine state in
the final action of the play.

The moral dramatists could thus use two sets of weapons – one
of which is associated with the temporary, worldly power of the
Vice, the other with the higher powers invoked at the end of the
action – to call attention to the two phases of their plays. Scenes
involving the dagger of lath or Moros' sword can be meaningful
and amusing in their own right yet still function as a part of a
larger pattern basic to the play as a whole. To cite another
example, the author of *The Trial of Treasure* provides three
scenes that span the play wherein: the hero, Just, 'bridles' the
Vice, Inclination; the other protagonist, Lust, unbridles the Vice
who subsequently leads Lust to his destruction; and, in the final
scene, Just rebridles Inclination to win Lady Trust. The dramatist
leaves us in no doubt about the point of this sequence: 'Thus
should every man that will be called Just, / Bridle and subdue his
beastly inclination, / That he in the end may obtain perfect trust, /
The messenger of God to give sight to salvation' (C2v). Again,
individual moments take on added meaning as part of a larger
pattern, here quite obvious.

Far less obvious is how such scenes would have been staged.
Although the reader can visualize with little difficulty the Vice's
use of his dagger, how would God's Plague or God's Judgment
deliver a blow against a foolish sinner? With a savage chop? or a
graceful, sweeping movement? or, in contrast to the Vice's comic

energy, a mere touch with the sword? For example, the signal for an execution in *Cambises* reads: '*Smite him in the neck with a sword to signify his death*' (C3r) wherein '*smite*' could suggest a powerful, 'real' blow but '*to signify his death*' could suggest a symbolic or stylized effect. A rare piece of external evidence is provided by an account of a lost play, *The Cradle of Security*, where R. Willis describes the arrival of 'two old men' representing 'the end of the world, and the last judgment' who bear a sword and a mace: 'the foremost old man with his Mace struck a fearful blow upon the Cradle; whereat all the Courtiers with the three Ladies and the vizard all vanished; and the desolate Prince starting up bare faced, and finding himself thus sent for to judgment, made a lamentable complaint of his miserable case.' However delivered, this 'fearful blow' (upon the cradle, not the protagonist) had an enormous impact upon at least one viewer, for Willis, some sixty or seventy years later, states: 'This sight took such impression in me, that when I came towards man's estate, it was as fresh in my memory, as if I had seen it newly acted.'[9] But neither this account nor various stage directions from other comparable plays nor information from dumb shows in plays like *Gorboduc* and *Jocasta* can confirm how verisimilar or how stylized would have been the original staging.

To consider scenes of stage violence in plays before the age of Shakespeare is therefore to end up with questions rather than answers. Of what value, then, are such moments from relatively obscure plays to the critic or director not particularly interested in theatrical history? After all, the plays of Shakespeare contain no cannons firing sweet powder and sweet water, no Virtues dropping roses upon Sins, no figures of heavenly judgment wielding irresistible swords or maces. I certainly am not arguing for an allegorical dimension for every stage duel in the age of Shakespeare, nor am I challenging all the conclusions of modern scholars. But as with my investigation of 'night' and 'place,' I *am* questioning the modern tendency to discuss such scenes solely in terms of verisimilar effects. When the overt allegory of the moral play became less fashionable, can we safely assume that the stagecraft and symbolic potential in such moments disappeared as well? Can we be confident that a blow in a non-allegorical Elizabethan play would be delivered with the speed, force, and timing of a similar blow in the street outside the theatre? Need a moment of stage violence at the Globe exist as an end in itself, adhering to a logic derived from an equivalent moment in 'real life,' or could it be linked to a symbolic or patterned logic relevant to the world of the play? Although examples from the moral plays cannot 'prove' anything about scenes from Marlowe, Heywood, and Shakespeare, this evidence should at least make us cautious about what we take for granted in the later, better plays.

As an introduction to the problem, consider first two moments from the plays of Heywood, a dramatist often praised for his 'realism.' In Part I of *If You Know Not Me You Know Nobody*, Princess Elizabeth, afraid for her life, falls asleep on stage. Heywood then provides a dumb show: '*Enter Winchester, Constable, Barwick, and Friars: at the other door, two Angels. The Friars step to her, offering to kill her: the Angels drive them back. Exeunt. The Angel opens the Bible, and puts it in her hand as she sleeps. Exeunt Angels, she wakes.*' The book, it turns out, is open to the passage: '*Whoso putteth his trust in the Lord, shall not be confounded*' (1, 228–9). The scene surely needs no explication. Note, however, the interesting parallel to a moment in Heywood's best known play, *A Woman Killed With Kindness*, a tragedy that lacks angels and dumb shows. After Frankford has discovered his wife in bed with Wendoll, Heywood directs the seducer to run '*over the stage in a Night-gown*' with the husband '*after him with his sword drawn*,' but the stage direction continues: '*the maid in her smock stays his hand, and clasps hold on him. He pauses for a while.*' After the pause, Frankford states: 'I thank thee maid, thou like the Angel's hand, / Hast stay'd me from a bloody sacrifice' (II, 138). This supernumerary maid has no assigned place in Frankford's fictional household (unlike the other servants who *are* developed as 'characters'). Rather, Heywood is again using a moment of threatened but prevented violence, this time with no obvious supernatural force, to call attention to the role of Heaven or mercy—reason in a decision at the heart of his play. Surely, neither the angel nor the maid should wrestle vigorously with the would-be violent figure, but, as in *The Castle of Perseverance*, the full effect is linked to the contrasting style and spirit of the alternative force. Rather than being a liability, this lack of 'realism' creates a special emphasis, a theatrical *italics*, that singles out such a moment for the viewer (as is also the case, although with a different emphasis, with the Nurse's intervention to prevent Romeo's suicide).

For another heavenly intervention in a non-allegorical play consider the climax of *The Atheist's Tragedy* where the villain, D'Amville, whose schemes have brought Charlemont and Castabella to the brink of public execution, chooses to take upon himself the role of headsman. Tourneur's stage direction reads: '*As he raises up the axe strikes out his own brains, staggers off the scaffold*' (v. ii. 241. s.d.). The speeches that follow leave no doubt about the significance of the violent event just witnessed. Thus, the atheist D'Amville can observe: 'There is a power / Above her [Nature] that hath overthrown the pride / Of all my projects and posterity' and 'yond' power that struck me knew / The judgment I deserv'd, and gave it' (ll. 258–60, 265–6). A judge then comments about 'the power of that eternal providence / Which overthrew his projects in their pride,' and Charlemont replies: 'Only to Heav'n I attribute the work' (ll. 271–5). Obviously, this scene defies any expectations linked to 'realism'; after all, how is a modern actor in the tradition of Ibsen and Stanislavski to play a character who 'strikes out his own brains' and then lives on for almost thirty lines, delivering two major speeches? But as in Heywood (or *The Castle of Perseverance*) the absence of 'realism' can be an asset rather than a liability. Indeed, the startling misdirection of the blow which unexpectedly brings justice to an apparently successful villain is the key to the final effect of this tragedy, a striking rebuttal to the claims and assumptions of this atheist who has relied solely upon his reason or 'brains.'[10] A less-spectacular conclusion might be more 'believable' to us but would drastically change the play, for Tourneur, like Heywood, has used theatrical *italics* to underscore the presence of a power above nature and beyond human reasoning.[11]

Less obvious to the reader but equivalent in effect are several scenes from Shakespeare's *1 Henry VI*. The links between Joan of Arc and the forces of Hell are spelled out late in the play when the fiends forsake her, ignoring her pleas for help against the English forces (v. iii), but earlier scenes could also provide a sense of the larger powers behind Joan's achievements. Thus, as the French seek to raise the siege at Orleans, Talbot, the symbol of English chivalry, pursues the Dauphin across the stage, but Joan then enters, driving the English soldiers in front of her. Talbot cannot understand this turn of events ('Where is my strength, my valor, and my force? / Our English troops retire, I cannot stay them') and consequently seizes the opportunity to 'have a bout' with Joan (whom he associates with the devil). But despite two such bouts ('*Here they fight* ... *They fight again*'), Joan emerges unscathed and defiant ('I scorn thy strength'), so that Talbot can only wonder at the larger forces at work ('Heavens, can you suffer hell so to prevail?') and try even harder to employ his manly strength ('My breast I'll burst with straining of my courage / And from my shoulders crack my arms asunder / But I will chastise this high-minded strumpet'). Joan's departure and the French victory leave Talbot alone on stage, confused, ashamed: 'My thoughts are whirlèd like a potter's wheel; / I know not where I am nor what I do. / A witch by fear, not force, like Hannibal, / Drives back our troops and conquers as she lists' (I. v. 1–22).

This confrontation can pose some difficult problems for the modern actor or director, for how does one choreograph a stage fight between a chivalric superhero and a seeming slip of a girl? Without question, the point of the scene lies in the surprising failure of the strength, valor, and force of the formidable hero and the equally surprising success of his apparently inferior opponent (who actually has larger powers behind her and therefore can scorn his strength). Such surprise or illogic is necessary for the scene to work. In the 1975 production at the Oregon Shakespearean Festival, Joan made several magical signs in the air with her sword before the combat; Talbot then fought at half speed, moving as if wading in molasses. Although I cannot offer any historical evidence, I would prefer to have Pucelle, a slight figure in armor who does not resemble a soldier in stature or expertise, wield a sword that need only touch her opponent or his weapon to achieve potent results. For me, such a strident violation of our expectations or sense of 'realism' would make far better theatrical sense of Talbot's failure and Joan's unexpected strength than would a Pucelle who could match Talbot move for move in battlefield tactics. Whether the emphasis falls upon Talbot's weakness or Joan's strength, the logic of both this scene and the play as a whole could be heightened if a mere touch from Joan's sword would have the effect of a sledge-hammer blow.

For a similar moment, consider the wrestling contest in *As You Like It* where the actors today must make an audience 'believe' that a slighter Orlando could best a giant Charles (indeed, I have seen at least one production in which Orlando looked incapable of 'throwing' Rosalind, much less Charles). The fight master must therefore seek a way for Orlando to triumph by skill or luck or trickery (which does not fit well with the character or context). But as with Joan's strength against Talbot, Shakespeare's point may lie in the image of a seemingly weaker figure triumphing over an apparently stronger one, perhaps linked to Orlando's references to 'the spirit of my father grows strong in me' (I. i. 64–5, 19–21), perhaps to the larger romance values of the comedy. At some point in the fight could Orlando, like Joan, show an unexpected surge of strength, surprising himself as well as the spectator? Somehow, this early confrontation between romantic hero and formidable opponent is designed to prepare us for the major images and oppositions that are to follow ('Sir, you have wrestled well, and overthrown / More than your enemies' – I. ii. 235–6), even though the only evidence provided in the Folio is '*wrestle*' (l. 194, s.d.). Is this match (or Joan versus Talbot) solely a matter for the fight master or should it be of equal concern to the imagist or thematic critic?

Such suggestions run counter to the verisimilar assumptions of most critics, editors, and directors. Thus, in his useful, practical study, Arthur Wise argues that 'the purpose of an authentic weapon is to kill' but 'the purpose of a theatrical weapon is to *appear* to do so.' For the last scene of *Hamlet* Wise would use a theatrical rather than an authentic weapon to deal the various death-inducing wounds: 'It is stretching the imagination of both audience and actor too far to expect them to believe that this can be done. It is not in the nature of that featherweight practice weapon, the modern fencing foil, to inflict two such wounds. An audience – and an actor – must be shown a weapon which, within the theatrical terms of reference, can be believed capable of performing what it is supposed to perform.'[12] No roses here.

But can Wise's arguments and assumptions account for the many weapons and combats found in Elizabethan plays? Consider two scenes in which a worthy English yeoman, armed only with a cudgel or staff, defeats two or three supposedly superior opponents armed with swords. First, in the final scene of *The Blind Beggar of Bednal Green* (I4v–K1r) the good and evil figures choose their weapons for a trial by combat before the king. All choose swords of different varieties except for Tom Strowd, the folk hero of the play (given special billing on the title page) who rejects such 'bars of Iron' and chooses instead 'an ashen Gibbet' or 'a good Cudgel' to fight the two figures who have abused him throughout the play. Tom then defeats his two tormentors and is singled out by the king as 'a lusty fellow' ('we have too few such Subjects in our Land'). Similarly, the hero of *George a Greene* traps three traitors by posing as a fortune-teller, and, after calling for his staff, challenges all three to combat: *'Here they fight, George kills Sir Gilbert, and takes the other two prisoners'* (ll. 741–2). The vanquished figures announce that they would rather bide the king's doom 'than here be murdered by a servile groom' (l. 747), but a neutral spokesman moralizes: 'Even as the cause, so is the combat fallen, / Else one could never have conquered three' (ll. 754–5). George's victory against odds therefore becomes a comment upon the justice of his cause and a display of native English prowess, as suggested in part through the weapon used.[13] The cudgel or staff as used by Tom Strowd or George a Greene can convey qualities or values that supersede the logic advanced by Wise.[14]

Unfortunately, many scenes which might derive added meanings from the use of a cudgel do not specify the weapon to be used. The best Shakespearean example is Edgar's fight with Oswald in *King Lear*. Oswald, who sees the blind, helpless Gloucester only as 'a proclaimed prize,' announces that 'the sword is out / That must destroy thee' (IV. vi. 222, 225–6), but Edgar, disguised as a peasant and using a stock stage accent, interposes, taking Gloucester's arm (ll. 227–31). The only evidence about Edgar's weapon is provided by his threat: 'Nay, come not near th'old man. Keep out, che vore ye, or Ise try whether your costard or my ballow be the harder' (ll. 235–7). Edgar has reasserted the bond with his father, summarized visually by the joined arms indicated in the text, and defeats a minor villain with a 'ballow' or cudgel, a weapon not of the court but from the world of unaccommodated man. Perhaps we should also take a cue from Edgar's reference to Oswald's 'costard' or head and his final threat – 'Chill pick your teeth, zir' (l. 240), both of which may indicate a blow to the head as the culmination of this fight. Oswald is certainly not a D'Amville figure of intellect and false reasoning who sees the truth only when his brains are dashed out, but a blow to the head of a minor schemer, delivered with a simple yet powerful weapon by a figure just emerging from his Poor Tom role, could have larger ramifications for the world of *King Lear* where ultimately an Edgar can defeat an Edmund.[15]

Nor need discussion be limited to combats in which cudgels are pitted against swords. Thus, as with Tom Strowd and George a Greene, victories against apparent odds can be theatrically spectacular and can display the justice of a cause. For example, in the climactic scene of *The Trial of Chivalry* two of the heroes who epitomize the chivalric values of the play (Ferdinand and Pembroke) take on two armies, while the third hero (Philip) disposes of the arch villain (Roderick) in single combat. As one observer later sums it up: 'Behold these two, which thousands could not daunt' (I4v). True chivalry has triumphed over villainy and misunderstanding, with the triumph and the inherent value of such chivalric qualities made emphatically clear through the disparity in numbers. Similarly, in *Cymbeline* four figures (Posthumus, Belarius, Guiderius, and Arviragus) stand off the Roman army and rally the faltering British forces to victory. The two stage directions read: '*The battle continues. The Britons fly; Cymbeline is taken. Then enter, to his rescue, Belarius, Guiderius, and Arviragus*'; and: '*Enter Posthumus, and seconds the Britons. They rescue Cymbeline and exeunt*' (v. ii. 10. s.d., 13. s.d.). The fleeing Britons, as represented by the lord of v. iii, undoubtedly seem to be well appointed, even soldierly, but the restoration and regeneration of Cymbeline's England require the virtues and qualities of the old man, the 'two striplings,' and the 'fourth man, in a silly habit' (v. iii. 19, 86) who, as later is said of Posthumus, 'promised naught / But beggary and poor looks' but provided 'precious deeds' (v. v. 9–10). As in *The Trial of Chivalry*, the greater the disparity in numbers in this combat, the more emphatic the theatrical point and effect (a non-allegorical equivalent to Faithful Few's insistence in *The Tide Tarrieth No Man* that, when good is on your side, 'weigh not then the number' of your opponents – l. 1511).

Also important for the combats cited so far is the element of surprise, especially when an apparently weaker or less-impressive combatant performs in an unexpectedly forceful way. Earlier in *Cymbeline* Shakespeare had provided two such moments. Thinking Imogen dead at his command, Posthumus takes off his Italian weeds upon his return to England and dresses as 'a Briton peasant' to let 'men know / More valor in me than my habits show' and to display 'the fashion, less without and more within' (v. i. 24, 29–30, 33). Following the British army *like a poor soldier,*' Posthumus *'vanquisheth and disarmeth Iachimo'* (v.ii. o. s.d.); the latter concludes that 'the heaviness and guilt within my bosom / Takes off my manhood'; otherwise, how 'could this carl, / A very drudge of nature's, have subdued me / In my profession?' (ll. 1–2, 4–6). Posthumus' weapon is not specified (although a cudgel would be appropriate); as with Edgar's defeat of Oswald, the triumph of a figure visually equated with peasantry or baseness over a more impressive-looking figure equated with cunning and the court is a prelude to some semblance of reordering in the kingdom. Earlier, in an even more obvious symbolic confrontation, the villainous Cloten, dressed resplendently in Posthumus' garments, had been defeated by a Guiderius scorned by Cloten as a 'rustic mountaineer' (IV. ii. 100). In a play that acts out the hollowness of a court epitomized by false assumptions about clothing and manners, the answers are provided by figures who show 'less without and more within.' In production, these stage combats underscore this major theme.

Of equal interest are scenes in which a figure's moral stature is called into question by his inability to defeat a supposedly inferior opponent (as with Iachimo's humiliating loss to the 'poor soldier'). Thus, in *Philaster* the hero, who has debased himself through his unjust suspicions of Arethusa and Bellario, has drawn his sword and wounded Arethusa when interrupted by a 'country-fellow' who accuses the prince of being 'a craven' for assaulting a woman. The country fellow is armed with a sword, not a cudgel (he brags that 'I made my Father's old Fox fly about his ears'); nonetheless, the contrast between the two combatants in bearing and costume should be striking. Philaster himself concludes: 'I am hurt. / The gods take part against me, could this Boor / Have held me thus else?' (I, 125–6). Here an apparently unequal fight produces a surprising result that in turn serves as a clear comment upon the degradation of the hero. Philaster's false use of his sword against Arethusa (and later against the sleeping Bellario) suggests a corruption of manhood and moral stature that can then be spelled out in his failure to best an apparently inferior opponent.

A far more suggestive example of the impugning of a hero through stage combat is to be found in the last scene of *Othello*. Earlier in the tragedy, Othello had twice stifled real or threatened violence by his stature or mere presence (I. ii, II. iii), but in Act v he appears briefly to cheer on a murder 'in the dark' and then departs to kill his innocent wife. After murdering Desdemona (with his hands, not a weapon), Othello is demonstrably no longer the man he once was. Near the end of the temptation sequence, the hero had bid farewell to 'the plumèd troop, and the big wars,' to 'the neighing steed and the shrill trump, / The spirit-stirring drum, th'ear-piercing fife, / The royal banner, and all quality, / Pride, pomp, and circumstance of glorious war' and had concluded: 'Farewell! Othello's occupation's gone!' (III. iii. 348–57). The effect of Iago's poison is then acted out in the ocular proof scene (IV. i), the brothel scene (IV. ii), and the hero's appearance in v. i. Lodovico, for one, calls attention to the change with his question: 'Is this the noble Moor whom our full Senate / Call all in all sufficient? Is this the nature / Whom passion could not shake?' (IV. i. 257–9).

To underscore this changed condition, Shakespeare then provides some striking stage business after the murder. In his soliloquy over the sleeping Desdemona the Moor had praised her 'balmy breath, that dost almost persuade / Justice to break her sword' (v. ii. 16–17); later, Emilia, cursing the murderer of her mistress, states: 'I care not for thy sword; I'll make thee known,/ Though I lost twenty lives' (ll. 166–7). After Emilia's revelations, Othello tries to use his sword against Iago (who has no difficulty fatally wounding his wife) only to lose that weapon to Montano ('take you this weapon, / Which I have here recovered from the Moor' – ll. 240–1); Othello concludes: 'I am not valiant neither; / But every puny whipster gets my sword' (ll. 244–5). The guilt-ridden hero then finds 'another weapon in this chamber' (l. 253) which he praises at length ('a better never did itself sustain / Upon a soldier's thigh') in a speech that stresses his heroic past: 'I have seen the day / That with this little arm and this good sword / I have made my way through more impediments / Than twenty times your stop.' But, he concludes ''Tis not so now. / Be not afraid, though you do see me weaponed'; rather, 'man but a rush against Othello's breast, / And he retires' (ll. 260–72). In a second assault upon Iago (which wounds but does not kill him), the Moor then loses this second weapon as well ('wrench his sword from him' says Lodovico – l. 288), and therefore must kill himself with a weapon snatched from someone else or, more likely, a knife secreted on his person (the weapon of an assassin, not a warrior). Since so much of importance is happening during this climactic scene, the reader can easily lose sight of the striking theatrical progression wherein Othello, who once might have triumphed over 'more impediments / Than twenty times your stop,' now twice loses his weapon to lesser men (including Montano, one of the figures controlled by the Moor in II. iii). In terms of the imagistic or symbolic progression, Othello at this point has lost his occupation, destroyed the best part of himself, and extinguished the light within, so that his sword, formerly the expression of his stature and strength, has become subject to 'every puny whipster.' Like the weapons of Courage or Moros, Othello's swords fail him in a bad cause, while his startling weakness (like Philaster's) serves as a climactic display of his descent.[16]

I can offer no evidence for how an Elizabethan actor would have played the surprising failure of an Othello or Philaster (or Macbeth after the final revelation from Macduff) as combatant. The effect for the viewer need not be as extreme as the shower of roses in *The Castle of Perseverance* or D'Amville's self-inflicted death, but if the scenes are to achieve their full impact, the staging should heighten the surprise and apparent illogic rather than conceal it. Remember, both Philaster and Othello (like Talbot and Iachimo) verbally call attention to their weakness and disappointment, thus italicizing the effect. Similarly, when a small group of figures holds off an entire army or when a less-impressive figure bests opponents superior in costume and bearing, the full effect can only be realized by emphasizing rather than softening the shock or surprise. In his advice to the players, Hamlet argues that the antics of the clown should not overshadow 'some necessary question of the play' (III. ii. 40). Any attempt to make moments based upon the logic of surprise compatible with our sense of 'realism' may also bury necessary questions that would be heightened if the staging were guided by a different logic.

This logic of surprise, however, is only one alternative to our prevailing logic of 'realism.' Thus, as with the twin Heywood scenes or D'Amville's fate, violent moments also lend themselves

readily to symbolic effects. Consider, for example, the blinding of
Gloucester in *King Lear*. One critic has argued that this scene 'is
painfully realistic; its cruelty has all the immediate horror of
everyday life ... By showing us directly this scene of almost
unbearable cruelty, Shakespeare is insisting that the evil at the
heart of the play is real and unmetaphoric' with Regan and
Cornwall acting out 'the farthest limit of human depravity.'[17] To
act out on stage this depravity, most actors and directors resort
instinctively to hands (or nails), seeking a direct physical
extension of this human animality. But the text directs otherwise,
at least for Gloucester's first eye; thus, Cornwall instructs his
servants: 'Fellows, hold the chair. / Upon these eyes of thine I'll set
my foot' (III. vii. 67–8). Since Shakespeare does not make clear
how a foot is to put out an eye (through a spur? the tip of a boot?),
the action implicit in this line seems physically awkward and
'unrealistic' to the modern actor.[18] But if we use a different logic,
the stage picture that follows from Shakespeare's signal can be
particularly rich in significance. If Gloucester, bound to a chair, is
lowered to the stage floor so that his head is under Cornwall's
foot, the audience will then witness a powerful symbolic tableau
that epitomizes not only injustice and oppression but, given the
associations with the head (as in D'Amville's dashing out his
brains), also acts out the failure of reason and 'cause' to deal with
the world of the storm. This visual image is linked to other
moments in the play (e.g., Tom 'throwing his head' in the
previous scene or Lear beating upon his head in I. iv. 262–3) and,
as with the blindness/sight motif, can generate meanings and
associations that inform the entire tragedy. If the logic of the
blinding is understood as symbolic rather than physiological, the
result again can be a kind of theatrical italics that transcends
verisimilitude to yield a larger, richer effect.

To confront this scene is to face several traps awaiting the
modern critic, editor, or director. Most obvious is the danger of
sidestepping the signals in the text ('upon these eyes of thine I'll set
my foot'), thus blurring the original poetic or visual language in
favor of more convenient modern assumptions. Equally dangerous, especially when dealing with any rich Shakespeare play, is
the isolation of one such moment from the flow of the entire play
so that a scene is viewed as an end in itself rather than as a
significant part of an informing pattern. Critics, actors, and

directors rarely make such a mistake about problems of 'character,' because, as heirs of the novel and Ibsen, we have been
conditioned to expect discrete speeches and actions, even of
minor figures, to be 'consistent' with a central psychological core
that can be inferred and analyzed. But the director or fight master
who designs stage combats for modern productions often is not
particularly concerned with such consistency but rather views
duels, battles, and violence in general as ends in themselves that
adhere to no larger logic than that which generates the most
suspense or titillation for the audience (a view supported by at
least some Elizabethan evidence). Thus, in a production of *King
Lear* at Stratford Festival Canada in 1972, the blinding scene was
drawn out interminably while Cornwall stripped down to a
leather tunic and then chose his gouging tool from a large rack of
gleaming instruments that had been wheeled onto the stage. In the
Oregon Shakespearean Festival production of 1976, both Edgar
and Oswald in iv. vi suddenly became savvy streetfighters,
employing tactics and expertise quite inconsistent with their
'character' as displayed elsewhere in the play. But, we should
remember, even the 'primitive' moral plays contain progressions
of scenes that use the Vice's dagger and the sword of heavenly
justice to establish a larger pattern. To treat any Elizabethan scene
as a discrete, separable event is to flirt with the danger of missing a
logic based upon patterned action that at times can supersede
our sense of verisimilitude or psychological realism.

To explore such a patterned presentation of violence let me
return to *King Lear*. Most critics and directors would agree that
the final confrontation between Edmund and Edgar is an important part of the climax of this tragedy, but less obvious are the
relevant moments that lead up to and prepare us for this climactic
combat, especially the carefully orchestrated activities of four
figures: Edgar, Edmund, Kent, and Oswald. Kent, already banished for his outspoken loyalty, has in disguise endeared himself
again to Lear by tripping up Oswald in front of the king;
meanwhile, Edmund's manipulative skills have been amply
demonstrated, especially in ii. i where he uses a mock combat and
a self-inflicted wound to set up the ocular proof necessary to have
Edgar outlawed and disinherited. An important new sequence
then begins with ii. ii when Kent confronts Oswald not before a
supportive Lear but in the domain of Cornwall and Regan.

Despite a series of insults and threats, Kent is unable to get Oswald to draw his sword and, by the end of the scene, only succeeds in getting himself stocked by Cornwall and Regan; the only physical combat, moreover, is between Kent and Edmund and takes place in front of the ranking figures. Thus, in response to Oswald's cries for help, the quarto reads: '*Enter Edmund with his rapier drawn, Gloster the Duke and Duchess*'; while the Folio directs: '*Enter Bastard, Cornwall, Regan, Gloster, Servants.*' Both editions agree that Edmund enters with the larger group and therefore has his bout with Kent before an audience that includes his father, Regan, and Cornwall.

I belabor this point because the editors of several widely used modern texts (the Variorum, the New Arden, the New Shakespeare, the Folger, and the Riverside) would have it otherwise. Here is the passage as printed in the Riverside edition:

OSWALD.	Help ho! murther, murther!
	Enter Bastard [Edmund, with his rapier drawn].
EDMUND.	How now, what's the matter? Part!
KENT.	With you, goodman boy, [and] you please!
	Come, I'll flesh ye, come on, young master.
	[Enter] Cornwall, Regan, Gloucester, Servants.
GLOUCESTER.	Weapons? arms? What's the matter here?
CORNWALL.	Keep peace, upon your lives!
	He dies that strikes again. What is the matter?

(II. ii. 43–9)

The note in the New Shakespeare edition (p. 180) justifies this change by arguing that 'Edmund would not take it upon himself to speak peremptorily to the brawlers if his seniors were present'; the logic of propriety or decorum is used to 'improve' a moment in the text that makes the editors uncomfortable. To the modern eye, moreover, Edmund's role here may appear gratuitous, a piece of dramatic filler. After all, why should a bastard son, recently wounded, be the one to intervene against Kent, especially if, as the Folio indicates, Cornwall's servants are on stage? Perhaps most puzzling is the question of timing. If Edmund enters as part of a larger group, even if his rapier is already drawn, why does it take so long for Gloucester and especially Cornwall to react and stop the combat? To the modern editor or director, then, the scene makes far more literal and theatrical sense if the entrance of the larger group is delayed.

But, as with Seyton's exit or the Nurse's intervention, such a change may distort or bury the logic of the original text based upon quite different assumptions. By this point, Kent has been carefully defined for us, with his speeches during the remainder of this scene, especially his comments on 'the holy cords,' clarifying his values even further. In the world epitomized by the new rulers, Cornwall and Regan, this worthy representative of an older order is unable to defeat an Oswald who will not fight or an Edmund who will. If we accept the original stage directions, Kent's failure to defeat either or both of these opponents is acted out in front of the figures who represent the new regime; his subsequent placement in the stocks then becomes an apt comment upon the helplessness and vulnerability of the qualities he embodies in the present world of the play. Meanwhile, Edgar (whom we saw in the previous scene with a sword drawn unsuccessfully against Edmund) has also become an outcast deprived of his identity, a juxtaposition that should be quite clear when Edgar, taking on his Poor Tom disguise, delivers his soliloquy (II. iii) while Kent is (or should be) visible, asleep in the stocks. As noted in chapter five, the modern director usually resorts to lighting to black out and draw attention away from Kent during Edgar's speech, but in the original production at the Globe the parallel straits of the two figures would have been obvious and emphatic. Kent's bout with Edmund, then, serves as an important symbolic comment upon what is working and what is failing in the world of Act II and, as such, can only take on its full meaning when staged before an audience that includes Cornwall and Regan.

The full implications of this moment, moreover, extend beyond the boundaries of Act II, especially when one recognizes the strong link forged in II. ii and II. iii between Kent and Edgar. Throughout the remainder of the tragedy Kent is a relatively helpless figure who can comfort his master but do little to reshape the world of the play. Rather, it is Edgar, after his descent to the Poor Tom level, who contributes most to whatever positive side is to be found in the resolution. A major part of that contribution comes when he defeats those same two figures Kent had fought but failed to best in II. ii. As noted earlier, the triumph of Edgar's ballow over Oswald's sword involves two scales of values as well as two weapons (and leads to the discovery of the letters that will help to undo Edmund). Then, in contrast to the abortive mock combat of II. i, Edgar's victory over his brother (who has been

told by Albany to 'trust to thy single virtue' – v. iii. 103) does yield
positive results, even though it does not save Cordelia. Like the
bout between Kent and Edmund, moreover, this climactic fight
takes place in front of the ranking figures in the play (Albany and
Goneril rather than Cornwall and Regan) with the presence of
Albany, which made the challenge possible in the first place,
marking a significant change from Act ii. The blocking of both
combatants and onlookers should therefore echo the earlier
scene; conversely, part of the logic behind the stage direction in
ii. ii that bothers some editors lies in the anticipation of this
climactic moment. Kent's bouts with two opponents, followed
closely by the juxtaposition of Kent in the stocks with Edgar in
flight, should set in motion a larger pattern that can only be
fulfilled when Edgar in the last two acts bests these same two
figures and what they stand for. The logic of the earlier and the full
meaning of the later scene cannot be understood in isolation but
can only be fully appreciated as part of a larger design that
supersedes social proprieties and stage realism.

For another example of the pitfalls in viewing scenes in isolation consider Marlowe's *Edward II*. After the king and Gaveston have been reunited, the Bishop of Coventry, who had played a
major role in exiling the favorite, comes on stage promising to
incense Parliament again. Enraged, Edward directs Gaveston to
'throw off his golden miter, rend his stole, / And in the channel
christen him anew,' while Kent pleads with the king ('lay not
violent hands on him') and Gaveston talks of revenge (ll.
187–92). Before our eyes, an elaborately attired symbol of the
religion that gives the king his legitimacy is being mocked,
stripped, degraded, and 'christened' with filthy water by two
figures who take sardonic pleasure in the act. But this early scene,
like Kent's bouts in ii. ii, should take on added meaning later in
the action. Thus, near the end of the play Edward II himself,
rather than the Bishop of Coventry, is degraded by two figures,
Matrevis and Gurney; when the king asks for water, he too is
offered 'channel water' and seemingly threatened, so that he
responds: 'Traitors away, what will you murder me, / Or choke
your sovereign with puddle water?' (ll. 2292–5). Edward's
struggles are ineffectual, for the stage direction reads: '*They wash
him with puddle water, and shave his beard away*' (l. 2310 s.d.).
This moment has obvious symbolic value, especially as an inver-

sion of the anointing of a king, an act of 'unkinging' linked to what Edward has done to himself and to his office. But if the staging also echoes the analogous treatment of the bishop, a more specific link may be forged between Edward's degradation of a figure who should have been a support to his crown and the king's similar degradation here. To add to the potential parallel, Kent, who had stood by helplessly in the earlier scene, also appears here only to be arrested and taken away to his fateful final meeting with Mortimer. If the critic or director perceives these two moments of violence and degradation as related rather than discrete, he may then recognize a symbolic cause-and-effect whereby the earlier action against the bishop condoned by Edward II has led to his helplessness here at the hands of two tormentors who act out a role visually analogous to that of the king and Gaveston in Act I. Such a link could heighten for the viewer Edward's own contribution to his present degradation, a responsibility he himself is not prepared to admit. But such an effect can only be realized through a logic that transcends the individual scene.[19]

Similar patterns that build upon moments of stage violence can be seen in two plays that span Shakespeare's career, *1 Henry VI* and *Coriolanus*, both of which display the vulnerability of a military hero who lacks the support of other elements in his society. In the earlier history play, many scenes act out divisions in England, especially the feuding between Gloucester and Winchester and between York and Somerset; the latter quarrel, moreover, is clearly linked to the demise of Talbot, the epitome of English heroic virtue. But Shakespeare also explores the limitations placed upon Talbot through a sequence of scenes analogous to the patterned violence in *King Lear*. As noted earlier, Talbot by himself was unable to defeat Joan in I. v, with the result that Orleans was temporarily lost to the French. But a major English victory at Orleans soon follows in II. i when Talbot, this time supported by Bedford and Burgundy, scales the walls and takes the town in one of Shakespeare's most spectacular battle scenes. In his New Arden edition, Andrew Cairncross observes that Burgundy 'is here introduced, unnecessarily, to prepare for his later part in the action' (p. 36). Quite the contrary, Burgundy's appearance *is* 'necessary' to set up a revealing sequence or larger pattern. As established in the dialogue (II. i. 28–34) the three figures ascend their scaling ladders simultaneously (Talbot presumably in the center, the other two at their respective 'corners') so that, in a very distinctive scene for the eye, the viewer witnesses the victory as a combined effort of three heroes acting together. Shortly thereafter the Countess of Auvergne is told that Talbot alone 'is but a shadow of himself' without his soldiers and supporters, 'his substance, sinews, arms, and strength' (ii. iii. 62–3). Starting, however, in ii. iv (the Temple Garden scene), the emphasis again is upon division rather than unity, an emphasis continued in Mortimer's legacy to York (ii. v) and the various arguments before the king in iii. i. Note then what happens to the component parts of that victorious combination that had scaled the walls in unison in ii. i. First, at the end of iii. ii, Bedford dies in his chair while watching the retaking of Rouen; heroic to the last, this old soldier refuses to be bestowed 'in some better place' but announces: 'Here will I sit, before the walls of Roan, / And will be partner of your weal or woe' (ll. 88, 91–2). In the next scene, Burgundy, the other major participant in the victory at Orleans, proves vulnerable to Joan's appeals and switches sides, an event displayed at length in iii. iii and emphasized again in iv. i. Old age and treachery have undermined Talbot's 'substance.' The spectacular wall-scaling of ii. i therefore functions not as an end in itself, a martial display for an audience demanding clamor and titillation, but rather as a means of setting up a winning combination of three figures, a group that by the end of iii. iii has been reduced to one – and, with the death of Talbot in Act iv, to none. There *is* a necessary logic behind Burgundy's appearance in ii. i and behind the scene as a whole, a logic not readily apparent to the modern interpreter who asks the wrong questions.

Late in his career Shakespeare uses an analogous device in i. iv of *Coriolanus* where the hero gains his name through his spectacular deeds. Much has been written about the staging of this scene, with modern assumptions often at odds with the evidence in the Folio. By appearing above at line 12, the two senators establish the rear tiring-house wall as the walls of Corioli, so that a stage door can represent the city gates from which issues the Volscian army at line 22. Exactly how the King's Men staged the ensuing battle remains murky, owing to some apparently authorial or 'fictional' signals (e.g., '*The Romans are beat back to their trenches*' – l. 29 s.d.) and the uncertain disposition of Titus

Lartius, but clearly, in the key moment of the scene, Caius Marcius follows the Volscian soldiers to the imagined 'gates' of the city, enters those gates, and '*is shut in*' (ll. 42–5). Less heroic (or foolhardy), the Roman soldiers hold back, telling Titus Lartius that Marcius, 'following the fliers at the very heels, / With them he enters, who upon the sudden / Clapped to their gates; he is himself alone, / To answer all the city' (ll. 49–52). Titus' premature epitaph is interrupted by the entrance of '*Marcius, bleeding, assaulted by the Enemy*' (l. 61 s.d.), so that the Roman forces now '*fight, and all enter the City*' (l. 62 s.d.).

At the heart of this scene, then, is the striking stage image of Caius Marcius isolated within the walls of Corioli. Shakespeare has provided the viewer with a vivid demonstration that under very special conditions, in wartime, with none of the demands of the give-and-take of politics, this overbearing hero can, for a moment, stand 'himself alone, / To answer all the city.' Here is the one moment when the hero lives up to his claim that he can stand alone 'as if a man were author of himself / And knew no other kin' (v. iii. 36–7). But the remainder of the play emphasizes the failure of Coriolanus either to be self-sufficient or to find a place in any city. Again and again he stands by himself, whether in his appearance before the senators (ii. ii. 34. s.d.) or in his gown of humility or waiting for Aufidius in iv. v, or he stands in opposition to family or plebeians. In response to the decree of banishment, he can tell the Roman tribunes and mob 'I banish you!' adding 'there is a world elsewhere' (iii. iii. 124, 136); in the final scene, again confronting an entire city (the supposed 'world elsewhere'), he can recall but not repeat his earlier victory ('alone I did it' – v. vi. 115). His capitulation to the three women and the boy in v. iii is the most obvious but by no means the only event to be measured against the striking triumph and independence of i. iv. In a manner analogous to the victory at Orleans by Talbot, Burgundy, and Bedford, Shakespeare has provided his tragic hero with a remarkable, eye-catching accomplishment early in the play that cannot be matched again, especially in peacetime in a world of politics, rhetoric, and cynicism, where the protagonist's heroic anger can be triggered by manipulation of key words ('boy,' 'traitor'). The spectacular battle scenes in both *1 Henry VI* and *Coriolanus* can thus generate symbolic possibilities and initiate larger patterns significant for the plays as a whole, but only when we ask the proper questions and sidestep misleading assumptions about 'realism.'

Throughout this chapter I have sought to be selective rather than exhaustive, suggestive rather than conclusive, so that a great deal of terrain has been left unexplored and many possibilities not pursued. For example, to what extent would the sequence of actions in an individual stage combat (e.g., Hal versus Hotspur) have been designed to comment upon the participants or upon some larger issues? To cite one more example from the moral plays, in the opening scene of *The Trial of Treasure* Lust and Just meet for the only time in the play to engage in a wrestling match. Lust appears '*to have the better at the first*' (A4r) but is eventually cast down and driven off by Just. Allegorically, we have witnessed 'the conflict of the Just, / Which all good men ought to use and frequent'; just so, every man should strive against lust: 'And though at the first he seem sturdy to be, / The Lord will convince him for you in the end' (A4v). Here, as with many battles in *The Faerie Queene*, both the sequence of events and the outcome have clear allegorical significance, but, lacking sufficient evidence, I find it difficult to determine the relevance of this technique to later plays that lack overt allegory and neat summaries.

To see both the potential and the difficulties in reconstructing Elizabethan stage violence, consider one last Shakespearean example, the rather unhelpful Folio stage direction for the final fight in *Richard III*: '*Alarum, Enter Richard and Richmond, they fight, Richard is slain.*' Clearly, this combat serves as an exciting climax to a long play, but '*they fight*' leaves open many possibilities. Thus, if the critic or director prizes the logic of patterning, the blow that kills Richard can echo unmistakably the thrust he asks for but does not receive from Lady Anne in i. ii (a link established in both the Stratford Festival Canada production of 1977 and the Oregon Shakespearean Festival production of 1978). If the emphasis is placed upon Richmond as God's captain (see especially v. iii. 109–18, 240–71), his blows could fall with more than human force upon Richard (as with my suggested staging for Joan's encounter with Talbot). If Richard eventually is killed with his own weapon (an often-used conclusion to modern stage fights), his fate could confirm Buckingham's assertion of the power of 'that high All-seer' who forces 'the swords of wicked men / To turn their own points in their masters' bosoms' (v. i. 20–4). If Richard dies when forsaken by Ratcliff or others in the final moments, his demise could be linked to Margaret's curse: 'Thy friends suspect for traitors while thou liv'st, / And take deep traitors for thy dearest friends' (I. iii. 222–3). If the staging suggests not Richmond's strength but Richard's weakness or surprising ineptness, the fight could be the final moment in a series started by the 'myself myself confound' oath (IV. iv. 397–405), where Richard pawns his future success, and continued in the 'coward conscience' soliloquy, with its emphasis upon guilt and revenging 'myself upon myself' (V. iii. 178–207).

Note that not all of these choices are incompatible with stage 'realism' nor are they all mutually exclusive, but each draws its potential meaning or force from a somewhat different logic, whether that logic is based upon patterning or surprise or symbolism or iterative imagery. From the limited evidence we cannot determine how this moment would have been staged in the original production, yet the director or critic who fails to consider such options may unwittingly be diminishing an important moment in a rich play by considering only those possibilities consonant with our prevailing tastes or assumptions. Rather, as with Edgar versus Edmund or Macduff versus Macbeth (or Hal versus Hotspur or Hamlet versus Laertes), a climactic Shakespearean fight, like a climactic Shakespearean speech, may weave together various threads into a highly theatrical yet intensely meaningful moment and may leave the audience with an epitome of what has gone before, a realization in action of central motifs or images or oppositions.

To realize the potential in such moments, however, the modern interpreter must recognize that Elizabethan stage violence is not solely the domain of today's fight master or naturalistic actor. Granted (as happens so often throughout this study), the surviving evidence about the original staging is scanty or non-existent. Granted, as with problems with 'night' and 'place,' strong modern reflexes may be pulling us away from the terms upon which the Elizabethan dramatists, actors, and spectators agreed to meet. But to appreciate the full range of drama in the age of Shakespeare, we should make every effort to grasp the assets of an alternative dramatic logic that can give meaning to moments otherwise puzzling or inexplicable. To travel too far down the road to 'realism' is to narrow the range of this great age of drama and to invite upon our heads a painful shower of roses or the sword of heavenly judgment.

7 · Theatrical metaphor: seeing and not-seeing

'I now am blind.'
'What's your conceit in this?'

(*The Duchess of Malfi*, I. i. 494)

To consider metaphoric or symbolic stage violence is inevitably to raise large (and often unanswerable) questions about Elizabethan playscripts, particularly those of Shakespeare. As noted throughout this study, the sparseness of stage directions in the extant manuscripts and printed texts continually frustrates attempts to link staging and imagery at key moments, so that I find it impossible to establish any firm connections between the staging of the death of a Richard III (or Richard II) in the 1590s and one or another iterative pattern woven through the fabric of the play. Even when stage directions do survive, they often do not make immediate sense in imagistic terms to today's critic or director and, as a result, may be bumped out of the text into the textual notes by the editor. Thus, as noted in chapter one, the Nurse's intervention to prevent Romeo's suicide as set forth in the first or 'bad' quarto was rejected by the editor of the New Arden edition as 'gratuitous and distracting' even though the resulting stage picture fits well with the emphasis in the dialogue upon a 'womanish' or 'effeminate' Romeo. The expanded sense of dramatic or theatrical imagery advocated by some recent critics[1] has here been rejected or ignored in favor of a literal-minded logic of interpretation that, especially on the part of an editor, can filter out some rich and potentially meaningful effects generated by the original scripts.

Consider too another moment cited earlier, Ophelia's entrance in the first quarto *'playing on a Lute, and her hair down singing'* (G4v). In his New Arden edition (1982), Harold Jenkins notes that 'Q1 no doubt records some contemporary staging.' Although he does point out that 'the hair down is conventional for madness,' he then (echoing Brian Gibbons on the Nurse's intervention) adds that 'the lute, uncalled for in the text and incongruous with the ballad snatches Ophelia spontaneously breaks into, looks like an actor's embellishment' (p. 348). Therefore, in this edition the stage direction reads '*enter Ophelia*' with the Q–1 signal to be found only in the dense textual notes in the middle of the page.

As Jenkins notes, the lute is not cited in the dialogue, so its absence from Q–2 and the Folio leaves no noticeable gap; moreover, even though I, for one, do not find such a musical instrument 'incongruous' with Ophelia's fragments of song, I would agree that, in practical terms, the lute is not 'necessary.' Yet in imagistic terms the lute would make excellent sense. Thus, the presence of such a musical instrument (as also in *Julius Caesar*, IV. iii and *The Taming of the Shrew*, II. i) can add to a spectator's sense of harmony violated (as Ophelia herself summed it up: 'sweet bells jangled, out of time and harsh' – III. i. 158). The image or concept of such an instrument, moreover, has already been orchestrated by Hamlet, first in his praise of those men like Horatio 'whose blood and judgment are so well commeddled / That they are not a pipe for Fortune's finger / To sound what stop she please' (III. ii. 66–8) and later in the same scene, with a recorder in his hand, in his critique of Guildenstern ('you would play upon me, you would seem to know my stops' – ll. 350–1). For the reader interested in linked ideas and images, especially those that draw upon more than just the words on the page, Q–1's stage direction sets up an on-stage configuration that reinforces and develops some highly significant motifs that may apply as well to Hamlet (who, according to some readers, may himself be an instrument to be played upon by the Ghost). 'Bad' quarto or not, to exclude or ignore this contemporary theatrical evidence is to do an injustice both to the stage historian and the imagist.

Consider another stage direction from the first quarto of *Romeo and Juliet*, this one included by Gibbons but excluded by some editors (e.g., Kittredge, Alexander, Bevington). Thus, after the discovery of the seemingly dead Juliet, the Friar and her family depart '*casting Rosemary on her and shutting the Curtains*' (I2v). As noted briefly in chapter two, on the Elizabethan stage such rosemary could be used to help signal '*as from a wedding*,' whether in stage directions or in the dialogue.[2] Here in *Romeo and Juliet*, the yoking together of death and marriage through the strewing of rosemary upon an apparent corpse makes particularly good imagistic sense. Thus, the close reader will call to mind Juliet's comment after first meeting Romeo ('If he be marrièd, / My grave is like to be my wedding bed' – I. v. 134–5); her lament to the Nurse after the death of Tybalt ('I'll to my wedding bed; / And death, not Romeo, take my maidenhead!' – III. ii. 136–7); Lady Capulet's comment upon her daughter ('I would the fool were married to her grave!' – III. v. 141); and, most important, the complex linking of love and death in the final scene. What at first may seem to us an odd or intrusive detail ('*casting Rosemary on her*') may have made excellent sense to the original audience and, metaphorically, could have enriched a meaningful network that runs throughout the play.

So that the reader will not conclude that such problems are limited to stage directions in the 'bad' quartos, consider the moment in *All's Well That Ends Well* when Helena, Diana, and the Widow, looking for the king, meet instead a gentleman who agrees to carry a message to his master. In most modern editions, the stage direction at v. i. 6 reads either '*enter a Gentleman, a stranger*' (New Arden, Signet, Ribner-Kittredge) or simply '*enter a Gentleman*' (Alexander, Pelican, Bevington). Yet our sole authority for this play, the Folio, reads: '*Enter a gentle Astringer.*' The OED, in turn, defines *astringer* (or *austringer* or *ostringer*) as 'a keeper of goshawks' – in short, a falconer. Most editors or annotators agree with G. K. Hunter that the Folio stage direction 'raises more difficulties than it avoids' (New Arden edition, p. 125); thus, although G. B. Evans in the Riverside edition provides '*Enter a [Gentleman, an] astringer,*' the annotator (Marie Edel) puzzles over 'why his profession should be stated, since it has no bearing on the action and is never mentioned in the dialogue' (p. 536). Finding little or no 'logic' in the Folio signal, most editors regard *astringer* as a compositor's misreading of *stranger*, so that, except for that dogged critic, actor or director who goes back to the Folio itself or reads the often inaccessible textual notes, this bit of evidence has, in effect, ceased to exist for most modern readers.

In a recent note, however, Alice Walker has argued that 'what Shakespeare intended' is best represented in the New Penguin edition (1970) by the addition of '*to the king*' to the original Folio signal. For her, 'the austringer sets the scene by his dress and equipment' (she suggests 'staff, glove, jesses, gamebag'), so that a spectator would infer that this figure 'was a member of the King's household' and 'that this was an outdoor scene on the King's Marseilles estate.' According to Walker, 'stripped of his occupational identity,' this gentleman 'cannot be "placed."' That when he later appears to deliver his message he is described only as '*a Gentleman*' (v. iii. 128. s.d.) should not surprise us, for 'it is doubtful whether he would appear indoors on a formal errand with his gear.'[3] So in this formulation the Folio's *astringer* signals a specific costume that in turn conveys to the spectator a locale for Helena's meeting with the gentleman, a costume and locale no longer relevant to the delivery of the message to the King in the final scene.

If indeed *astringer* is not a misprint for *stranger*, then, as Walker suggests, the point behind this curious signal lies in what the original spectator would have seen (costume, properties). Although the link between costume and locale fits well with my argument in chapter five, in this instance I do not see why the suggestion of 'an outdoor scene on the King's Marseilles estate' is of particular importance or interest. In more general terms, a sense of the hunt or a hunt would fit well with Helena's aggressive pursuit of Bertram, although falconry seems somewhat less appropriate (unless we are to envisage Helena as a Petruchio 'taming' her Bertram–Katherina).

To pursue my logic of imagery (and perhaps try the patience of my reader) let me extend Walker's inventory of the *astringer's* accoutrements and suggest that this figure, both when meeting Helena *and* when delivering the message to the king two scenes later, could be carrying a hawk or falcon. Remember that the Folio stage direction from 2 *Henry VI* (ii. i. o. s.d.) brings in a group of figures '*with Falconers halloaing*,' but the equivalent stage direction in the quarto calls for the same group to enter '*as if they came from hawking*' and specifies that Queen Margaret is to enter '*with her Hawk on her fist*'[4] (C1v). If Shakespeare, for whatever reason, wished to introduce a falconer and his falcon, such an effect is at least possible (and was incorporated into the Royal Shakespeare Company production of 2 *Henry VI* in 1977–8). What then would happen to v. i and especially to v. iii if the gentleman who delivers Diana's letter to the king remains on stage (the Folio provides no exit) holding a falcon, particularly a hooded falcon? Keep in mind the striking effect set up by

Marlowe in *Edward II* where a Mower, presumably carrying a scythe, stands in the background during Edward's capture and at the end reminds the arresting figure to 'remember me' (see ll. 1913, 1984). Could an astringer with bird on hand offer such a symbolic or metaphoric context, whether for v. i or the final moments?

Although I can offer no firm answers, such questions generated by the Folio stage direction strike me as valid and worth pursuing. Thus, I find no significant cluster of bird images in this play (Helena's early reference to Bertram's 'hawking eye' in i. i. 90 could be suggestive), but, not unexpectedly, references to hood-winking and muffling are plentiful during the exposure of Parolles, while in the two pivotal scenes (ii. iii and v. iii) great emphasis is placed upon eyes and seeing. Thus, Bertram's first reaction to Helena's choice is to ask the King 'in such a business give me leave to use / The help of mine own eyes'; moments later, a chastened Bertram begs pardon and agrees to 'submit / My fancy to your eyes,' adding, in terms appropriate to falconry, that 'honor / Flies where you bid it' (ii. iii. 106–7, 166–9). References to seeing abound in the play, with the key exchange coming with the climactic appearance of Helena:

> KING.   Is there no exorcist
> Beguiles the truer office of mine eyes?
> Is't real that I see?
> HELENA.   No, my good lord,
> 'Tis but the shadow of a wife you see,
> The name and not the thing.
> BERTRAM.   Both, both; O, pardon!
>   (v. iii. 301–5)

Bertram, who in the dark accepted an unseen Helena as a substitute for Diana, here 'sees' his wife for the first time with unfettered eyes, a throwing off of blinkered vision that recalls the blindfolded Parolles of iv. iii who also came to see the truth. Earlier in this scene Bertram had referred to his eyes and his view of Helena and Maudlin in a superficial, self-serving fashion (ll. 47, 54), but now, for the first time, 'the truer office' of his eyes can take him beyond the mere 'name' or 'the shadow of a wife' to 'the thing' itself. An astringer standing by with a hooded falcon could recall the clear analogue to a Parolles who transcended his blindfold and his foolery and could bring into strong theatrical focus the imagery of sight and blindness.

Undoubtedly, my inferences and suggestions about the Folio's *'Enter a gentle Astringer'* will not satisfy many readers of this problematical comedy, nor do I advance the presence of a hooded falcon during the climax of the play with any great confidence. But given appropriate staging, this signal, like Ophelia's lute or the Nurse's intervention or the rosemary, could make excellent sense to a spectator according to the logic of imagery. Trapping such particles in the editorial filter can eliminate some potentially suggestive and meaningful evidence, at least for some readers. Given the imagistic potential in the astringer (however interpreted) or his possible function of 'placing' the action of v. i, should not the text confronted by today's interpreter at least include this puzzle?

In most cases, however, no stage directions at all have survived for many rich and puzzling moments (another reason to treat the extant signals with due respect), so what may have been interesting and provocative images in the original productions may for us have melted into thin air, leaving not a rack behind. For example, while talking to the Doctor, Macbeth calls three times for his armor (and once for his staff – v. iii. 33, 36, 48), then tells Seyton 'pull't off, I say' (l. 54), and finally, in his exit speech, commands 'bring it after me!' (l. 58). Both 'pull't off' and 'bring it after me' could refer to the armor; in this interpretation, the spectator would see an impatient Macbeth (Seyton has told him ''tis not needed yet' – l. 33) donning, then discarding his armor (a provocative action in its own right), then having it brought after him. Or the final 'bring it after me' could refer to Macbeth's staff or sword that then would be carried off by Seyton.

But at least one critic has suggested that 'pull't off' and 'bring it after me' refer not to the armor but more specifically to the helmet.[5] Thus, 'heads' figure prominently in this tragedy, starting with the account of Macbeth's killing of Macdonwald and subsequent placing of the rebel's head on the battlements (i. ii. 22–3), building to the first apparition, *'an Armed Head'* (iv. i. 68. s.d.), and climaxing with Macduff's entrance *'with Macbeth's head'* (v. viii. 53. s.d.). In imagistic terms, just before the arming by Seyton, Macbeth had asked the Doctor 'Canst thou not minister to a mind diseased' or 'raze out the written troubles of the brain,' eliciting the telling response: 'therein the patient / Must minister to himself.' Throughout the play we find emphasis upon the vulnerability of the head to 'the insane root / That takes the reason prisoner' (I. iii. 84–5) or the ability of passion to 'outrun the pauser, reason' (II. iii. 107). To have Macbeth depart in armor but have his helmet carried behind by Seyton (Satan?) is to act out for the spectator the failure of 'head' and reason also being orchestrated in the major speeches. Here an ambiguous or indeterminate 'it' may cloak a potentially rich and striking effect.

Or consider another potentially provocative stage image in the final scene of *All's Well That Ends Well* that may elude the reader. Thus, at the end of Act IV Lavatch describes the arrival of Bertram off-stage 'with a patch of velvet on's face,' adding: 'Whether there be a scar under't or no, the velvet knows, but 'tis a goodly patch of velvet; his left cheek is a cheek of two pile and a half, but his right cheek is worn bare.' Lafew's comment – 'a scar nobly got, or a noble scar, is a good livery of honor; so belike is that' – then elicits Lavatch's rejoinder: 'But it is your carbonadoed face' (IV. v. 88–95). Here, as I read the passage, Shakespeare uses theatrical *italics* to prepare the audience for something soon to be seen and provides in advance three different ways to evaluate that sight. Most obvious is Lafew's inference that the velvet patch worn by this 'young noble soldier' (l. 97) covers 'a noble scar' or 'a good livery of honor,' a worthy emblem of heroic deeds (the kind of scar one associates with Coriolanus). In contrast, Lavatch's cynical reference to 'your carbonadoed face' suggests that under the patch lurks a scar of less-worthy origins, an incision 'made to relieve syphilitic chancres' (G. K. Hunter's gloss in his New Arden edition, p. 124). The third (and, for me, the most suggestive) possibility is supplied in the clown's comment: 'Whether there be a scar under't or no, the velvet knows, but 'tis a goodly patch of velvet.' Bertram's left cheek, like his right, may be bare of any scar at all.

In the absence of any further references to patch or scar, what are we to conclude? Parolles, under extreme pressure, describes Bertram as 'a dangerous and lascivious boy, who is a whale to virginity' and is 'very ruttish' (IV. iii. 206–7, 201) but does not associate him with venereal disease. Lafew's 'noble scar' is in keeping with Bertram's martial exploits in Florence, but the verbal emphasis, starting in II. iii, has been upon the hero's less than honorable behavior. Thus, in a major speech after Bertram's rejection of Helena, the king comments at length upon 'dropsied honor' (II. iii. 127), while the countess notes that her son's 'sword can never win / The honor that he loses' by deserting Helena (III. ii. 91–2). Repeatedly, Bertram's honor is called into question in Act IV, especially in his dialogue with Diana about the ring that is associated with 'an honor 'longing to our house, / Bequeathèd down from many ancestors, / Which were the greatest obloquy i'th'world / In me to lose' (IV. ii. 42–5). Note too that Parolles, who is associated with 'snipped-taffeta' and 'villainous saffron' (IV. v. 1–2), scarves, and fashions ('the soul of this man is his clothes' – II. v. 42–3), tries to fake an honor he has not earned: 'I would the cutting of my garments would serve the turn, or the breaking of my Spanish sword' (IV. i. 44–5). His subsequent exposure forestalls any further equation between honor and mere surfaces: 'I will never trust a man again for keeping his sword clean, nor believe he can have everything in him by wearing his apparel neatly' (IV. iii. 136–8). Both the general comments on honor and the specific analogy to Parolles seem to me to preclude Lafew's generous inference about the velvet patch and to suggest instead a Bertram who is using that patch to direct attention away from his shameful treatment of Helena (and his loss of the ring).

To sum up, at the end of IV. v, before we see the returning Bertram, Shakespeare signals the presence of a velvet patch and provides three possible interpretations, one of which (that it, like Parolles' scarves and military bearing, covers nothing of substance) follows from a well-developed cluster of images. But no further mention of patch or scar is to be found in the Folio. As a result, critics and editors rarely if ever comment upon the patch's presence or role in the final scene; directors either ignore the problem completely or cut the Gordian knot by eliminating Lavatch's lines in IV. v (quite difficult to follow anyway) or provide some token resolution (in the 1977 Stratford Festival Canada production, Nicholas Pennell wore a tiny black spot the size of a 'beauty mark'). But what if Bertram *is* wearing such a patch, particularly a large patch (large enough perhaps to recall Parolles' blindfold of IV. iii)? If then at some point during the climactic scene that patch should fall off or be taken off (by Bertram, by Helena, by someone else) to reveal no scar beneath, this loss of the last symbol of 'dropsied honor' would then be juxtaposed with the 'new' Bertram who accepts Helena and transcends his former self, just as Parolles' blindfolded state, once transcended, led to new insight and new status. The loss of the patch, moreover, would be offset by the regaining of the ring, the symbol of true, lineal honor, and with the restitution of Helena as wife, thus undoing the sin against honor that, as noted by various figures, had offset any chivalric gains (so I can envisage Helena putting the ring on Bertram's finger and taking off the patch). Reunion with Helena, not a velvet patch covering a non-existent scar, brings honor back to Bertram. Although I have no way to 'prove' such a staging, an italicized presence and removal of the patch could reinforce key images, ideas, and analogies and buttress the 'change' in Bertram that troubles so many readers (especially if linked to an astringer holding a hooded falcon).

Investigation of Macbeth's 'it' or Bertram's patch underscores the importance of respecting the surviving signals and viewing them in theatrical rather than solely literary terms. Although difficult for some editors and critics, such an approach would appear to be second nature to the theatrical professional who, presumably, would best be able to resolve such puzzles. But, for a variety of practical and conceptual reasons, today's director often sidesteps these apparent anomalies by omitting them from the acting script (a common fate for Lavatch's description of the patch). Such cuts, moreover, are most likely to occur when a combination of practical necessity and a modern sense of 'realism' supersede an Elizabethan logic of imagery or analogy.

I have yet to see a production of *Richard III* in which Richard and Buckingham actually do enter '*in rotten armor, marvellous ill-favored*' (III. v. o. s.d.) as called for in the Folio. On the one hand, the strange humor of the subsequent scene, where Richard and Buckingham first compare notes on acting and then outdo themselves in front of the Mayor, is affected significantly by the image presented to the spectator. The more bizarre the appearance of the two actors, the more of a sardonic twist is given to their scarcely believable claims about Hastings and to the intimidated Mayor's acceptance of 'all your just proceedings in this cause' (l. 66). But, as with my suggestions in chapters five and six, a larger pattern may also be at work here. Overall, Richard's decline and fall in the final movement are linked to the failure of tactics that earlier had served him well. Thus, the same arguments that had succeeded with Lady Anne in I. ii fail with Queen Elizabeth in IV. iv (for me, the turning point of the play). The tactics that had eliminated a series of enemies and roadblocks (the Greys, Hastings, the two princes, Buckingham) no longer work against Richmond and what he stands for in Act v. The mocking or manipulation of religion so blatant in Act iii (e.g., the violation of sanctuary, the use of a bishop to fetch strawberries, the use of clergymen as stage properties to establish his supposed piety in the eyes of the Mayor and citizens) is seen in a new light when Richard, in the terms of the imagery of Act v, must face God's captain who calls upon the powers above to 'make us thy ministers of chastisement' (v. iii. 109–14). Just so, the ungainly armor mockingly thrust on against non-existent enemies reappears as the armor that cannot protect Richard in Act v against Richmond's sword (and much can be made on-stage of the arming of these two figures). The Folio's rotten armor, then, should have both an immediate impact upon the tone and meaning of iii. v and a larger meaning in terms of the total movement of the play, especially if a production (or *any* interpretation) is giving full credit to Shakespeare's design.

For a more obvious imagistic cut, consider Prince Hal's speech upon finding his father threatened by Douglas at Shrewsbury:

> Hold up thy head, vile Scot, or thou art like
> Never to hold it up again. The spirits
> Of valiant Shirley, Stafford, Blunt are in my arms.
> It is the Prince of Wales that threatens thee,
> Who never promiseth but he means to pay.
>
> (*1 Henry IV*, v. iv. 38–42)

Within a week in August 1979 I saw two quite different productions of this play, one in Stratford, Ontario, the other in Highpoint, North Carolina, both of which altered this moment. In North Carolina, all these lines were gone; Hal entered, saw his father fighting with Douglas, and attacked. In Ontario, Richard Monette spoke the first line and a half and then rescued his father. One can understand how all or most of these lines might drop out in rehearsal as impediments to the flow of the action or violations of plausibility. After all, from a 'realistic' point of view, would a son, seeing his father in danger, go through five blank verse lines before coming to the rescue? In response to my query, moreover, the director in Canada told me that the line starting 'It is the Prince of Wales …' was, in his terms, a 'white gloves' passage with a formal or prissy ring to it out of keeping with the scene and with Hal's character. So in both productions the climactic lines disappeared, with few spectators aware of their absence.

What then can be said in behalf of these five lines? Throughout the play, a wide range of figures, including Falstaff, the king, and the rebels, are associated with not paying their debts and not keeping their promises. In contrast, Prince Hal does honor his debts and promises, whether those made in his early soliloquy (where he vows to 'pay the debt I never promisèd') or in his reply to Falstaff in the major tavern scene ('I do, I will') or in the interview with his father (where he vows, among other things, to force Hotspur to 'exchange / His glorious deeds for my indignities'). Here, just before his climactic fight with Hotspur, the prince appears as a vengeful warrior, visibly bloodied, who embodies in his arms 'the spirits' of those who have already fallen (Shirley, Stafford, Blunt). But note that in this speech he describes himself not as Hal or Prince Henry or the prince but as 'the Prince of Wales,' the crown prince, the heir to Henry IV, the role that epitomizes the debt he never promised, and note also that he further characterizes that Prince of Wales as one who, unlike almost everyone else in the play, 'never promiseth but he means to pay.' Both in action (this rescue of his father) and in metaphor, Hal here fulfills a role, a debt, a promise that is central to the final movement of Part I (and of Part II as well). To cut these lines is then to achieve a modest gain in the flow of the battle and to avoid what might or might not be a 'white gloves' passage, but at the cost of losing a major signpost that should be pointing both the actor and the spectator toward some distinctive meanings embodied in Hal's emergence as the Prince of Wales and eventually as Henry V. Indeed, for anyone interested in the imagistic or metaphorical potential of the final movement of this play, these lines could be considered indispensable.

This brief discussion can serve at best as an introduction to the many problems associated with theatrical images and metaphors in the age of Shakespeare. Note that some of my examples are linked to stage directions often excluded from modern editions (the Nurse's intervention, Ophelia's lute, the Capulets' rosemary); some are associated with moments often pared down or eliminated in modern productions (the rotten armor, Hal's speech to Douglas); some are usually overlooked even as possibilities because they do not capture the attention of the average reader of a text[6] (the astringer's falcon, Macbeth's helmet, Bertram's patch). Other related moments, however, do stand out as problems too striking to ignore. So for that reader not convinced of a significant interpretative problem in the gentle astringer or Bertram's patch or Macbeth's 'it,' let me turn to a puzzling moment in that most problematic of plays, *Hamlet*, where, at the height of the closet scene, the Ghost interrupts Hamlet's tirade against Gertrude with a brief speech heard by Hamlet and the audience but not by the queen. When Hamlet asks his mother 'do you see nothing there?' she responds: 'Nothing at all; yet all that is I see' (III. iv. 132–3). Generations of readers and playgoers have then asked the obvious question: why does Gertrude *not* see and hear the Ghost? Given the focus of this study, I would like to press the matter even further. How are we, today, to go about answering such a question? In seeking our answer, what constitutes valid evidence? And to what extent are our twentieth-century assumptions about 'psychology' or 'dramatic illusion' or 'realism' appropriate for solving such a problem?

As will be evident from the previous chapters, my own sense of method calls for the placing of Shakespearean problems, whenever possible, in a larger context of scenes and effects provided by other dramatists (and, at times, by Shakespeare himself). To suggest such a context for Gertrude's not-seeing, let me start then with scenes from two moral plays from the first half of Queen Elizabeth's reign. First, in *The Tide Tarrieth No Man* (1576) Christianity (wearing the symbolic armor described by St. Paul) and Faithful Few, the play's chief spokesman for virtue, are on stage when the dramatist provides the stage direction: '*Courage and Greediness enter as though they saw not Christianity*' (l. 1520 s.d.). Here Courage is the Vice, the allegorical tempter, villain, and comedian; Greediness is a usurer whose materialism is undermining Christianity. To the modern reader, this scene and indeed this stage sermon as a whole are obvious, heavy-handed. Yet the signal '*enter as though they saw not Christianity*' represents a melding of allegory and good theatre that deserves closer consideration, for here the dramatist is conveying moral or spiritual blindness through a striking bit of stage business wherein Figure A does not or cannot see Figure B because Figure A is blind to what Figure B stands for. A director today might seek to make this entrance more 'believable' by having

Greediness and the Vice looking the wrong way or by distancing
the two sets of figures. But then the dramatist's point would be
lost or blurred, for the effect is keyed to a 'not-seeing' that would
be immediately recognized and appropriately interpreted by a
spectator. Indeed, the more 'unrealistic' the moment, the more
effective would be the allegorical point, so I would have Greediness and Courage walk right through Christianity as if he did not
exist (and an instinctive resistance to such a suggestion on the part
of many modern readers may reveal something distinctive about
the gap between us and the 1570s).

Consider next a comparable scene from *The Longer Thou
Livest the More Fool Thou Art* (1559) where Moros, the clownish
protagonist, is nearing the end of his long career of folly and vice.
God's Judgment, wearing '*a terrible visure*' (presumably an ugly,
frightening mask), now enters (l. 1758 s.d.), first to provide a
sermon for the audience that stresses Moros' folly and denial of
God and then, in a climactic action, to strike Moros with the
sword of vengeance. What is of particular interest here is that
Moros, unlike the spectator, never sees or hears this figure of
God's judgment. Rather, to explain his sudden distress after the
blow he refers to the palsy or the falling sickness and calls for a
cup of wine. Such blindness and deafness, in this theatrical
formulation, seal off this sinner from God's grace and act out his
spiritual condition. Thus, a higher truth and an answer to the
dilemma are audible and visible to the audience but not the
foolish, morally blind protagonist who is incapable of seeing,
hearing, or understanding God's Judgment.

Although modern readers regularly dismiss such scenes as
primitive or quaint, consider for the moment the *assets* of such a
technique. When Figure A fails to see Figure B, that failure tells
the spectator, swiftly and emphatically, something important
about A's moral status or spiritual condition or way of life.
Narrative allegory in general and allegorical theatre in particular
work best when thesis and action are wedded in this fashion. At
such moments, our sense of 'character' and 'motivation' may be
quite irrelevant. Rather, both scenes convey successfully the inner
states of key figures through highly visible and highly emphatic
stage actions that carry their own distinctive logic and force
regardless of our notions of 'realism.' Indeed, the element of
surprise in such moments, the initial *il*logic (when we first realize

that Greediness and Moros do not see what we see), provides a theatrical *italics* that underscores the dramatist's point. Like an italicized phrase, such a device calls attention to itself and provides a clear signal that something of importance is happening, thus encouraging a thinking precisely on the event. The effect, especially in a staged action, is equivalent to what Angus Fletcher calls the 'silences' in allegory which, for him, 'mean as much as the filled-in spaces.' According to Fletcher, 'by bridging the silent gaps between oddly unrelated images' the reader of allegory reaches 'the sunken understructure of thought.'[7] On stage, the equivalent to such 'silences' can be even more striking.

Although figures like Christianity and God's Judgment fade from sight, examples of moral, spiritual, and psychological 'blindness' do recur in the drama of the age of Shakespeare, often accompanied by clear verbal signals. For example, the blindness to higher forces found in Moros is discussed by the Friar in *'Tis Pity She's a Whore* where he argues against man being 'led alone / By Nature's light – as were philosophers / Of elder times,' rather telling Giovanni: 'but 'tis not so: then madman, thou wilt find / That Nature is in Heaven's positions blind' (II. v. 30–4). The inability of foolish figures to 'see' the truth staring them in the face is explained to Volpone by Mosca:

> True, they will not see't.
> Too much light blinds 'hem, I think. Each of 'hem
> Is so possess'd, and stuff'd with his own hopes,
> That anything, unto the contrary,
> Never so true, or never so apparent,
> Never so palpable, they will resist it –   (v. ii. 22–7)

Or, as Imogen notes, 'our very eyes / Are sometimes like our judgments, blind' (*Cymbeline*, IV. ii. 301–2). No one needs reminding of the many pregnant passages in *King Lear*, starting with Kent's 'see better, Lear' in the opening scene, ranging through Gloucester's 'I stumbled when I saw,' and concluding with Lear's final lines. And for the related issue of metaphoric deafness, one need only turn to Falstaff, who confesses to 'the disease of not listening, the malady of not marking' (2 *Henry IV*, I. ii. 115–16).

Since many readers are at home with verbal metaphors, such imagistic treatment of blindness or 'seeing' causes few if any problems. Rather, the challenge comes from moments like those in the two moral plays where the metaphor is translated into stage action or into what I term theatrical metaphor. Thus, the modern reader can readily grasp a discussion of how a figure is 'blind to' Heaven or to some truth he would prefer to ignore, but that same reader may have great difficulty accepting the acting out of such a metaphor, wherein before his eyes a figure is clearly unable to 'see' something that *is* visible to the spectator and to someone else on stage. Such scenes, moreover, *are* to be found in the age of Shakespeare, although the figure not seen is more likely to be a ghost or devil or angel than a Christianity or God's Judgment. Thus, a version of this theatrical technique was still available, still potentially meaningful, presumably as an italicized signal that some form of blindness or myopia was central to the scene.

A good example of this device is to be found in Heywood's 2 *Edward IV*, a play roughly contemporary with *Henry V* and *Julius Caesar*. Here a clergyman, Doctor Shaw, the man responsible for the interpretation of the prophecy that led to the death of Clarence, is on stage with the ghost of Friar Anselm, who has returned to curse Shaw for falsely interpreting that prophecy. When a messenger arrives to summon Shaw to Richard III, the Doctor, in great distress, says he cannot come, but suggests instead: 'I pray thee, take that Friar; / For he can do it better far than I.' The messenger responds: 'A friar, M. Doctor, I see none,' setting up Shaw's comment: 'No: thy untainted soul / Cannot discern the horrors that I do' (1, 164). In contrast to the two scenes from the moral plays, 'seeing' here is associated with guilty knowledge and 'not-seeing' with innocence. Regardless, a larger metaphoric point is made in striking theatrical fashion, without figures named Christianity or God's Judgment. Again, what an on-stage figure sees or fails to see provides a telling comment upon his spiritual condition, his values, his fate — a highly visible summary of his state of mind or soul. The messenger's failure to see a ghostly friar visible to the audience clearly singles out Doctor Shaw as a guilty, tainted figure. If our theatrical logic then prevents us from appreciating such a technique, the fault may lie in us rather than in the 'primitive' technique of Heywood and his predecessors.

Consider another example from Heywood, this time from 2 *The Iron Age* (1612), that clearly echoes the closet scene in *Hamlet*. Thus, Heywood provides a son (Orestes) standing by the body of the man he has just killed (Egistus) while berating his mother (Clitemnestra) and praising his dead father (Agamemnon). When the queen denies any role in Agamemnon's death, Orestes calls upon 'you powers of Heaven' to 'give me some sign from either fiends or angel.' The stage direction then reads: '*Enter the Ghost of Agamemnon, pointing unto his wounds: and then to Egistus and the Queen, who were his murderers, which done, he vanisheth.*' Although the ghost (unlike Hamlet's father) has no lines, Orestes addresses this 'godlike shape' that, in his terms, has provided 'that sacred testimony, / To crown my approbation.' But when the son calls for his mother to 'see,' she responds: 'See what? thy former murder makes thee mad.' Again, when he asks: 'saw you nothing?' she responds: 'what should I see save this sad spectacle, / Which blood-shoots both mine eyes' (i.e., the body of Egistus). 'And nothing else?' he asks. 'Nothing' is the response. He concludes: 'Mine eyes are clearer sighted then, and see / Into thy bosom.' The action concludes with Orestes wounding his mother, her admission of guilt ('heavens are just'), and her death (III, 422–3). Unlike the situation in *Hamlet* (where the wrong man lies dead and Gertrude is not an accomplice to murder), Heywood's point is never in doubt. Both Orestes and the spectator accept the clear signal from the ghost as an answer to his plea, while the queen is blind to what she cannot or will not see but rather can only see the 'sad spectacle' of her dead lover. As with Doctor Shaw and the messenger, such a disparity in 'seeing' between two on-stage figures signals a deeper disparity in guilt or understanding, with the blindness of one figure italicizing a larger blindness or guilty sight.

Several Jacobean and Caroline plays use such disparities to signal a distinction between earthly and heavenly vision. Thus, several tragedies devoted to martyrdom and miraculous conversions (e.g., *Herod and Antipater*, *The Martyred Soldier*, *The Virgin Martyr*) provide such seeing and not-seeing moments to underscore the distinctive vision of a saintly figure. For example, in Dekker and Massinger's *The Virgin Martyr* the heroine Dorothea, just before her execution, talks to and is reassured by an angelic figure while two other on-stage observers comment: 'what object / Is her eye fix'd on?' and 'I see nothing' (IV. iii. 125–6); again, in the final scene the converted Theophilus has an elaborate vision that brings on stage his martyred victims, a vision not shared by Diocletian and others hostile to Christianity. The best example of such privileged seeing is to be found in *Henry VIII* when the sleeping Queen Katherine, near death, is visited by six vizarded figures dressed in white who dance about her, curtsy to her, and crown her with a garland (the Folio heads the long stage direction with: *The Vision*). When the Queen awakes, she identifies these figures as 'spirit[s] of peace' and 'a blessed troop' who 'promised me eternal happiness' (IV. ii. 83, 87, 90). But the two other on-stage figures, Griffith and Patience, have seen nothing, so when Katherine asks: 'Saw ye none enter since I slept?' the answer is 'None, madam' (and moments later Griffith adds: 'I am most joyful, madam, such good dreams / Possess your fancy'). Here again, the effect is keyed to a disparity in seeing – this time the spectator and a figure near death versus on-stage observers impervious to a transcendent vision.

Rather than pursuing more examples from little-known plays[8] (other than *Henry VIII*), let me turn to three of the best-known tragedies of this period, each of which makes telling use of the theatrical potential in the seen and the unseen. First to be considered is *Doctor Faustus*, a play with more than its share of the supernatural. Any analysis of this play is immediately complicated by the murky textual situation caused by the two extant versions: the shorter A text of 1604 and the longer B text of 1616. Indeed, a major distinction between the two versions lies in their quite different approaches to the problem of seeing and not-seeing.[9]

On many matters the A and B texts do agree. For example, both provide key passages that refer to things seen by a figure on stage but not by the spectator. Thus, after kissing Helen, Faustus says: 'Her lips suck forth my soul, see where it flies' (B 1877, A 1360). Similarly, the Old Man tells Faustus: 'I see an Angel hovers o'er thy head, / And with a vial full of precious grace, / Offers to pour the same into thy soul' (A 1320–2, B 1835–7). Again, Faustus in his final moments calls out: 'See see where Christ's blood streams in the firmament' (A 1463, not in B) and 'And see where God stretcheth out his arm, / And bends his ireful brows' (A 1468–9, abbreviated in B 2053). Especially in the A text, the heavenly dimension (as represented by Faustus' soul, the angel with the vial of grace, Christ's blood, or God's arm) cannot be seen by the audience but rather must be imagined or accepted on faith.

In contrast, the forces of Hell are far more visible. Mephostophilis, of course, is seen by Faustus and the audience throughout the play, while Lucifer and Belzebub appear in scene vi to
intimidate Faustus and bring on the Seven Deadly Sins. Both texts
call for devils to frighten the clown in scene iv, to bring on rich
apparel in scene vi, and to drag Faustus off to Hell.

But the two texts vary significantly on other points. Scene iii in
the A text begins: '*Enter Faustus to conjure*'; but the stage
direction in B reads: '*Thunder. Enter Lucifer and four devils,
Faustus to them with this speech.*' Thus, in the A text Faustus is
alone when he first invokes Mephostophilis, but, in B, five devils
look on, unseen by Faustus, a presence that could have a considerable effect upon our view of the protagonist's stature and
autonomy. Again, in A the famous speech that constitutes the
tragic hero's final hour follows immediately the exit of the
scholars to pray for Faustus, but, in strong contrast, B provides a
brief but significant exchange with Mephostophilis and then
some thirty-five lines from the two angels (cited in chapter three)
in which a heavenly throne descends, Hell is discovered, and,
overall, the two alternative routes are elaborately mapped. At no
point does the A text provide a clear equivalent to the heavenly
throne found in B – that is, a tangible, unequivocal manifestation
of the heavenly alternative. Rather, in A the reader or spectator
must depend upon the words of the Old Man, the Good Angel,
and Faustus himself, along with ambiguous signs like the *homo
fuge* warning and the congealed blood.

Perhaps the most telling difference between the two texts comes
after Faustus departs with Helen. Here A provides a summary
comment by the Old Man who then triumphs over the devils who
seek to torment him. B omits this passage entirely but instead
brings in Lucifer, Belzebub. and Mephostophilis to mark how
Faustus demeans himself during his final moments (and no *exeunt*
is indicated for these devils). The presence (B text) or absence (A
text) of two or three devils can then have a radical effect upon the
moments that follow. For example, in both texts the scholars urge
Faustus to call upon God, and he responds: 'On God whom
Faustus hath abjured, on God, whom Faustus hath blasphemed,
ah my God, I would weep, but the devil draws in my tears, gush
forth blood, instead of tears, yea life and soul, Oh he stays my
tongue, I would lift up my hands, but see, they hold them, they

hold them.' When the scholars ask 'Who Faustus?' he responds *'Lucifer* and *Mephostophilis'* (A 1414–22, B 1949–56). Again, in his final speech Faustus calls out:

> O I'll leap up to my God: who pulls me down?
> See see where Christ's blood streams in the firmament,
> One drop would save my soul, half a drop, ah my Christ,
> Ah rend not my heart for naming of my Christ,
> Yet will I call on him, oh spare me *Lucifer*!
> Where is it now? 'tis gone: (A 1462–7, B 2048–52)

In the B text, during both of these passages Lucifer and Belzebub are (presumably) on stage. Even if they do not menace Faustus overtly, their presence underscores their power over him. In this version the untainted scholars remain unaware of the hellish presence, but only Faustus, whose choices have given Hell this power, and the spectator can see the devils. Remember Doctor Shaw's line to the messenger: 'thy untainted soul / Cannot discern the horrors that I do.' If indeed the devils are on stage during the final speech, the B text provides a striking, highly visible demonstration of what stands between Faustus and Christ's blood, so that 'where is it now? 'tis gone' has a special poignancy.

But if we read the A text, no such devils are visible, at least to the spectator, during these final scenes. Rather, Faustus' allusions to the devils are similar in kind to his allusions to his soul being sucked forth or Christ's blood in the firmament or God's arm. Because the devils are cited but not seen in the A text, the spectator can never be sure whether Hell is actually exerting control over the protagonist, actively preventing his repentance, or whether the blockage is purely internal, a self-imagined constraint that Faustus only believes to be external control. In particular, when Faustus cries out: 'I would lift up my hands, but see, they hold them, they hold them,' the scholars in both texts respond: 'Who Faustus?' In the B text the audience would see the devils while the innocent scholars, who lack Faustus' special bond with Hell, would see nothing; but in the A text neither the scholars nor the spectators would see anything corresponding to the protagonist's vision of devils holding him back. Each version has its own particular power and horror. The A version, by providing less, perplexes us the more, for what is 'real' becomes inextricably intertwined with what is real in Faustus' mind. Both versions find distinctive yet somewhat different ways of building upon the metaphoric value of the seen and the unseen to enhance our understanding of this tragedy of damnation. Again, to draw upon Angus Fletcher, the 'silences' or 'silent gaps' in either version encourage us, even force us to explore Faustus' relationship to the powers above and the forces below.

Let me turn now to two justly famous moments in Shakespearean tragedy. First, both Macbeth and Lady Macbeth have their versions of the A text Faustus who sees what is invisible to the audience. In a much-discussed moment, Macbeth sees 'the air-drawn dagger' (III. iv. 62) which he glosses as 'a dagger of the mind, a false creation / Proceeding from the heat-oppressèd brain' (II. i. 38–9). Remember too his alternatives: 'Mine eyes are made the fools o'th'other senses, / Or else worth all the rest' (ll. 44–5). He may conclude that 'there's no such thing' (l. 47), but clearly, for him, the vision has a reality and validity. Similarly, during her sleep-walking, Lady Macbeth's 'eyes are open' yet 'their sense are shut' (v. i. 22–3). Here she sees (and smells) blood on her hands and, in her re-enactment of earlier moments, sees Macbeth ('wash your hands, put on your nightgown, look not so pale ... give me your hand' – ll. 57–8, 62). Thus, twice in this tragedy key figures have visions that suggest an interior reality not directly visible to the spectator.

But a third moment, the richest of all, poses a more complex problem. Thus, during the banquet scene Macbeth, like Heywood's Doctor Shaw or Orestes, sees a ghost that is visible to the audience but remains invisible to other figures on stage. Like Doctor Shaw, Macbeth is the possessor of guilty knowledge that enables him to see horrors not apparent to the innocent thanes or even to his wife who is not involved in Banquo's murder.

In the light of my examples so far, consider then Shakespeare's use of Banquo's ghost as a metaphoric device linked to the major issues of the play, a means to bring Macbeth's tragedy into focus. Earlier, Macbeth had defended his decision not to kill Duncan with: 'I dare do all that may become a man; / Who dares do more is none' (I. vii. 46–7). Here and later (e.g., with the two murderers in III. i) an implicit sense of *man* and *manhood* governs his actions (a concept in his mind associated with *do*, *dare*, *deed*). But when faced with a ghost that he alone can see, his single state of man is badly shaken, so that Lady Macbeth can ask him: 'Are you a man?' (III. iv. 58). His major speech of the scene follows the second appearance of the ghost:

> What man dare, I dare.
> Approach thou like the rugged Russian bear,
> The armed rhinoceros, or th'Hyrcan tiger;
> Take any shape but that, and my firm nerves
> Shall never tremble. Or be alive again
> And dare me to the desert with thy sword.
> If trembling I inhabit then, protest me
> The baby of a girl. Hence, horrible shadow!
> Unreal mock'ry, hence! Why, so; being gone,
> I am a man again.   (ll. 99–108)

Macbeth both sees and is unmanned by sights not shared by the others on stage. His question as to how the others 'can behold such sights' and not be 'blanched with fear' elicits Ross's telling response: 'What sights, my lord?' (ll. 112–16), an interchange that recalls the 'Who Faustus?' of the scholars. Macbeth's limited sense of manhood has led him to dare two murders, to pawn his eternal jewel, and to jump the life to come to gain a crown. His privileged seeing at the banquet has set him off from everyone else, isolated him as the tragic hero, and shattered his basic premises about his manhood and his dare. In her next appearance, Lady Macbeth says, with tragic irony: 'What need we fear who knows it, when none can call our power to accompt?' (v. i. 34–5). Shakespeare has not presented a figure named God's Judgment to strike down a sinner at the height of his power, but he has played off the seen against the unseen so to dramatize with great power the central conflict in the tragedy and to explore what it is to be a man. Again, the disparity in seeing italicizes the moral or spiritual state of the protagonist and acts out that combination of tragic vision and blindness that epitomizes Macbeth. His privileged seeing should surprise us, leap out at us, tease us into thought.

Now, after much travail, let me return to Hamlet's 'Do you see nothing there?' and Gertrude's 'Nothing at all; yet all that is I see.' The situation in the closet scene is more complex than any of the moments cited so far, for Hamlet's relationship to his dead father, his mother, Claudius, the Ghost, and the dead Polonius have all been explored throughout the play and epitomized here, in speech and action. As far back as his first soliloquy, Hamlet had been remembering his father and berating his mother; in the same scene he had announced to Horatio that 'methinks I see my father,' although only 'in my mind's eye.' The issue of 'seeing' then becomes basic to the evolution of the tragedy and of particular importance in Act III. Thus, Claudius is eventually moved and shocked by 'The Murder of Gonzago' (as enhanced by Hamlet's comments), but does not react to the dumb show and, in a sense, may not 'see' it. Although actors often play the king looking the other way (or embracing Gertrude), Claudius may be looking directly at the pantomime (I find no evidence he does not) but not be able to 'see' it as relevant to himself or his crime (as he is later brought to 'see' that crime in the prayer scene). Then, in III. iii, Hamlet 'sees' Claudius kneeling, apparently in prayer, and therefore decides not to kill him ('why, this is hire and salary, not revenge') – understandably reacting on the basis of what he 'sees.' But in the couplet that concludes the scene, heard by the spectator but not by Hamlet, Claudius reveals that his prayers were ineffectual, so that what appeared to be a momentary state of grace was, in fact, only a façade, a pose without substance. Moments later, hearing a noise, Hamlet runs his sword through the arras, hoping to find the king. In this arras, Shakespeare provides an obvious symbol for a surface that prevents one from seeing the truth, a surface that epitomizes the seeming world of Denmark and helps set up a major tragic error.

If one iterated image then predominates in the closet scene, it is that of seeing (and, to a lesser extent, of hearing). Initially, Hamlet's goal with Gertrude is to 'set you up a glass / Where you may see the inmost part of you,' a clear echo of 'the mirror up to nature' that is 'the purpose of playing.' After the murder, the famous portrait speech forces the queen to 'look here upon this picture, and on this,' to 'see' the graces of Hamlet Senior, and then to 'look you now what follows.' The twice repeated 'have you eyes?' calls into question (in Hamlet's eyes) 'what judgment / Would step from this to this?' and leads to 'what devil was't / That thus hath cozened you at hoodman-blind?' Hamlet concludes: 'Eyes without feeling, feeling without sight, / Ears without hands or eyes, smelling sans all, / Or but a sickly part of one true sense / Could not so mope.' Gertrude reveals the efficacy of her son's words: 'O Hamlet, speak no more. / Thou turn'st mine eyes into my very soul, / And there I see such black and grainèd spots / As will not leave their tinct.' Moments later, she adds: 'O, speak to me no more. / These words like daggers enter in mine ears.' As Hamlet rages on about Claudius, the Ghost enters, eliciting questions from Hamlet ('do you not come your tardy son to chide') and 'Alas, he's mad' from the queen. The Ghost enjoins: 'Do not forget. This visitation / Is but to whet thy almost blunted purpose,' then adding 'but look, amazement on thy mother sits.' The queen's amazement, needless to say, arises from her inability to see and hear the figure Hamlet is addressing. Thus, she asks her son: 'Alas, how is't with you, / That you do bend your eye on vacancy.' To her question, 'Whereon do you look?' Hamlet responds: 'On him, on him! Look you, how pale he glares!' Then follows a particularly revealing exchange:

QUEEN.   To whom do you speak this?
HAMLET.   Do you see nothing there?
QUEEN.   Nothing at all; yet all that is I see.
HAMLET. Nor did you nothing hear?
QUEEN.   No, nothing but ourselves.
HAMLET. Why, look you there! Look how it steals away!
         My father, in his habit as he lived!
         Look where he goes even now out at the portal!
                                              (III. iv. 132–7)

To Gertrude, Hamlet's vision of the Ghost 'is the very coinage of your brain. / This bodiless creation ecstasy / Is very cunning in.' Hamlet, however, denies 'ecstasy' or madness, instead telling his mother: 'Lay not that flattering unction to your soul, / That not your trespass but my madness speaks,' for that excuse, he claims, 'will but skin and film the ulcerous place / Whiles rank corruption, mining all within, / Infects unseen.'

Shakespeare's web of references to seeing, looking, eyes, and mirrors admits of no easy summary. Such seeing has its positive connotations here (self-knowledge, true judgment, a son's recognition of his father), but also its pejorative side (madness or ecstasy, corruption lurking unseen, corrupted judgment, the wife who cannot 'see' her idealized husband). But to the reader and particularly the spectator, one question leaps out: why is Gertrude unable to see and hear her former husband? For some, the puzzle is easily resolved. Thus, whoever rewrote this scene for the German adaptation (*Fratricide Punished*) had Hamlet respond to Gertrude's 'I see nothing' with: 'I indeed believe that you see nothing, for you are no longer worthy to behold its form.'[10] This Hamlet then storms off-stage, leaving his mother with the impression he is mad. Rather than singling out her unworthiness, one might find the key in the queen's memory. As Hamlet has noted several times (with savage force), her former husband has, in her mind, been eclipsed by Claudius, while, in contrast, Hamlet has not only promised to 'remember thee' but, in addition, has been provoked by thoughts beyond the reaches of his soul. The tragic hero, who has already been strongly affected by his earlier interview with the Ghost, can therefore 'see' what Gertrude cannot, however one defines that 'seeing' (tragic vision? privileged insight? a tainted mind? the very coinage of his brain?).

Taken together, the obvious presence of the Ghost, Hamlet's reactions, and Gertrude's failure to 'see' italicize theatrically a striking blindness or obtuseness. Given such a noteworthy moment, our logic of interpretation compels us to seek reasons within the queen's character or situation for this not-seeing (and such reasons are not hard to find). But is this logic, this approach, valid or fruitful? After all, despite this startling failure to see the Ghost, the focus of this pivotal scene is upon Hamlet, not Gertrude. Remember that at the Ghost's entrance Hamlet is castigating Claudius as a king of shreds and patches and berating his mother for her sexual crimes against the memory of his dead father, while he himself is standing in the vicinity of the body of a man he has just killed, a man not implicated in the death of Hamlet Senior. The death of Polonius, moreover, will set in motion a chain of events that will eventually destroy Ophelia, Laertes, and Gertrude, not to mention Claudius and Hamlet himself. Gertrude's failure to see is underscored by the dialogue and the stage business (and in at least one recent production the Ghost and the queen were almost touching at her 'Nothing at all'). But what about the logic of theatrical metaphor? What about the model set by the moral drama and by my other examples, each admittedly less complex than this scene?

So, at the risk of muddying the waters even further, I propose that this striking anomaly – Gertrude's failure to see and hear the Ghost – is designed primarily to *italicize* the larger issue of *not*-seeing in this scene and in the tragedy as a whole. If we confront the *issue* rather than the *character*, we recognize immediately that the pivotal not-seer is not the queen but Hamlet. Gertrude does not see the Ghost but can confidently state 'all that is I see.' In contrast, Hamlet does see (and remember) the Ghost and hears the speech about his almost blunted purpose. But here, as elsewhere, Hamlet does not 'see' all that the spectator sees. He does not see the truth behind the arras or behind the façade of Claudius kneeling in prayer. Most important, he does not 'see' the body of Polonius and the full implications of what he inadvertently has done. Between his discovery of Polonius behind the arras ('Thou wretched, rash, intruding fool, farewell! / I took thee for thy better' – ll. 32–3) and his next acknowledgment of the body ('For this same lord, / I do repent' – ll. 173–4) fall one hundred and forty lines, a gap I find very revealing. Equally revealing is his 'I'll lug the guts into the neighbor room' and his final, sardonic comments on the 'foolish prating knave.' Moreover, much depends upon staging choices here, for if Polonius' body, suitably bloodied, is in full view during those one hundred and forty lines and if Hamlet, for even part of the time, is waving a bloody sword, an image of a Pyrrhus-like revenger is juxtaposed with his accusations against Gertrude for *her* crimes and not-seeing. Given his previous errors in 'seeing' with the kneeling Claudius and the voice behind the arras, can we expect Hamlet to see what he has done, what he has become? As I understand it, Gertrude's blindness is then a major signal that should alert us to Hamlet's blindness to himself and to the full implications of his actions. If this scene is indeed a mirror, that mirror is being held up not to Gertrude or to a generalized Nature but to Hamlet himself, so that the queen's striking behavior becomes a theatrical metaphor that provides a strong signal that the scene as a whole is keyed to such blindness (or forgetting).

Lacking Shakespeare's program notes or a videotape of a Globe performance, I cannot hope to satisfy the modern reader of *Hamlet* with my metaphoric interpretation. Indeed, I find myself cast in the role of Iago who first asks Othello 'Where's satisfaction? / It is impossible you should see this' and then comments: 'But yet, I say, / If imputation and strong circumstances / Which lead directly to the door of truth / Will give you satisfaction, you may have't' (III. iii. 401–2, 405–8). Having no 'ocular proof,' I can only offer, like Iago, 'imputation and strong circumstances' – in this case, comparable scenes from less-complex plays. My argument, moreover, is affected by several of the significant puzzles created in Act III: the nature of the Ghost (now that Eleanor Prosser has set up for us the diabolic argument[11]); the reason for the Ghost's appearance in the closet scene; the degree of Hamlet's distraction or feigned passion or madness; the disposition of Polonius' body. Citing analogous scenes from plays spanning roughly fifty years certainly cannot 'prove' that Gertrude's failure to see is primarily a means to italicize Hamlet's tragic blindness, his inability to 'see' the body of Polonius.

But recourse to other scenes and plays can force a modern reader to consider a wider range of possibilities, more things in heaven and earth than were dreamt of in his or her original philosophy. According to our prevailing logic of interpretation, Gertrude's failure to see and hear the Ghost is to be explained largely in terms of her individual limitations or weaknesses, as would also be true for other figures who fail to see sights visible to the spectator (e.g., Lady Macbeth and the banquet guests, the scholars who accompany Doctor Faustus in the B text, Griffith and Patience). Our logic, our sense of theatrical conventions, thereby sets real but often invisible limits upon our range of interpretation. But from the later moral drama through *Macbeth*, I find another kind of logic at work, one often linked to moral thesis or metaphoric action, whereby a striking, often surprising stage direction calls attention to itself in such a way as to establish or underscore a larger symbolic or metaphoric effect ('*Enter as though they saw not Christianity*'). As evident throughout this study, such metaphoric actions need not be limited to failures to see or to privileged seeing, for the logic of surprise has many uses (as with Othello's loss of his weapon to lesser men twice in his final moments or other such instances of metaphoric stage violence). In the realm of stage metaphor, many different kinds of 'silences' or 'silent gaps' are available. Yet since many theatrical conflicts are based upon faulty or limited sight ('see better, Lear'), such acting out of metaphoric blindness or guilty seeing can be especially rich and meaningful and can lead to the kind of illumination described by Rosemund Tuve wherein 'the enclosed meaning explodes in a firework of suddenly grasped metaphorical relations.'[12] My examples of this technique (which range from the Chester Balaam play to *The Martyred Soldier* of 1638) cannot 'prove' my reading of the closet scene, but to screen out such possibilities is to limit our perspectives, narrow our range of vision, and leave us, as modern readers of Shakespeare, dangerously close to Gertrude who admits that she sees 'Nothing at all' but still claims confidently: 'yet all that is I see.'

8 · Conclusion: Elizabethan playscripts and modern interpreters

What's past is prologue

(*The Tempest*, II. i. 247)

To focus upon 'seeing' and 'not-seeing' is then to return to the questions raised in my earlier chapters about today's criticism, editing, production, and stage history. Admittedly, the myriad approaches to how we 'see' Shakespeare (on the page, on the stage, on television, in the classroom) defy any tidy categories, but, in the broadest sense, the most basic divisions fall between the 'historians' and the 'modernists,' those committed to 'Shakespeare the Elizabethan' and those primarily interested in 'Shakespeare our contemporary.' This study falls squarely in the 'historical' camp, not only because of the many references to Elizabethan, Jacobean, and Caroline plays but also because of my advocacy of the assets in recovering the original 'logic' of presentation (as opposed to the emphasis much in evidence today upon the decoding of texts by the contemporary reader).

But even the reader with some 'historical' sympathies will note many omissions in this study. Thus, no claims are advanced here for new insights into Shakespeare's links to the intellectual climate of his age or into his relations with other writers. Despite all my theatrical evidence, moreover, I have offered no new proposals about theatrical architecture, the shape of the stage, the number of stage doors, the presence of 'flying' machinery, or other issues that continue to bedevil the stage historian. In addition, I am certainly not the first to argue for the potential importance of the original stage conventions (Muriel Bradbrook's pioneer study is nearing its fiftieth anniversary) or the rewards to be gained by treating the plays as scripts rather than literary texts (a position argued eloquently by Harley Granville-Barker and J. L. Styan, to name only two). Finally, my treatment of stage conventions and the original 'logic' of presentation has been selective rather than exhaustive. Thus, although I have dealt with boots, nightgowns, disheveled hair, and rosemary, I have not commented upon other equivalent signals (e.g., figures who enter '*muffled*' or with halters about their necks[1]), nor, despite my concern with 'night' and 'place,' have I discussed the analogous problem of 'time.'[2]

Nonetheless, with due regard for the patience of the reader, I have sought to present in the preceding chapters a series of categories and examples – some perhaps familiar, others decidedly less so, a few surprising, even startling (the cutting off of a nose 'in the dark' in Massinger's *The Guardian* can serve as one extreme) – in the hope of building a fuller context for understanding the best plays. In this selective process, moreover, my continual emphasis upon what may appear oddities or anomalies to the modern eye has been quite deliberate. Thus, the first response of the 'modernist' to the arrow in Nessus or roses as weapons or the astringer or the presence of an on-stage banquet while Adam and Orlando complain of starving may be to block out the problem or pass over it in embarrassed silence (Shakespeare, like Homer, may nod). But from the historian's point of view such moments can be of critical importance in that they call attention to the fact (easily obscured by great artistic achievement) that Shakespeare is *not* our contemporary and therefore can serve as windows through which the reader open to such possibilities can begin to see a well-developed craft of the theatre taken for granted by some of the finest dramatists in our language but now largely lost or submerged. From this angle, such 'historical' insights can function not as a strait-jacket for the modern interpreter but as a liberating device that can expand our sense of the potential for stage metaphors or meaningful juxtapositions or other striking effects factored into the original equations.

The more striking the anomaly, then, the more that may be revealed about the gaps between then and now that often lurk under the surface of familiarity. For example, when R. B. Graves suggests that actors at the Globe may not even have lit their tapers (because such flames would be hard to maintain on windy days, while the actual light would be negligible, even counterproductive), the reader's first reaction may be amusement or incredulity, yet further consideration may help to pinpoint something of importance that was shared by players and spectators then as opposed to what is taken for granted now about 'illusion' or 'going to the theatre.' In the terms advanced by Sir Walter Greg: 'Every item of historical evidence performs a two-fold function: positively it enlarges the basis we have to build on, and enables us to extend the structure of valid inference; negatively it is often of even greater service in limiting the field of admissible conjecture.'[3] Here Greg has in mind the few surviving playhouse documents, but the accumulated force of the stage directions cited throughout this study can also aid in developing valid inferences and admissible conjectures, especially for those instances where no clear signals have survived. Granted, despite my canvas of many plays, the evidence is rarely definitive or fully satisfying, with gaps often occurring in just those scenes that most interest the modern reader. Rather, as various scholars have noted, Elizabethan dramatists were writing their playscripts not for us but for actors who already knew how to present '*as from dinner*' or '*ravished*' or '*in prison.*' The scholarly mind may yearn for order and proof, but as Harley Granville-Barker aptly observed about the untidiness of the evidence about the Elizabethan stage, 'such a creature is unlikely to have behaved itself with any consistent regard for the interests and habits of the historian.'[4]

Given the absence of tidy formulations or orderly findings, what then are the implications of this study for the modern interpreter of Shakespeare? First, the material presented in the preceding chapters should provoke the editor to reconsider the presentation of stage directions and, in particular, whether the logic behind decisions about words is appropriate for decisions about the theatrical evidence. Thus, when an editor must choose one word ('scallion' versus 'scullion' versus 'stallion'), he or she must rely upon a logic of exclusion that eliminates B (and sometimes C) in favor of A on the basis of some yardstick (e.g., which text has greatest 'authority'? what did the author intend?). But how appropriate is this logic (wherein 'authority' quite logically is linked to the 'author') to decisions about stage directions? Thus, in terms of theatrical evidence (rather than poetry and prose) all three versions of *Hamlet* carry their own somewhat different 'authority': the play as (presumably) envisaged by the author when writing it; the same play as altered or conditioned by the King's Men for performance; and a version of the play as remembered by actors who had been involved in some production of unknown auspices. For readers with varying interests, *all* of the stage directions in all three versions of *Hamlet* are of value; even though Q–2 as a text may be closest to the 'author,' all of these signals have 'authority' as theatrical evidence; all should therefore be preserved for the potential user (actor, director, costumer, stage historian, cultural historian, antiquarian) in some kind of accessible form. In such cases, inclusion rather than exclusion should be the practice, because editorial decisions to exclude (or change or sanitize) may undermine the value of the evidence for at least part of the readership, many of whom will *not* read the textual notes.

Admittedly, many of the theatrical signals with which an editor must wrestle remain puzzling, even indecipherable. Granted too that scholars can cite dramatists like Jonson and Berkeley who preferred to present their plays in printed texts freed from the concessions made (grudgingly?) to the playhouse. But I know of no evidence for such a sense of division between page and stage on the part of Shakespeare. To devalue in any way the surviving stage directions when editing the plays is then to run the risk of imposing an inappropriate or anachronistic logic upon some potentially valuable evidence and, in the process, to screen out what may be a lost but recoverable code from those readers (theatrical professionals, stage historians, cultural historians) who might be able to solve it. Why should the reader be spared the puzzlement (and perhaps the enlightenment) provoked by the king's astringer, the Nurse's intervention, the Capulets' rosemary, Ophelia's lute, and the Ghost's nightgown?

Like the editor preparing an edition, the director mounting a production must confront many varied problems in any Shakespeare play and, understandably, may prefer to dispense with obvious anomalies by cutting or reshaping the acting script. Many of these changes result from practical concern with budget, personnel, running time, and the physical resources at hand, not to mention problems with continuity, plausibility, and obscurity. Thus, even more than the editor concerned with the reader, the director must worry about murky syntax, hard words, obscure allusions, and seemingly confused narrative, any one of which can place an immediate and potentially damaging strain upon a spectator's attention. In addition, actors are often resistant to 'historical' explanations that will not 'play' for a modern audience (that lacks access to the learned notes that can be supplied by the editor).

But, as noted throughout this study, post-Elizabethan assumptions about verisimilitude, continuity, and imagery can have a strong impact upon any Shakespeare play, especially if those assumptions lead to significant omissions or alterations. Admittedly, few plays will suffer from the elimination of a few lines of verse or the excision of some mythological allusions or the telescoping together of some attendant lords, yet more substantial changes, supposedly to make matters easier for an audience, may, in fact, end up diminishing the experience. Sidestepping Shakespeare's juxtaposition of Adam–Orlando with the banquet or Edgar with Kent in the stocks may appear to smooth over some rough spots in *As You Like It* and *King Lear* but may actually blot out some distinctive and potentially revealing parts of the original design. In his account of a memorable production of *Othello*, Kenneth Tynan notes that in the rendition of v. i 'Othello's brief and dramatically pointless appearance is cut, in accordance with sound theatrical custom.'[5] To observe such a custom (as has happened in just about every production I have seen) is then to ensure that Othello's relationship to other murders 'in the dark' *remains* 'dramatically pointless,' for any opportunity (or incentive) to explore the original links and metaphors has disappeared. Again, a director told me that he cut the striking clock at the end of *Richard III* (v. iii. 276. s.d.) because for him such a sound or phenomenon seemed out of place on a battlefield, a decision that allows a verisimilar sense of 'place' to take precedence over a potentially powerful image at a moment when time clearly is running out for Richard. I find a considerable difference between the paring down of murky or opaque passages and the elimination of images, actions, or juxtapositions meaningful then and still potentially meaningful today given an expanded sense of the logic of presentation.

The director aware of such alternative possibilities, on the other hand, may not only include such moments but conceivably find ways to make them exciting and fruitful. To cite but one example, in his Royal Shakespeare Company production of the *Henry VI* trilogy (1977–8) director Terry Hands decided 'not to do even our own usual reshaping of a few corners and reorganizing the occasional speech' but chose rather 'just to put it all very crudely, very naively down on the stage – everything that was there, warts and all, in the hope that one or two of them would turn out to be beauty spots. There was something to learn.'[6] From this 'naive' approach emerged a stunning production that was both a great success at the box office and a revelation to students of the history plays. Granted, most directors lack the resources and skills of the RSC; as already noted, moreover, many cuts or changes are slight, even negligible. But when an actor or director makes a major change, whether to smooth out the play or sustain a particular 'concept,' what has happened to the process of interpretation? As Stanley Wells asks: 'where does the borderline come between interpretation and fresh creation?'[7] There is a large gap between the 'good' quarto of *Romeo and Juliet* and *West Side Story*, but, along that spectrum, at what point do production and interpretation turn into rewriting, even translation? To be aware of the original conventions and logic of presentation is not to resolve such questions but at least to widen the framework within which directors will make their many practical, artistic, and conceptual choices. Such awareness need not lead to 'museum theatre' (a barren, uninviting reconstruction of the past) but (as in the Terry Hands *Henry VI*) can result in an exploration and, in some cases, a re-invention of appropriate theatrical conventions, a development of the terms upon which *we* agree to meet.

As for the critic, even though the trumpet calls heralding the treatment of plays as scripts rather than literary texts have now become commonplace, the full implications of such an approach to Shakespeare have yet to be explored. Any interpreter must face some recurring questions – for example, why does a character use a particular phrase or engage in a particular action or even wear a particular costume (the Ghost's nightgown in the closet scene)? – but answers to such questions often are not readily forthcoming on the basis of modern 'logic' and verisimilar assumptions but may require tools available only through some kind of 'historical' study. Sometimes the questions themselves, in Hamlet's terms, 'would be scanned' (III. iii. 75), for too rigid an approach ('where' does the last scene of *Coriolanus* take place?) can belie the flexibility of Elizabethan staging and overall presentation. As others have pointed out, studies of imagery need not be limited to the words on the page but should include costume and properties, including some not specified in the scanty stage directions but (presumably) there in the original productions. Especially in the collision between Elizabethan and modern notions of 'night' and 'place,' moreover, some of the original metaphors or metaphoric actions may be buried under the accumulated strata of post-Elizabethan accretions. Similarly, the linking of moments in various parts of a play may have been heightened then by recurring effects highly visible to the viewer's eye based upon various narrative conventions involving such items as boots, nightgowns, and keys (a property of potential interest in *Measure for Measure*). Critical investigations of both imagery and structure cannot be divorced from the original logic of presentation without risk of distortion.

If the language of the theatre does include more than the words on the page, then editor, director, and critic should recognize that the on-stage language available to Shakespeare included terms and phrases that made excellent sense then but at best are dimly understood today. Perhaps we will never unravel all the components of that lost language, but even without a Rosetta stone we can expand our sense of links and meanings and further develop our interpretative reflexes so to include moments designed to surprise us, tease us into thought, make unexpected connections, or even sacrifice what we consider of prime importance (motivation, plausibility, continuity) for something else that seemed more important to the dramatist (a 'sacrifice' that in turn may reveal a great deal about the goals or logic of a given play). If indeed Shakespeare crafted his plays according to a set of conventions or a sense of design that we ignore or make no effort to understand, how can we expect to realize the full extent of his characters, images, and meanings?

At the end of a previous study I argued that, if every good story needs a villain, then the villain who stands between Everyreader and Understanding Shakespeare is Realism, 'that complex of expectations and assumptions about character, plot, and overall logic brought to Elizabethan drama by the modern reader nurtured by the novel and the mainstream of drama since Ibsen.'[8] Similarly, throughout this study I have quarreled with assumptions and verdicts that proceed from an overly literal or verisimilar approach to the dialogue, stage directions, and staging of these plays. But the villain of the piece now seems to me not any

one set of assumptions that can be neatly labeled but rather what
Leontes calls the 'wide gap of time' (v. iii. 154) that separates us
not only from the words but also from the playhouses, players,
properties, spectators, conventions, and climate of ideas in the
age of Shakespeare. Granted, given much recent emphasis upon
the autonomy of the reader, many modernists feel no such gap (or
even welcome it). But as a partisan who has pitched his tent in the
'historical' camp, I am continually reminded of how much has
been lost, because, for me, the fullest enjoyment of the plays
comes from those glimpses of the characters, actions, and metaphors functioning as the artist himself designed them to function
in the terms upon which dramatist, players, and spectators
originally agreed to meet.

Behind many of the decisions by critics, editors, and directors
that I have cited lies the problem of *trust*. Despite the universal lip
service (Macbeth calls it 'mouth honor'), how many of us in the
universities or the theatre *really* trust Shakespeare's knowhow
and skills to the extent that we feel a responsibility to *dis*cover and
*re*cover his techniques and meanings? When making alterations
in the original playscripts in order to facilitate understanding by
readers and viewers, editors and directors regularly raise the
question: 'does it work?' Even if the original signals did make
sense then, can they be intelligible to the untutored now? Like that
Roman pragmatist Dolabella, asked by a Cleopatra remembering
an Antony larger than life 'Think you there was or might be such a
man / As this I dreamt of?' many Shakespeareans would answer:
'Gentle madam, no' (v. ii. 93–4). To eliminate the anomalies, the
warts, is then to simplify matters and to make a smoother voyage
for the reader, the actor, or the spectator. But to do so may also be
to limit the discoveries, the insights, the full range of meaning.
Rather, the more arduous but more fruitful path for critic, editor,
or director is based upon a greater trust in Shakespeare. In answer
to the question 'does it work?' let us oppose Prospero's comment
at the first meeting of Ferdinand and Miranda: 'It works' (I. ii.
494). Such an affirmation, however, requires trust. Thus, if
Shakespeare, like Hermione, is to be brought back to life, we must
remember what Paulina told Leontes: 'it is required / You do
awake your faith.'

Notes

1 The arrow in Nessus: Elizabethan clues and modern detectives

1 *Dynamics of Drama* (New York, 1970), p. 3
2 James Black, ed., *The History of King Lear*, Regents Restoration Drama Series (Lincoln, Neb. 1975), p. 1
3 'Preface, the Grounds of Criticism in Tragedy,' *Of Dramatic Poesy and Other Critical Essays*, ed. George Watson (London and New York, 1962), Vol. I, p. 240
4 *The Thurber Carnival* (New York and London, 1945), pp. 60–3
5 Brian Gibbons, ed., *Romeo and Juliet* (London and New York, 1980), p. 180
6 George Walton Williams, 'The Year's Contributions to Shakespearian Study: Textual Studies,' *Shakespeare Survey* 34 (1981), 188
7 Alan Brissenden, '*Romeo and Juliet*, III. iii. 108: The Nurse and the Dagger,' *Notes and Queries*, NS 28 (1981), 126–7
8 The Padua *Macbeth*, a Folio text apparently annotated for use in a seventeenth-century amateur performance, does add to or expand the original stage directions, especially in Act V, but does not indicate an exit and re-entry for Seyton here. See G. Blakemore Evans, ed., *Shakespearean Prompt-books of the Seventeenth Century* 5 vols. (Charlottesville, Va., 1960), vol. I, part i
9 Morris Palmer Tilley, *A Dictionary of the Proverbs in England in the Sixteenth and Seventeenth Centuries* (Ann Arbor, 1966)
10 *Shakespeare at the Globe 1599–1609* (New York, 1962), pp. 161–2. My study is heavily indebted to this book, especially Beckerman's chapters three and five
11 *Henslowe's Rose: The Stage and Staging* (The University Press of Kentucky, 1976), p. 164
12 *Drama from Ibsen to Brecht* (London, 1968), pp. 12–16. For more general treatments of 'convention' (not limited to theatrical contexts), see David K. Lewis, *Convention: A Philosophical Study* (Cambridge, Mass., 1969); and Lawrence Manley, *Convention 1500–1750* (Cambridge, Mass. and London, 1980). In an early classic study, M. C. Bradbrook defines *convention* 'as an agreement between writers and readers, whereby the artist is allowed to limit and simplify his material in order to secure greater concentration through a control of the distribution of emphasis' (*Themes and Conventions of Elizabethan Tragedy*, Cambridge, 1935; rep. 1960, p. 4). For a recent provocative study with an

emphasis upon 'character' and 'reality' see Robert R. Hellenga, 'Elizabethan Dramatic Conventions and Elizabethan Reality,' *Renaissance Drama*, NS 12 (1981), 27–49

13 'An Apologie for Poetrie,' *Elizabethan Critical Essays*, ed. G. Gregory Smith, 2 vols. (Oxford, 1904), vol. 1, p. 197

14 *Theatre for Shakespeare* (Toronto, 1955), p. 52

15 For other 'difficult' scenes involving fire and water, see Heywood's rendition of Horatius at the bridge (*The Rape of Lucrece*), Fletcher's version of a battle at sea (*The Double Marriage*), Nero looking on while Rome burns (*The Tragedy of Nero*), and, perhaps strangest of all, the on-stage rescue by a ship of a man marooned on a rock (*The Hector of Germany*)

2 Interpreting stage directions

1 See Gāmini Salgādo, *Eyewitnesses of Shakespeare: First Hand Accounts of Performances 1590–1890* (Sussex University Press, 1975), pp. 16–48. For Forman's accounts, see pp. 31–3; for a reproduction of the Peacham drawing mentioned on my p. 19, see Salgādo, p. 17

2 For such inferences see Hal H. Smith, 'Some Principles of Elizabethan Stage Costume,' *Journal of the Warburg and Courtauld Institutes*, 25 (1962), 240–57

3 John R. Elliott, Jr., 'Medieval Rounds and Wooden O's: The Medieval Heritage of the Elizabethan Theatre,' *Medieval Drama*, ed. Malcolm Bradbury and David Palmer, Stratford-upon-Avon Studies no. 16 (London and New York, 1973), pp. 245–6

4 Thus, recently (in an argument that has not won favor with reviewers) Ernest L. Rhodes has sought to prove the existence of five stage doors at the Rose. See *Henslowe's Rose: The Stage and Staging* (The University Press of Kentucky, 1976), pp. 28–35

5 Eleanor Prosser, for one, argues that the power of the moment 'is destroyed by a grotesque jump down to Laertes' level in the trap' and notes that 'inevitably one hears a stifled "Oof!" from the audience, and often a snort of laughter. It is all too apparent that someone must have landed on Ophelia's stomach' (*Hamlet and Revenge*, Stanford, 1967, p. 225)

6 See Sir Edmund Chambers, ed., *The Shakspere Allusion-Book: A Collection of Allusions to Shakspere from 1591 to 1700* (London, 1932), vol. 1, p. 272

7 In listing these four categories, I have oversimplified a very complex situation. Thus, Fredson Bowers sets forth thirteen possible classes of printer's copy, 'some of them speculative' (*On Editing Shakespeare and the Elizabethan Dramatists*, Philadelphia, 1955, pp. 11–12). According to Sir Walter Greg, when we seek to determine the probable source of printer's copy, 'we enter … a misty mid region of Weir, a land of shadowy shapes and melting outlines, where not even the most patient inquiry and the most penetrating analysis can hope to arrive at any but tentative and proximate conclusions' (*The Shakespeare First Folio*, Oxford, 1955, p. 105)

8 'Preface,' *The Plays and Poems of William Shakspeare*, 10 vols. (London, 1790), vol. 1, p. lviii

9 'Playhouse Interpolations in the Folio Text of *Hamlet,*' *Studies in Bibliography,* 13 (1960), 42
10 *Shakespearean Staging, 1599–1642* (Cambridge, Mass., 1971), p. 8
11 'Sir William Berkeley's *The Lost Lady,*' *The Library,* 4th Series, 17, (1937), 407–8. Bald also notes that 'when one finds an obvious prompter's direction in a printed text, it is by no means safe to assume that all such directions have been reproduced. In fact, the evidence points rather in the other direction, and indicates that there was a tendency to rid the text of them should they be present' (p. 409)
12 'What is a Text?' *Research Opportunities in Renaissance Drama,* 24 (1981), 4. The dearth of references in this study to the plays of Jonson therefore should not be attributed to any lack of interest (especially from one who has published a book on Jonson's comedies) but rather to a working assumption that this author (as opposed to Shakespeare) carefully transformed the original theatrical scripts into literary texts for a reader, in the process often screening out evidence about staging and stage practice. For example, the first printed versions of *Volpone* (the 1607 quarto) and *The Alchemist* (the 1612 quarto) have between them *one* stage direction ('*Dol is seen*' at II. iii. 210 of the latter), for Jonson, modeling his practice upon editions of Plautus, Terence, and Aristophanes, eschews even *enter* and *exit.* Jonson's meticulous care in preparing the quartos and particularly the 1616 Folio reveals much about his sense of style, punctuation, typography, and scene construction but undercuts the value of the evidence for the stage historian
13 'What is a Text?' pp. 3–4
14 Bernard Beckerman's review in *Renaissance Drama,* NS 4 (1971), 243, 239–40. See also John Freehafer's review in *Shakespeare Studies,* 9 (1976), 337–43
15 'The Elizabethan Printer and Dramatic Manuscripts,' *The Library,* 4th Series, 12 (1931), 270–2
16 *Bibliographical Studies in the Beaumont and Fletcher Folio of 1647* (Oxford, 1938), p. 75. Similarly, in the two versions of *The Humourous Lieutenant,* the stage directions 'in the folio are more precise, and every now and then make provision for properties or noises off stage of which the manuscript knows nothing' (p. 76). See pp. 74–9 for Bald's discussion of the differences in stage directions in five of Fletcher's plays (*The Honest Man's Fortune, Beggar's Bush, The Woman's Prize, The Humourous Lieutenant, Bonduca*). Lest the reader, however, conclude that sound effects are always an accurate yardstick, consider Daborne's *The Poor Man's Comfort.* In his Malone Society edition (1955), Kenneth Palmer concludes that 'there is good evidence that the quarto was printed from the prompt-copy, and some evidence that the manuscript is derived, at one or more removes, from Daborne's foul papers' (p. xii). With regard to sound effects, Palmer's conclusion is supported by one passage where '*Horn within*' announces a messenger in the quarto (E4r) but not the manuscript (l. 1324) but this criterion does not work in the final scene when challengers to combat are twice signaled by a '*Tucket*' in the manuscript (ll. 2202, 2222) with only silence at the equivalent point in the quarto
17 *Dramatic Documents from the Elizabethan Playhouses,* 2 vols. (Oxford, 1931) vol. I, 86–7, 208, 213. Greg also notes (p. 208) that 'even

manuscripts showing no connexion with the playhouse at all contain at times distinctively theatrical terms and phrases.' In his discussion of an otherwise unknown edition clearly used as a playhouse book, Charles Read Baskervill finds the carelessness in the entries 'almost inconceivable,' but is forced to conclude that 'the apparent fact that the book was in use for many years and that a number of people contributed to the preparation of it suggests that a disregard for errors and inconsistencies in the text was not unusual.' See 'A Prompt Copy of *A Looking Glass for London and England,*' *Modern Philology,* 30 (1932), 51

18 'The Gallery over the Stage in the Public Playhouse of Shakespeare's Time,' *Shakespeare Quarterly,* 8 (1957), 16–17. Earlier, McKerrow ('The Elizabethan Printer and Dramatic Manuscripts,' pp. 273–4) had noted that we should not 'regard the use of the words "within", "aloft", or "above" – though, of course, they belong properly to the language of the stage – as in any way suggestive of actual stage copy,' for 'there seems no reason to doubt that an author might use them in his own manuscript' if he 'had in his mind a clear idea of how his play was to be staged.' McKerrow asks, quite sensibly: 'what could be more natural than that a skilled dramatist closely connected with the theatre and writing, not with any thought of print, but with his eye solely on a stage production, should give stage directions in the form of directions to the actors (as they might appear in a prompt-book), rather than as descriptions of action viewed from the front of the theatre?'

19 Hosley, 'The Gallery over the Stage in the Public Playhouse of Shakespeare's Time,' p. 19, n. 8. Since he finds a total of only nine allusions to such windows in Shakespeare's plays, Hosley considers it likely 'that permanent windows over the public-theatre stage would not have been sufficiently useful to justify their expense,' so he doubts their presence. For a recent attempt to use dialogue evidence to demonstrate the presence of windows at the Rose, see Rhodes, *Henslowe's Rose,* pp. 86–7

20 'The Elizabethan Printer and Dramatic Manuscripts,' p. 266

21 'The Reconstruction of Stage Action from Early Dramatic Texts,' *The Elizabethan Theatre V,* ed. G. R. Hibbard (Hamden, Conn., 1975), p. 91

22 'Re-Enter the Stage Direction: Shakespeare and Some Contemporaries,' *Shakespeare Survey* 29 (1976), 124. In this brief section, Honigmann deals with *stand forth, music still* and *silence;* elsewhere in his essay he discusses misplaced stage directions, asides, '*all*' speeches, and what he calls 'crypto-directions' (e.g., the use of 'O!–O!')

23 For other extensive sound effects associated with the hunt, see the opening of *Patient Grissil,* Act II of *The Brazen Age,* and Act I of *The Royal King and the Loyal Subject.* In *A Maidenhead Well Lost,* '*Sound Horns within*' is followed by the on-stage comment: 'It seems the Duke is Hunting in the Forest' (IV, 122)

24 See R. A. Foakes and R. T. Rickert, eds., *Henslowe's Diary* (Cambridge, 1961), p. 317, ll. 20–1

25 See, for example, *Philaster, Thierry and Theodoret, The Martyred Soldier, 3 Henry VI, James IV, Patient Grissil,* and *A Maidenhead Well Lost*

26 See, for example, *The Custom of the Country, 1 Edward IV, The Downfall of Robert Earl of Huntingdon, The Humourous Lieutenant, The Brazen Age,* and *The Golden Age*

27 Thus, for an obvious alternative to disheveled hair, the quarto of *2 Henry VI* provides: '*The Cardinal is discovered in his bed, raving and staring as if he were mad*' (F1v). In the quarto of *Troilus and Cressida*, Cassandra enters not with her hair about her ears but '*raving*' (D2v). In *The White Devil*, Webster first calls for Flamineo to enter '*as distracted*' (III. iii. o. s.d.); then specifies that the speeches of the dying Bracciano '*are several kinds of distractions and in the action should appear so*' (v. iii. 82. s.d.); and finally directs Cornelia to deliver her dirge '*in several forms of distraction*' (v. iv. 82. s.d.)

28 For Shakespearean examples, see *2 Henry VI*, IV. vi. 6. s.d. and *3 Henry VI*, II. iii. 5. s.d.; see also *Edmond Ironside*, *1 The Fair Maid of the West*, *The Bondman*, and *The Valiant Welshman*. The 'plot' of *2 The Seven Deadly Sins* provides '*to them Lucius running*' and '*to him Will Fool running*' (ll. 44, 62–3). For other figures who enter '*in haste*' see *The Captives*, *The Wounds of Civil War*, and *The Valiant Welshman*

29 See also *Perkin Warbeck*, v. i. o. s.d.; *A Yorkshire Tragedy*, l. 296; *The Picture*, I. i. o. s.d.; *1 Edward IV*, I, 39; *The Witch*, ll. 909–10; and *The Noble Gentleman*, VIII, 188. The OED defines *safeguard* (no. 8): 'an outer skirt or petticoat worn by women to protect their dress when riding.' For other wands and rods for the men, see *Amends for Ladies*, IV. iii. 16; *Wit Without Money*, II, 170; *King Leir*, ll. 398–9, 408–9

30 For just a few examples, see *Wit Without Money*, II, 166–7; *The Widow's Tears*, III. i. o. s.d.; *A Woman Killed With Kindness*, II, 133; *Two Lamentable Tragedies*, D4r, F1r; *James IV*, l. 557; *1 Edward IV*, I, 48. For an illustration from Holinshed depicting a booted messenger, see Martin Holmes, *Shakespeare and His Players* (London, 1972), p. 60. Holmes notes that 'the man's long boots, spurs and high-collared cloak fastened at the neck indicate that he is dressed for hard riding, and would at once give that impression if seen upon the stage.'

31 For '*as from bed*' and related signals, see *2 The Iron Age*, III, 381; *The Lovers' Progress*, v, 128; *Dick of Devonshire*, l. 1286; *The English Traveller*, IV, 33; '*Tis Pity She's a Whore*, II. i. o. s.d.; *The Bashful Lover*, v. i. 71. s.d.; *Thierry and Theodoret*, x, 30; *The Coxcomb*, VIII, 325; *Claudius Tiberius Nero*, l. 2064; *A Woman Killed With Kindness*, II, 141; and *Tom a Lincoln*, 37a. For '*unready*' figures, see *Match Me in London*, I. iii. o. s.d.; *The Rape of Lucrece*, v, 226; and *The Coxcomb*, VIII, 323

32 *Costume in the Drama of Shakespeare and his Contemporaries* (Oxford, 1936), pp. 184–5. In her booklet, *English Dress in the Age of Shakespeare* (Folger Shakespeare Library, 1958), Virginia A. LaMar concludes that nightgowns 'were apparently dressing gowns and were often so similar to the gowns worn publicly by men and women that they could be worn abroad at the owner's discretion' (p. 11). She adds: 'Though some of the wealthy had special garments for night wear, it is very likely that most people slept naked or in their shirts or smocks.'

33 For other references to 'night attire' see *Tom a Lincoln*, 25b; *The Coxcomb*, VIII, 361; *The Fatal Contract*, D4v; *Lust's Dominion*, II. iii. 91. s.d.; *The Two Maids of More-Clacke*, E3v; and *Sophonisba*, I. ii. o. s.d. For 'night clothes' see *A Match at Midnight*, H2r and *The Little French Lawyer*, III, 416; for nightcaps alone see *The Custom of the Country*, I, 363–4. Gowns along with slippers appear in *2 If You Know*

Not Me You Know Nobody, I, 302, 309; 2 *The Iron Age*, III, 385; and *The Captain*, V, 296

34 An interesting divergence from the source may support the analogy suggested here. Thus, Holinshed has Ross and Willoughby join Boling-broke earlier at Ravenspurgh (as suggested by Northumberland at the end of II. i), but Shakespeare separates the two lords from Northum-berland between II. i and II. iii, a change that sets up a highly visible entrance of two figures newly committed to the duke. The effect could be further enhanced if the bearers of bad tidings to Richard II in III. ii (Salisbury and Scroop) are unbooted and different in demeanor from Ross and Willoughby with their newly fired commitment

35 See, for example, Norman Rabkin, *Shakespeare and the Common Understanding* (New York, 1967), pp. 105–14

36 As some readers may have noticed, throughout this chapter I have avoided using the terms *prompt-book* and *prompter*, neither of which is an Elizabethan term (*book* and *book-holder* would be their closest equivalent). The use of *prompt-book*, I have discovered, plays at least some part in the furtherance of a set of anachronistic conceptions drawn from nineteenth- and twentieth-century practice where such theatrical playbooks do show the kind of regularity and care for detail often missing in Elizabethan playhouse manuscripts (as noted by Greg, McKerrow, Baskervill, and others). Using terms *not* of an age to describe a phenom-enon *of* the age (my pet example is *morality play*, a term from the mid eighteenth century) is an invitation to distortion

37 *On Shakespeare's Stage* (Boulder, 1967), p. 8. With the exception of his treatment of the 'inner stage,' Reynolds' *The Staging of Elizabethan Plays at the Red Bull Theater 1605–1625* (New York, 1940), along with Beckerman's *Shakespeare at the Globe*, remains one of the basic books for anyone dealing with Elizabethan stages and staging

3   The logic of 'this' on the open stage

1 For Styan, 'stage-centred criticism is that which characteristically checks text against performance, and does not admit critical opinion as fully valid without reference to the physical circumstances of the medium.' Such criticism, in his terms, 'assesses the intention, the conception, behind a play from a reconstruction of performance before a particular audience,' makes adjustments when subsequent productions reveal more of the play's qualities, and eventually 'is modified and refined to greater accuracy, until at some unseen vanishing point the focus is felt to be exact and the play defined' (*The Shakespeare Revolution: Criticism and Per-formance in the Twentieth Century*, Cambridge, 1977, p. 72). For many suggestive comments about the staging and interpretation of Shake-speare's plays, see also Styan's *Shakespeare's Stagecraft* (Cambridge, 1967)

2 See *Drama of the English Renaissance*, ed. Russell A. Fraser and Norman Rabkin (New York and London, 1976), vol. I, The Tudor Period, p. 350. Fraser comments: 'Most editors append the gratuitous direction "Gives a ring."'

3 *Holinshed's Chronicles of England, Scotland and Ireland*, 6 vols. (London, 1807), vol. II, p. 586. The relationship between known sources

(e.g., Holinshed, North's Plutarch) and the actual staging of Shakespeare's plays is a murky area yet to be explored adequately. To cite but one example, if Holinshed cites eight murderers along with Exton, what (if anything) does such a specification mean about Shakespeare's staging of the death of Richard II? For some helpful distinctions and comments, see Ann Pasternak Slater, *Shakespeare the Director* (Brighton and Totowa, NJ., 1982), pp. 185–9

4 Many more Shakespearean passages can be cited. Thus, in *The Merchant of Venice* Gratiano promises Bassiano not to 'hood mine eyes / Thus with my hat' during grace (II. ii. 179–80); Achilles, as he sheathes his sword after killing Hector, says it 'thus goes to bed' (*Troilus and Cressida*, v. viii. 20); and Cassio, describing Bianca, says 'she falls me thus about my neck' (*Othello*, IV. i. 134)

5 See, for example, *Richard II*, III. iii. 4; *The Tempest*, I. ii. 180; v. i. 137, 161; *Pericles*, II. i. 102; II. iii. 85, 89; v. iii. 20, 23. Remember also the many 'cloud' passages, the most famous being Hamlet's query for Polonius: 'Do you see yonder cloud that's almost in shape of a camel?' (III. ii. 361–2)

6 *The Staging of Elizabethan Plays at the Red Bull Theater 1605–1625* (New York, 1940), p. 43

7 See chapter seven for a fuller discussion of what the spectator sees or does not see in the two versions of *Doctor Faustus* and the significant difference for any interpretation of the tragedy

8 See R. A. Foakes and R. T. Rickert, eds., *Henslowe's Diary* (Cambridge, 1961), p. 320, l. 74. Such a property was then, presumably, used for a discovery in *The Downfall of Robert Earl of Huntingdon*: '*Curtains open, Robin Hood sleeps on a green bank, and Marian strewing flowers on him*' (ll. 1490–1); conceivably, special effects in other plays may require such a 'bank' (e.g., see *The Wisdom of Doctor Dodypoll*, a play in the repertory of the Children of Paul's). But I see no evidence that 'this bank' in *Dream* or *Merchant* requires anything more than an actor's gesture in concert with the spectator's imagination

9 For a very different formulation, that uses dialogue and '*at a window*' to argue in favor of a penthouse, see Ernest L. Rhodes, *Henslowe's Rose: The Stage and Staging* (The University Press of Kentucky, 1976), pp. 86–7

10 In the hope of avoiding Macbeth's dismay ('will the line stretch out to th'crack of doom?' – IV. i. 117), I will not try the reader with the hundreds of examples from Shakespeare's plays alone

11 'Some Textual Implications of Tyrone Guthrie's 1953 Production of *All's Well That Ends Well*,' *Shakespeare Quarterly*, 25 (1974), 56. As G. K. Hunter observes, on the open stage the locale is 'whatever the actions and assumptions of the characters have made it'; thus, an actor may move 'from the main stage to the upper level' saying 'I'll to bed' and 'at a later point the same actor may make the same movement and cry defiance to the besiegers.' See 'Flatcaps and Bluecoats: Visual Signals on the Elizabethan Stage,' *Essays and Studies*, 33 (1980), 22–3

12 For Fletcher's version of the same effect, see *Rule a Wife and Have a Wife* (III, 179, 202–3) and especially *The Maid in the Mill* (VII, 65–6) where the king keeps asking 'what rooms are these?' and 'this little Room?' until the hidden Florimel is discovered. As a general practice, such repeated use

of the gestic *this* suggests to me not that the object or phenomenon is in view but rather that the house or forest is to be 'created' through 'imaginary forces.' If we can already 'see' the house, tree, cave, or castle, would such gestic emphasis be necessary?

13 For a recent exchange of views on this passage, see Winifred L. Frazer, 'King Lear's "Good Block,"' *Shakespeare Quarterly*, 28 (1977), 354–5 (for Frazer, *block* means 'scheme' or 'stratagem'); and George Walton Williams, 'Second Thoughts on Lear's "Good Block,"' *Shakespeare Quarterly*, 29 (1978), 421–2 ('block' is Lear's headdress)

14 See, for example, York's warning to Bolingbroke not to forget 'the heavens are over our heads' (III. iii. 17) and Richard's assertion that 'the breath of worldly men cannot depose / The deputy elected by the Lord' (III. ii. 56–7)

15 Thus, well before Jacobi's Hamlet, Eleanor Prosser, for one, argued against 'the stage tradition that has Hamlet yank out his tables and frantically write down Claudius's villainy lest he forget it' and praised instead 'a Hamlet who jabbed the picture into his brain with a rigid finger.' For Prosser, 'the imagery indicates that the "tables" are not in his pocket but in his mind' (*Hamlet and Revenge*, Stanford, 1967, p. 138, n. 36)

4 Elizabethan darkness and modern lighting

1 For example, in her New Mermaid edition of *The Duchess of Malfi* (New York, 1965), Elizabeth Brennan argues that at the Blackfriars 'the main light on stage is provided by candles or lanterns which the speakers hold,' so that 'darkness and confusion' result 'when only one or two speakers are present' (pp. 114–15). Such logic therefore 'explains' why Bosola mistakenly kills Antonio in v. iv

2 'Elizabethan Lighting Effects and the Conventions of Indoor and Outdoor Theatrical Illumination,' *Renaissance Drama*, NS 12 (1981), 56–7

3 'Shakespeare's Lighting Effects,' *Speech Monographs*, 15 (1948), 83. Similarly, Graves notes 'that despite the attempt to suggest darkness, there had to be enough light on stage for the audience to see what kind of lighting utensil was brought on, as well as to see other important signals of time, place, and character which had nothing to do with light' ('Elizabethan Lighting Effects,' p. 58)

4 *Shakespearian Production* (London, 1964), pp. 64–5

5 'Shakespeare's Outdoor Stage Lighting,' *Shakespeare Studies*, 13 (1980), 243, 248

6 Knight, *Shakespearian Production*, pp. 65–6

7 'The Duchess of Malfi at the Globe and Blackfriars,' *Renaissance Drama*, NS 9 (1978), 209, 202

8 For other suggestive uses of metaphoric darkness see *Romeo and Juliet*, II. i–ii and v. iii and *Julius Caesar*, I. iii, III. iii, and IV. iii. See also Graves' comments on various scenes in Webster's two tragedies in 'The Duchess of Malfi at the Globe and Blackfriars'

9 Thus, Graves ('The Duchess of Malfi at the Globe and Blackfriars,' p. 208) argues that if Othello's flickering candle is the only light at the outset, 'the audience might have difficulty seeing Desdemona's horrified

reactions to Othello's accusations.' For him, 'the theatrical point of "Put out the light" resided more in the poetry and acting than in the lighting.'
10 Graves, *'The Duchess of Malfi* at the Globe and Blackfriars,' p. 209

5   The logic of *'place' and locale*

1 'Preface,' *The Plays and Poems of William Shakespeare*, 10 vols. (London, 1790), vol. i, pp. lviii-ix
2 For an excellent brief discussion of this problem, see Gerald Eades Bentley, *Shakespeare and His Theatre* (Lincoln, Neb., 1964), pp. 53–63. Bentley traces 'the great confusion' back to Nicholas Rowe's edition of 1709 in which the editor 'invented places in which he thought the scenes of Shakespeare's plays should take place, and for early eighteenth-century readers and playgoers these suggested settings (since they conformed to the accustomed place convention) seemed not only normal, but inevitable' (p. 56)
3 *Shakespeare and His Theatre*, p. 57
4 *Shakespeare at the Globe 1599–1609* (New York, 1962), pp. 66, 108. More recently, G. K. Hunter in an important brief essay has argued that the first soliloquy in *Hamlet 'could* be delivered in the room of state, and scenic productions are obliged to make it so. But there is no reason to suppose that it is: Hamlet is not energizing any locale and gives the audience no requirement to imagine a scenic location.' Rather, when Horatio, Bernardo, and Marcellus enter, 'we are now in a world of friendly and relaxed relationships, somewhere between the formal world of the court and the anguished solitariness of the soliloquy. The place is any place where such relationships can be easily imagined. It becomes, that is, whatever the actions and assumptions of the characters have made it' ('Flatcaps and Bluecoats: Visual Signals on the Elizabethan Stage,' *Essays and Studies*, 33, 1980, 23)
5 For other examples of such outside–inside transitions see *Julius Caesar*, iv. ii–iii, *Titus Andronicus*, v. iii, and J. L. Styan, *Shakespeare's Stagecraft* (Cambridge, 1967), p. 45. According to Styan, 'relationships and not localities matter,' for, 'as a problem, the convention of place seems hardly to have entered Shakespeare's conscious mind' (p. 46)
6 For other examples of changes of 'place' without a clearing of the stage see Beckerman, *Shakespeare at the Globe*, p. 175 (especially the example from *The Miseries of Enforced Marriage*) and *Alphonsus, King of Aragon* where, after a lengthy court scene, Fausta is directed to *'make as though you were a going out'* and is met by Medea who asks: *'Fausta*, what means this sudden flight of yours? /Why do you leave your husband's princely Court, / And all alone pass through these thickest groves . . . ?' (ll. 1094–8). The alternative view is defended by John Cranford Adams who argues that in Shakespeare's plays after 1595 'any unit of the multiple stage shall represent only one locale during the course of a given scene (i.e. from one "clear stage" to the next)' ('Shakespeare's Use of the Upper Stage in *Romeo and Juliet*, iii. v,' *Shakespeare Quarterly*, 7, 1956, 146)
7 *Theatre for Shakespeare* (Toronto, 1955), pp. 24–5
8 'The Use of a "Fit-Up" Booth in *Othello*,' *Shakespeare Quarterly*, 12 (1961), 362–3. For a wealth of material on beds and bed scenes, see Richard Hosley, 'The Staging of Desdemona's Bed,' *Shakespeare Quar-*

terly, 14 (1963), 57–65. In G. K. Hunter's terms, entering characters 'make their presence real by claiming position in that field of force that the open stage represents.' Beds and thrones could be pushed out onto the stage 'and there claimed their relationship to the world around them. If in modern drama environment is presented as the creator of character, in Elizabethan drama the character, his entry and his movement create, in so far as we are required to assume one, the environment that is appropriate to his deeds. The actor did this by projecting upon the neutral or generalized diagram of stage space the shape of his fictional life, and the audience then supplied the visual particularities' ('Flatcaps and Bluecoats,' pp. 21–2). Hunter cites Harley Granville-Barker's comment that the fixed features of the Elizabethan stage 'had, so to speak, no life and no rights of their own,' but rather 'the true landscape lay in the characters and the tale of themselves that they told' ('A Note Upon Chapters xx. and xxi. of *The Elizabethan Stage,*' *Review of English Studies,* 1, 1925, 63–4)

9 'Tree Properties and Tree Scenes in Elizabethan Theater,' *Renaissance Drama,* ns 4 (1971), 69–92. Clearly, some plays do require stage trees to set up a particular effect. For example, in *Old Fortunatus* Dekker has Vice '*bring out a fair tree of Gold with apples on it*' and Virtue '*bring a tree with green and withered leaves mingled together, and little fruit on it*' (i. iii. o. s.d.); the dialogue then indicates that these trees are 'planted' on stage (ll. 2–3, 11–12). But more typical of the general practice are the many scenes in which the dialogue calls for only a momentary effect, so that, a few lines later, the presence of a stage tree would be intrusive or counterproductive. Thus, on-stage figures regularly speak lines such as 'hang him on this tree' (*Titus Andronicus,* v. i. 47; *The Massacre at Paris,* ll. 496–7); 'tie him to this tree' (*Beggar's Bush,* ii, 247; *The Coxcomb,* viii, 331, 339); 'take the shadow of this tree' (*King Lear,* v. ii. 1); or 'as I did sleep under this yew tree here' (*Romeo and Juliet,* v. iii. 137). For a recent reappraisal of the evidence about on-stage properties like trees, tents, and mansions, see Michael Hattaway, *Elizabethan Popular Theatre* (London, 1982), pp. 34–40. 'In the absence of definitive evidence' about 'houses,' booths, and other large properties, Hattaway concludes, 'we have to be open-minded' (p. 39)

10 'An Apologie for Poetrie,' *Elizabethan Critical Essays,* ed. G. Gregory Smith, 2 vols. (Oxford, 1904), vol. i, p. 197

11 As noted by Richard Hosley ('The Discovery-Space in Shakespeare's Globe,' *Shakespeare Survey* 12, 1959, 41–6), some 'shop' and 'study' scenes may call for significant properties combined with 'the convention of discovery by opening a door' (e.g., *Thomas Lord Cromwell, Eastward Ho, Satiromastix*). Nonetheless, many relevant moments could have been staged by means of the *as in* technique rather than through the introduction of booths or furniture. Thus, a series of scenes in *The Fair Maid of the Exchange* (ii, 40, 44, 64) establishes two alternating shops by bringing on figures (like Jane) at work ('*Enter Boy in a Shop, cutting up square parchments*'; '*The Cripple at work*'; '*Enter Cripple in his shop*') and by providing gestic passages ('this is the shop: / And in good time the *Cripple* is at work'). For a recent overview on 'discovery' scenes, see Hattaway, *Elizabethan Popular Theatre,* pp. 27–9

12 The exception, as already noted, is the bar for trial scenes that is cited both in manuscripts and printed texts associated with the playhouse

(although the vast majority of courtroom scenes do not mention this property). The presence of such a bar may have had less to do with 'placing' the action than with the practical theatrical advantages for staging the legal attack and defense (as opposed to the limited advantages offered by a stage tree or grate or shipboard ropes)

13 For some representative tavern scenes, see 1 *The Fair Maid of the West, Look About You, Eastward Ho, The Queen of Corinth, The Coxcomb,* and *A Match at Midnight*; for a typical inn scene, see *The Merry Devil of Edmonton*

14 See, for example, *The Puritan, The Revenger's Tragedy, The Atheist's Tragedy, The Fleer, A Woman Killed With Kindness,* and *When You See Me You Know Me*

15 *Elizabethan Prisons and Prison Scenes,* 2 vols., Salzburg Studies in English Literature (Salzburg, 1974), vol. II, p. 306

16 See Pendry, *Elizabethan Prisons and Prison Scenes,* pp. 315–17

17 See, for example, Dick Pike, the king in *The Island Princess,* Eugenius in *The Martyred Soldier,* Sir Charles Mountford in *A Woman Killed With Kindness,* Captain Thomas Stukeley, and the victims in *Lust's Dominion*

18 See *Sir Thomas Wyatt, Thomas Lord Cromwell, Sir John Oldcastle, Sir Thomas More,* 1 *If You Know Not Me You Know Nobody,* 2 *Edward IV,* and *Richard III*

19 Thus Pendry, drawing upon external rather than internal evidence, notes that 'illustrations of gaolers in real life show that they were easily recognizable from the conspicuous bunches of keys – and, apparently, truncheons or wands – which they carried' (*Elizabethan Prisons and Prison Scenes,* p. 318). Truncheons or other accoutrements may well have been used on stage (as with properties associated with the hunt or tavern), but I have found no conclusive evidence, as opposed to the wealth of material on keys. Pendry also cites the Revels Accounts under Edward VI for a payment for 'great and small keys for the Jailers'

20 Thus, one recent critic has argued that 'Isabella is consistently developed in ways Shakespeare's original audience would have found consonant with her continuing appearance in the robes of the order of St. Clare.' In this view, 'her novice's robes and the meanings they imply' continually remind the audience of her essential nature, so that her final decision on behalf of Mariana would probably be signaled by 'the removal of some part of Isabella's own monastic habit.' See Darryl J. Gless, '*Measure for Measure,' The Law, and the Convent* (Princeton, 1979), pp. 141, 211, 213

21 *Shakespeare at the Globe,* p. 159

22 See Bradley, *Shakespearean Tragedy* (London, 1904), p. 260; and Rosenberg, *The Masks of King Lear* (Berkeley and Los Angeles, 1972), p. 151

23 See Reynolds, 'Two Conventions of the Open Stage (As Illustrated in *King Lear?*),' *Philological Quarterly,* 41 (1962), 87. For a good brief analysis of the links between Kent and Edgar, see Mark Rose, *Shakespearean Design* (Cambridge, Mass., 1972), pp. 28–30

24 For a possible but by no means certain non-Shakespearean example of such on-stage counterpoint consider Act V of *Volpone* where, in the midst of the trial sequence, Jonson provides a 'cross-cut' to Volpone (and eventually Nano, Castrone, and Androgyno) in some other undefined 'place.' Most readers and editors assume here an *exeunt* for the figures in

the court scene at the end of v. x and a re-entry of this same group at the beginning of v. xii after the departure of Volpone, but Jonson provides his reader with no such signals (and, indeed, according to his usual practice, would have omitted an *exeunt* even if the King's Men in their production *had* cleared the stage at the end of v. x). Jonson's transformation of the original playscript into a literary text has here created a puzzle for the modern reader, but it is at least possible that a spectator at the Globe would have seen Volpone and his three bizarre servants on one part of the large stage while the figures 'in the courtroom' were still in view, a potentially meaningful juxtaposition analogous to the moments in *As You Like It* and *King Lear*

6 The logic of stage violence

1 Clearly, some dramatists left the implementation of stage fights to the players, perhaps assuming a standard choreography, perhaps thinking of such fights as a practical way of filling time. For some early examples: in *The Tide Tarrieth No Man*, several figures are directed to fight '*to prolong the time*' while an off-stage actor makes a difficult costume change (l. 1214 s.d.); in *Horestes*, Pickering directs: '*Go and make your lively battle and let it be long ere you can win the City*' and later: '*strike up your drum, and fight a good while*' (ll. 861–8, 919–23). Two decades later we still find such signals as in '*they fight a good while and then breathe*' (*Orlando Furioso*, l. 1536) or in a rescue of the protagonist from two opponents '*after a good pretty fight*' (*Captain Thomas Stukeley*, ll. 1170–3)
2 Robert E. Morsberger, *Swordplay and the Elizabethan and Jacobean Stage*, Salzburg Studies in English Literature (Salzburg, 1974), p. 5. See also Thornton S. Graves, 'The Stage Sword and Dagger,' *South Atlantic Quarterly*, 20 (1921), 206, and Martin Holmes, *Shakespeare and His Players* (London, 1972), pp. 132–4. As supporting evidence, scholars often cite the description of the fight between Palemon and Arcite in a play performed before Queen Elizabeth at Oxford in 1566 (see W. Y. Durand, '*Palaemon and Arcyte, Progne, Marcus Geminus* and the Theatre in Which They Were Acted, as Described by John Bereblock [1566],' *PMLA*, 20, 1905, 511) and the fact that the author of *The Rich Cabinet* (1616) includes 'skill of weapon' among the 'many excellent qualities' of the player (see W. C. Hazlitt, ed., *The English Drama and Stage Under the Tudor and Stuart Princes 1543–1664*, London, 1869, p. 230). In his analysis of Benvolio's account of Mercutio's death, Horace S. Craig stresses Shakespeare's expertise in swordplay ('Dueling Scenes and Terms in Shakespeare's Plays,' *University of California Publications in English*, 9, 1940, 14)
3 In addition to the comments from Sidney and Jonson cited in chapter one, the Prologue to *The Two Merry Milkmaids* (1619) asks the spectator to forgo his usual pleasures ('to expect no noise of Guns, Trumpets, nor Drum, / Nor Sword and Target') but to appreciate a 'reform'd' stage 'free / From the loud Clamors it was wont to be, / Turmoil'd with Battles' (A4v). Twenty years later, James Shirley, in his Prologue to *The Doubtful Heir* (a play intended for the Blackfriars but presented at the Globe) tells his 'grave understanders' that 'what you most delight in' will not be found in his play, for 'here's no target-fighting / Upon the Stage, all work for Cutlers barr'd.'

4 For a recent useful analysis of Shakespeare's battle scenes, see Jean MacIntyre, 'Shakespeare and the Battlefield: Tradition and Innovation in Battle Scenes,' *Theatre Survey*, 23 (1982), 31–44. MacIntyre notes 'four ways to stage a pitched field' at the time Shakespeare began writing his plays: 'to separate speech and fighting, which the actors managed at will; to limit battle to a duel between leaders, accompanied by offstage sound; to represent the battle by offstage sounds alone, with or without onstage observers; to order simultaneous or successive duels, flights, and pursuits, introduced and followed by speeches and accompanied by sound effects.' She also notes 'a tradition of comic recruits or clowns as soldiers, who fight among themselves but seldom effectively participate in battles, and perhaps also a tradition of indicating the loser by bringing him in wounded' (p. 37)

5 One recent critic who does confront this question is Huston Diehl, 'The Iconography of Violence in English Renaissance Tragedy,' *Renaissance Drama*, NS 11 (1980), 27–44. She argues that acts of stage violence often 'function as symbolic icons, embodying abstract ideas through conventional visual images' (that range 'from bloody daggers, impaled hearts, and dismembered bodies to banquets of human flesh and demonic physical tortures') in the process creating 'striking stage pictures, rich in associative meaning, which further the plays' central themes' (p. 44). See also Martha Hester Fleischer, *The Iconography of the English History Play*, Salzburg Studies in English Literature (Salzburg, 1974)

6 For the account of the show at Deptford, see John Gough Nichols, ed., *Literary Remains of King Edward the Sixth* (London, 1857), vol. II, p. 279; for the re-enactment at Kenilworth, see F. J. Furnivall, ed., *Robert Laneham's Letter: Describing a Part of the Entertainment Unto Queen Elizabeth at the Castle of Kenilworth in 1575*, New Shakspere Society, series 6, no. 14 (London and New York, 1907), pp. 26–7, 31–2

7 John Nichols, ed., *The Progresses and Public Processions of Queen Elizabeth*, 3 vols (London, 1823), vol. II, p. 319

8 *The Medieval Theatre in the Round* (London, 1957), p. 198

9 *Mount Tabor, or Private Exercises of a Penitent Sinner* (London, 1639), pp. 112–13

10 For an extended treatment of both the play and this scene see Huston Diehl, ' "Reduce Thy Understanding to Thine Eye": Seeing and Interpreting in *The Atheist's Tragedy*,' *Studies in Philology*, 78 (1981), 47–60. She argues that D'Amville's bizarre death 'is rich in symbolic associations,' for 'the axe is traditionally an iconographic symbol of death' (so the villain's 'desire to use it may associate him and his atheism with death, with what is life-denying') and, since the head traditionally is linked to Reason, the 'self-inflicted blow may therefore call to mind the conventional belief that the atheist in his denial of God murders his own God-given reason' (p. 55)

11 For obvious reasons, scenes that underscore the efficacy of such higher powers (as opposed to the inadequacy of merely human efforts) appear regularly in plays that depict martyrdom or conversions to Christianity (e.g., *The Two Noble Ladies*, *A Shoemaker a Gentleman*, *The Martyred Soldier*). Thus, in *The Virgin Martyr* Dorothea is bound to a pillar and assaulted with cudgels, but, protected by an angelic figure only seen by her, she remains invulnerable to the blows of her tormentors ('these bats

have power down to fell giants, / Yet her skin is not scarr'd' – IV. ii. 105–6)

12 *Weapons in the Theatre* (New York, 1968), pp. 18–19

13 See also *The Shoemakers' Holiday*, where the shoemakers oppose their clubs or cudgels to the swords of Hammon's group; *Locrine*, where the old warrior Corineus bests Hubba and Segar, two giant Scythians, with his club; and *Henry V*, v. i, where Fluellen cudgels Pistol

14 The apotheosis of this weapon is achieved in the exploits on- and especially off-stage of the celebrated Dick Pike. According to the *DNB*, the English adventurer Richard Pike or Peake was captured at Cadiz in 1625 and later questioned by the Spanish. Given an opportunity to display his prowess, he bested a Spanish champion with rapier and poniard. 'There-upon, armed with a quarter-staff, which he described as his national weapon, he gave battle to three Spaniards armed with rapiers and poniards. He killed one of his foes and disarmed the other two.' Honored and freed by the Spaniards, Pike returned to England in 1626 and in July published his account of his victory (*Three to One*); his exploits were soon brought on stage in *Dick of Devonshire*. Throughout both pamphlet and play, the quarterstaff is referred to as 'mine own country weapon' or 'my old trusty friend.' Pike's exploits, we should remember, occurred over three decades after *George a Greene*, a chronology that raises some interesting speculations about life imitating art

15 For valuable contexts for this and other cudgel scenes, see A. L. Soens, 'Cudgels and Rapiers: The Staging of the Edgar–Oswald Fight in *Lear*,' *Shakespeare Studies*, 5 (1969), 149–58. According to Soens, 'Shakespeare makes Edgar into a popular champion by arming him with the plebeian cudgel, and pitting his English techniques against the aristocratic rapier and the Italian technique of Oswald' (p. 150). Soens also observes that Shakespeare's fights 'are as much a part of his dramatic vocabulary as is his poetry, and we should no more disregard fencing technique than we should disregard blank verse' (p. 153)

16 Other Shakespearean passages provide glosses on such symbolic weakness. For example, in *The Merry Wives of Windsor* Falstaff explains his acceptance of the fairies: 'I was three or four times in the thought they were not fairies; and yet the guiltiness of my mind, the sudden surprise of my powers, drove the grossness of the foppery into a received belief, in despite of the teeth of all rhyme and reason, that they were fairies' (v. v. 119–24). In *The Tempest*, Prospero easily disarms Ferdinand, describing the latter (inaccurately) as one 'who mak'st a show but dar'st not strike, thy conscience / Is so possessed with guilt' (I. ii. 471–2). Such instances of symbolic weakness, whether in action or dialogue or both, are quite common. See, for example. *A King and No King*, I, 193, 204; *The Queen of Corinth*, VI, 69; *The Knight of Malta*, VII, 148; *A New Way to Pay Old Debts*, v. i. 361–5; *The Parliament of Love*, IV. ii. 90–1; and *The Costly Whore*, E3r–v

17 Maurice Charney, 'The Persuasiveness of Violence in Elizabethan Plays,' *Renaissance Drama*, NS 2 (1969), 62–3

18 As a result, one interpretation I have often heard from theatrical professionals is that Cornwall intends to set his foot – i.e., trample upon – Gloucester's eyes once they have been put out. In this reading, the foot has nothing to do with the actual blinding. Such an interpretation, however,

admits no connection between 'upon these eyes ...' and the immediately preceding 'fellows, hold the chair.' Rather, as I understand the passage, Cornwall is ordering his men to hold the chair *so that* he can place his foot upon Gloucester's eyes

19 For fuller discussions of such analogous actions or scenes, see Richard Levin, *The Multiple Plot in English Renaissance Drama* (Chicago and London, 1971); Lawrence L. Levin, 'Replication as Dramatic Strategy in the Comedies of Ben Jonson,' *Renaissance Drama*, NS 5 (1972), 37–74; and Alan C. Dessen, *Elizabethan Drama and the Viewer's Eye* (Chapel Hill, NC, 1977), pp. 50–70

7   Theatrical metaphor: seeing and not-seeing

1 See, for example, R. A. Foakes, 'Suggestions for a New Approach to Shakespeare's Imagery,' *Shakespeare Survey*, 5 (1952), 81–92; Maurice Charney, *Shakespeare's Roman Plays: The Function of Imagery in the Drama* (Cambridge, Mass., 1961); Dieter Mehl, 'Visual and Rhetorical Imagery in Shakespeare's Plays,' *Essays and Studies*, 25 (1972), 83–100; Alan C. Dessen, *Elizabethan Drama and the Viewer's Eye* (Chapel Hill, NC, 1977), pp. 71–109; and Ann Pasternak Slater, *Shakespeare the Director* (Brighton and Totowa, NJ, 1982), especially pp. 3–7, 193–201

2 For relevant stage directions, see *The Woman's Prize*, VIII, 2; *Eastward Ho*, D2r; *A Match at Midnight*, H4r; and *A Fair Quarrel*, v. i. 36. s.d. For similar signals in the dialogue, see *The Pilgrim*, v, 229; *The Scornful Lady*, I, 235; and especially *A Fair Quarrel*, v. i. 40–2, 119, 123–4; 133–4

3 'Six Notes on *All's Well That Ends Well*,' *Shakespeare Quarterly*, 33 (1982), 342

4 Not surprisingly, contemporary illustrations depicting falconers often provide such a bird in addition to the accoutrements cited by Walker. For two examples from George Turberville's *The Book of Falconry* (1575), see Virginia A. LaMar, *English Dress in the Age of Shakespeare* (Folger Shakespeare Library, 1958), illustrations 5 and 14

5 See John Doebler, *Shakespeare's Speaking Pictures: Studies in Iconic Imagery* (Albuquerque, 1974), pp. 137–9

6 Consider also the disposition of the body of Sir Walter Blunt during the battle scenes that climax *1 Henry IV*. Since the quarto provides no signal for the removal of the body, some editors add their own stage direction after Falstaff's speech that ends what is v. iii in modern editions, a speech that includes the last reference to the corpse ('I like not such grinning honor as Sir Walter hath'). Directors too prefer to clear the stage at this point to free as much space as possible for the two combats that follow. Yet if a counterfeit version of Henry IV ('semblably furnished like the king himself' – v. iii. 21) remains on stage during the king's confrontation with Douglas, the rescue by Hal, and Hal's standing over two other prostrate bodies (Hotspur and Falstaff), the resulting stage picture is rich in imagistic potential, whether to remind the spectator that 'a borrowed title hast thou bought too dear' (v. iii. 23) or to comment upon Falstaff's 'counterfeit' speech (v. iv. 112–23) or to suggest Hal's triumph not only over Hotspur's limitations and Falstaff's sense of time but also Henry IV's tainted status

7 *Allegory: The Theory of a Symbolic Mode* (Ithaca and London, 1964), p. 107

8 See, for example, *A Knack to Know a Knave* (where only Bishop Dunstan can see the devil Astoroth); *The Wounds of Civil War* (where only the dying Scilla can see and hear his Genius); and *The Birth of Merlin* (where Joan but not the clown can see the devil, Merlin's father). For an especially elaborate example (heavily indebted to Shakespeare) see William Sampson's *The Vow Breaker* in which the protagonist, guilty of her lover's death, has *three* different scenes with a ghost no one else can see (with many clear echoes of the relevant scenes in *Hamlet* and *Macbeth*). For another possible Shakespearean example (comparable, perhaps, to Queen Katherine's vision in *Henry VIII*) consider Pericles' vision of Diana. Most editors insert here their own exeunt and re-entry for Helicanus, Lysimachus, and Marina (see v. i. 240. s.d., 252. s.d. in the Pelican), thus leaving the sleeping king alone, but the quarto provides no such signals. Granted, Lysimachus' 'so, leave him all' (l. 238) suggests either an exeunt or a withdrawal to another part of the stage, but if the figures move away but stay in view, the configuration seen by the spectator would parallel the Marina–Pericles reconciliation (where, apparently, the onlookers withdraw but do not depart), with Diana replacing Marina and Pericles now asleep rather than in his speechless state. The contrast between the vision of Pericles and the not-seeing of the other observers, moreover, would then repeat the situation a few lines earlier when he but not the others had heard the music of the spheres. In contrast to that moment, however, no lines here call attention to the gap between Pericles' privileged seeing and their normal sight, so the presence of this device must remain uncertain

9 For an important reassessment of the relationship between competing texts and interpretations, see Michael J. Warren, '*Doctor Faustus*: The Old Man and the Text,' *English Literary Renaissance*, 11 (1981), 111–47

10 See Ernest Brennecke, ed., *Shakespeare in Germany 1590–1700* (Chicago and London, 1964), p. 275

11 See *Hamlet and Revenge* (Stanford, 1967), especially chapters four and five

12 *Allegorical Imagery* (Princeton, 1966), p. 246

8   Conclusion: Elizabethan playscripts and modern interpreters

1 '*Muffled*' usually carries with it associations of conspiracy or suspicious behavior, as suggested in *Julius Caesar*, ii. i. 73–85. Traditionally, halters are associated with suicide or despair (as in the example from *The Spanish Tragedy* cited in chapter three), but in quite a few historical plays (e.g., 2 *Henry VI*, *Edward III*, *Captain Thomas Stukeley*) figures enter with halters or strangling cords about their necks to place their lives in the hands of an authority figure who must decide whether to pardon or kill them

2 For two suggestive (and quite different) treatments of time see Emrys Jones, *Scenic Form in Shakespeare* (Oxford, 1971), pp. 41–65; and David Riggs, 'The Artificial Day and the Infinite Universe,' *Journal of Medieval and Renaissance Studies*, 5 (1975), 155–85

3 *Dramatic Documents from the Elizabethan Playhouses*, 2 vols. (Oxford, 1931), vol. I, p. x
4 'A Note Upon Chapters xx. and xxi. of *The Elizabethan Stage*,' *Review of English Studies*, 1 (1925), 61
5 '*Othello*': *The National Theatre Production* (New York, 1967), p. 11
6 Quoted in Homer D. Swander, 'The Rediscovery of *Henry VI*,' *Shakespeare Quarterly*, 29 (1978), 149
7 'Shakespeare's Text on the Modern Stage,' *Shakespeare Jahrbuch West* (Heidelberg, 1967), p. 189. For some suggestive comments about the director and Shakespeare, see this essay and Bernard Beckerman, 'The Flowers of Fancy, the Jerks of Invention, or, Directorial Approaches to Shakespeare,' in *Shakespeare 1971*, ed. Clifford Leech and J. M. R. Margeson (Toronto and Buffalo, 1972), pp. 200–14
8 *Elizabethan Drama and the Viewer's Eye* (Chapel Hill, NC, 1977), p. 158

List of plays and editions

The following list includes all plays (other than those by Shakespeare) quoted or cited in the preceding chapters. Titles and authors are drawn from *Annals of English Drama*, ed. Alfred Harbage, rev. S. Schoenbaum (London, 1964), although I have chosen to sidestep problems growing out of doubtful or multiple authorship. Thus, I have listed some plays under title rather than putative author; I have attributed several plays to Munday for which he provided only a part; and I have collapsed Beaumont, Massinger, and others into the category 'Fletcher.' Readers looking for an unfamiliar title listed earlier with volume and page number should look first at the Fletcher and Heywood entries where the plays cited from those two editions are listed in alphabetical order (a practice I have also followed with Dekker, Jonson, Marlowe, and Massinger).

Abbreviations

Folger The Folger Shakespeare Library, Washington, DC
MSR Malone Society Reprints, published by Oxford University Press
Revels The Revels Plays, published by Manchester University Press and The Johns Hopkins University Press
RRD Regents Renaissance Drama Series, published by University of Nebraska Press
STC A. W. Pollard and G. R. Redgrave, *Short-Title Catalogue* (London, 1946), followed by the number and date of publication
TFT Tudor Facsimile Texts edited by John S. Farmer
Wing Number designated in Donald Wing's *Short-Title Catalogue*, 3 vols. (New York, 1972), followed by the date of publication

Alphonsus Emperor of Germany, ed. Herbert F. Schwarz, New York and London, 1913.
Armin, Robert, *The Two Maids of More-Clacke*, TFT, 1913.
Barnes, Barnabe, *The Devil's Charter*, TFT, 1913.
Berkeley, William, *The Lost Lady*, Folger manuscript J.b.1.
    The Lost Lady, STC no. 1902, 1638.
The Bloody Banquet, ed. S. Schoenbaum, MSR, 1962.
Captain Thomas Stukeley, ed. Judith C. Levinson, MSR, 1975.

The Castle of Perseverance, in *The Macro Plays*, ed. Mark Eccles, EETS no. 262, Oxford, 1969.

Chapman, George, *An Humourous Day's Mirth*, ed. W. W. Greg, MSR, 1938.

The Widow's Tears, ed. Akihiro Yamada, Revels, 1975.

Chapman, Jonson, and Marston, *Eastward Ho*, TFT, 1914.

Chettle, Henry, *The Tragedy of Hoffman*, ed. Harold Jenkins, MSR, 1951.

Claudius Tiberius Nero (The Tragedy of Tiberius), ed. W. W. Greg, MSR, 1915.

Clyomon and Clamydes, ed. W. W. Greg, MSR, 1913.

Cooke, John, *Greene's Tu Quoque*, TFT, 1913.

The Costly Whore, STC no. 25582, 1633.

Daborne, Robert, *The Poor Man's Comfort*, ed. Kenneth Palmer, MSR, 1955.

The Poor Man's Comfort, Wing D-101, 1655.

Davenport, Robert, *The City Nightcap* in *Old English Plays*, ed. A. H. Bullen, vol. III, rpt. New York, 1964.

Day, John, *The Blind Beggar of Bednal Green*, TFT, 1914.

The Travels of the Three English Brothers in *Works*, ed. A. H. Bullen, London, 1881.

Dekker, Thomas, *The Dramatic Works*, ed. Fredson Bowers, 4 vols., Cambridge, 1953–61. Plays cited: 1 *The Honest Whore*; *Lust's Dominion*; *Match Me in London*; *Northward Ho*; *Old Fortunatus*; *Patient Grissil*; *The Roaring Girl*; *Satiromastix*; *The Shoemakers' Holiday*; *Sir Thomas Wyatt*; *The Virgin Martyr*; *Westward Ho*; *The Witch of Edmonton*; *The Wonder of a Kingdom*.

Dick of Devonshire, ed. James G. and Mary R. McManaway, MSR, 1955.

Edmond Ironside, ed. Eleanore Boswell, MSR, 1928.

Edward III, TFT, 1910.

Fair Em, ed. W. W. Greg, MSR, 1928.

The Fair Maid of Bristow, TFT, 1912.

Field, Nathan, *The Plays*, ed. William Peery, Austin, 1950. Plays cited: *Amends for Ladies*; *A Woman is a Weathercock*.

Fletcher, John, *Beggar's Bush*, Folger manuscript J.b.5.

Demetrius and Enanthe, ed. Margaret McLaren Cook and F. P. Wilson, MSR, 1951.

Sir John van Olden Barnavelt, ed. T. H. Howard-Hill, MSR, 1980.

The Woman's Prize, Folger manuscript J.b.3.

The Works of Francis Beaumont and John Fletcher, ed. Arnold Glover and A. R. Waller, 10 vols., Cambridge, 1905–12. Plays cited: *Beggar's Bush*; *The Captain*; *The Coxcomb*; *Cupid's Revenge*; *The Custom of the Country*; *The Double Marriage*; *The Fair Maid of the Inn*; *The Honest Man's Fortune*; *The Humourous Lieutenant*; *The Island Princess*; *A King and No King*; *The Knight of Malta*; *The Little French Lawyer*; *The Lovers' Progress*; *Love's Pilgrimage*; *The Maid in the Mill*; *The Night Walker*; *The Noble Gentleman*; *Philaster*; *The Pilgrim*; *The Prophetess*; *The Queen of Corinth*; *Rule a Wife and Have a Wife*; *The Scornful Lady*; *The Spanish Curate*; *Thierry and Theodoret*; *The Two Noble Kinsmen*; *Valentinian*; *Wit at Several Weapons*; *Wit Without Money*; *The Woman's Prize*; *Women Pleased*.

Ford, John, *Love's Sacrifice*, STC no. 11164, 1633.

Perkin Warbeck, ed. Peter Ure, Revels, 1968.

'Tis Pity She's a Whore, ed. Derek Roper, Revels, 1975.

Fulwell, Ulpian, *Like Will to Like*, TFT, 1909.

George a Greene, ed. F. W. Clarke, MSR, 1911.

Greene, Robert, *Alphonsus, King of Aragon*, ed. W. W. Greg, MSR, 1926.

    Friar Bacon and Friar Bungay, ed. W. W. Greg, MSR, 1926.

    James IV, ed. A. E. H. Swaen and W. W. Greg, MSR, 1921.

    Orlando Furioso, ed. W. W. Greg, MSR, 1907.

Greg, W. W., *Dramatic Documents from the Elizabethan Playhouses*, 2 vols, Oxford, 1931. 'Plots' cited: *The Battle of Alcazar*; *The Dead Man's Fortune*; *2 The Seven Deadly Sins*; *Troilus and Cressida*.

Haughton, William, *Englishmen for My Money*, ed. W. W. Greg, MSR, 1913.

Hemming, William, *The Fatal Contract*, Wing H-1422, 1653.

Heywood, Thomas, *The Captives*, ed. Arthur Brown, MSR, 1953.

    The Dramatic Works, 6 vols., London, 1874. Plays cited: *The Brazen Age*; *1* and *2 Edward IV*; *The English Traveller*; *The Fair Maid of the Exchange*; *1 The Fair Maid of the West*; *Fortune by Land and Sea*; *The Four Prentices of London*; *The Golden Age*; *1* and *2 If You Know Not Me You Know Nobody*; *1* and *2 The Iron Age*; *The Late Lancashire Witches*; *Love's Mistress*; *A Maidenhead Well Lost*; *The Rape of Lucrece*; *The Royal King and the Loyal Subject*; *The Silver Age*; *The Wise Woman of Hogsdon*; *A Woman Killed With Kindness*.

The Honest Lawyer, TFT, 1914.

How a Man May Choose a Good Wife from a Bad, TFT, 1912.

John of Bordeaux, ed. William Lindsay Renwick, MSR, 1936.

Jonson, Ben, *Ben Jonson*, ed. C. H. Herford and Percy and Evelyn Simpson, 11 vols., Oxford, 1925–52. Plays cited: *The Alchemist*; *Every Man In His Humour*; *Sejanus*; *Volpone*.

    Every Man Out of His Humour, ed. F. P. Wilson and W. W. Greg, MSR, 1921.

King Leir, ed. W. W. Greg, MSR, 1908.

A Knack to Know a Knave, ed. G. R. Proudfoot, MSR, 1964.

Kyd, Thomas, *The Spanish Tragedy*, ed. Philip Edwards, Revels, 1959.

Locrine, ed. Ronald B. McKerrow, MSR, 1908.

Lodge, Thomas, *The Wounds of Civil War*, ed. J. Dover Wilson, MSR, 1910.

Look About You, ed. W. W. Greg, MSR, 1913.

Markham, Gervase and Sampson, William, *Herod and Antipater*, STC no. 17401, 1622.

Marlowe, Christopher, *Marlowe's 'Doctor Faustus' 1604–1616*, ed. W. W. Greg, Oxford, 1950.

    The Works, ed. C. F. Tucker Brooke, Oxford, 1910. Plays cited: *Edward II*; *The Jew of Malta*; *The Massacre at Paris*; *2 Tamburlaine.*.

Marston, John, *Antonio and Mellida*, ed. W. W. Greg, MSR, 1922.

    The Insatiate Countess, STC no. 17476, 1613.

    The Malcontent, ed. G. K. Hunter, Revels, 1975.

    Sophonisba or The Wonder of Women, STC no. 17488, 1606.

Massinger, Philip, *Believe as You List*, ed. Charles J. Sisson, MSR, 1928.

    The Plays and Poems, ed. Philip Edwards and Colin Gibson, 5 vols., Oxford, 1976. Plays cited: *The Bashful Lover*; *The Bondman*; *The Duke of Milan*; *The Emperor of the East*; *The Fatal Dowry*; *The Great Duke of Florence*; *The Guardian*; *A New Way to Pay Old Debts*; *The Parliament of Love*; *The Picture*; *The Renegado*; *The Unnatural Combat*.

The Merry Devil of Edmonton, TFT, 1911.

Middleton, Thomas, *No Wit, No Help Like a Woman's*, ed. Lowell E. Johnson, RRD, 1976.

The Witch, ed. W. W. Greg and F. P. Wilson, MSR, 1950.

Middleton, Thomas and Rowley, William, *The Changeling*, ed. N. W. Bawcutt, Revels, 1958.

A Fair Quarrel, ed. George R. Price, RRD, 1976.

Munday, Anthony, *The Death of Robert Earl of Huntingdon*, ed. John C. Meagher, MSR, 1967.

The Downfall of Robert Earl of Huntingdon, ed. John C. Meagher, MSR, 1965.

John a Kent and John a Cumber, ed. Muriel St. Clare Byrne, MSR, 1923.

Sir John Oldcastle, ed. Percy Simpson, MSR, 1908.

Sir Thomas More, ed. W. W. Greg, MSR, 1911.

Nashe, Thomas, *Summer's Last Will and Testament* in *Selected Writings*, ed. Stanley Wells, Cambridge, Mass., 1965.

Nero, STC no. 18430, 1624.

Peele, George, *Edward I*, ed. W. W. Greg, MSR, 1911.

Pickering, John, *Horestes (The Interlude of Vice)*, ed. Daniel Seltzer, MSR, 1962.

Porter, Henry, *The Two Angry Women of Abingdon*, ed. W. W. Greg, MSR, 1913.

Preston, Thomas, *Cambises*, TFT, 1910.

The Puritan, TFT, 1911.

Rowley, Samuel, *When You See Me You Know Me*, ed. F. P. Wilson, MSR, 1952.

Rowley, William, *All's Lost by Lust*, STC no. 21425, 1633.

The Birth of Merlin, TFT, 1910.

A Match at Midnight, STC no. 21421, 1633.

A New Wonder, a Woman Never Vexed, STC no. 21423, 1632.

A Shoemaker a Gentleman, STC no. 21422, 1638.

Sampson, William, *The Vow Breaker*, STC no. 21688, 1636.

Shakespeare, William, *The Complete Pelican Shakespeare*, gen. ed. Alfred Harbage, Baltimore, 1969.

The Norton Facsimile: The First Folio of Shakespeare, ed. Charlton Hinman, 1968.

Shakespearean Prompt-books of the Seventeenth Century, ed. G. Blakemore Evans, vol. 1, part i. Charlottesville, Va., 1960.

Shakespeare's Plays in Quarto, ed. Michael J. B. Allen and Kenneth Muir, University of California Press, 1982.

Sharpham, Edward, *The Fleer*, ed. Hunold Nibbe, Louvain, 1912.

Shirley, Henry, *The Martyred Soldier*, STC no. 22435, 1638.

Shirley, James, *The Doubtful Heir*, Wing S-3466, 1652.

Smith, Wentworth, *The Hector of Germany*, ed. Leonidas Warren Payne, Jr., Publications of University of Pennsylvania, Series in Philology and Literature, Philadelphia, 1906.

Suckling, Sir John, *Brennoralt* in *The Plays*, ed. L. A. Beaurline, Oxford, 1971.

Swetnam the Woman-Hater Arraigned by Women, TFT, 1914.
Tailor, Robert, *The Hog Hath Lost His Pearl*, ed. D. F. McKenzie, MSR, 1972.
The Taming of a Shrew, TFT, 1912.
The Telltale, ed. R. A. Foakes and J. C. Gibson, MSR, 1960.
Thomas Lord Cromwell, TFT, 1911.
The Thracian Wonder, Wing T-1078A, 1661.
Tom a Lincoln, British Library manuscript Add., 61745.
Tourneur, Cyril, *The Atheist's Tragedy*, ed. Irving Ribner, Revels, 1964.
    The Revenger's Tragedy, ed. R. A. Foakes, Revels, 1966.
The Trial of Chivalry, TFT, 1912.
The Trial of Treasure, TFT, 1908.
The True Tragedy of Richard III, ed. W. W. Greg, MSR, 1929.
The Two Merry Milkmaids, TFT, 1914.
The Two Noble Ladies, ed. Rebecca G. Rhoads, MSR, 1930.
The Valiant Welshman, TFT, 1913.
Wager, W., *The Longer Thou Livest the More Fool Thou Art* and *Enough Is as Good as a Feast*, ed. R. Mark Benbow, RRD, 1967.
Wapull, George, *The Tide Tarrieth No Man*, ed. Ernst Ruhl, *Shakespeare Jahrbuch*, 43 (1907), 1–52.
A Warning for Fair Women, TFT, 1912.
The Wasp, ed. J. W. Lever, MSR, 1976.
Webster, John, *The Devil's Law-Case*, ed. Frances A. Shirley, RRD, 1972.
    The Duchess of Malfi, ed. John Russell Brown, Revels, 1964.
    The White Devil, ed. John Russell Brown, Revels, 1960.
Wilkins, George, *The Miseries of Enforced Marriage*, ed. Glenn H. Blayney, MSR, 1964.
Wilson, Arthur, *The Swisser*, ed. Albert Feuillerat, Paris, 1904.
Wilson, Robert, *The Three Ladies of London*, TFT, 1911.
The Wisdom of Doctor Dodypoll, ed. M. N. Matson, MSR, 1965.
Woodstock (1 Richard II), ed. Wilhelmina P. Frijlinck, MSR, 1929.
Yarington, Robert, *Two Lamentable Tragedies*, TFT, 1913.
A Yorkshire Tragedy, ed. Sylvia D. Feldman, MSR, 1973.

Index